Uniforms of the Union Volunteers of 1861:

Mid-Atlantic States

for the

"First Defenders."

Washington, DC, 2016

To Whom It May Concern:
The Company of Military Historians takes great pride in endorsing *Uniforms of the Union Volunteers of 1861: The Mid-Atlantic States* as a standard reference in American military history.

Craig D. Bell,
President
Review Board:
William O. Adams, Chairman
Thomas Arliskas
Joseph G. Bilby
Official: David M. Sullivan,
Administrator.

Ron Field

Uniforms of the Union Volunteers of 1861: Mid-Atlantic States

Schiffer Publishing Ltd
4880 Lower Valley Road • Atglen, PA 19310

Library of Congress Control Number: 2018937041

Type set in Scotch Modern, Latin MT, Egyotian, Clarendon & Univers.

ISBN: 978-0-7643-5622-3

Printed in China

Published by Schiffer Publishing, Ltd.
4880 Lower Valley Road
Atglen, PA 19310
Phone: (610) 593-1777; Fax: (610) 593-2002
E-mail: Info@schifferbooks.com
Web: www.schifferbooks.com

CONTENTS

INTRODUCTION

Named for Maj. Samuel Ringgold—the first American soldier to lose his life in combat during the Mexican War in 1846—the Ringgold Light Artillery of Reading was organized and equipped in 1850 under Capt. James McKnight. Photographed at the Washington Navy Yard in April 1861, they drill as infantry as part of "the First Defenders" to reach the federal capital. Enlisted men wear uniform jackets, or "roundabouts," with nine-button front and a blind buttonhole on standing collar. Their forage caps have oil cloth covers. Three officers wear 1851-pattern frock coats, while a fourth—probably Capt. McKnight—wears a non-federal-pattern caped great coat. All ranks have wide seam stripes on their trousers. Three 12-pound howitzers were assigned to the company for the purpose of defending the Navy Yard, and the entire unit did duty there with the exception of twelve men who were detached to guard the Short Bridge, which was vital to the defense of the federal capital. *Albumen print, Pennsylvania State Archives*

The first state troops to reach Washington, DC, following the initial call from President Abraham Lincoln for three-month volunteers on April 15, 1861, were from Pennsylvania. During the early hours of April 18, five companies amounting to 530 men—consisting of the Ringgold Light Artillery of Reading, the Logan Guards of Lewistown, the Allen Rifles of Allentown, and the Washington Artillery and National Light Infantry of Pottsville—reached the capital city. In a letter published in the *Lowell Daily Courier* dated April 28, a Massachusetts volunteer observed that many men in these companies were in "citizen dress," although the Ringgold Light Artillery were described by another source as being in "entirely new uniforms."[1]

In Washington, the *National Republican* reported that some of these men had been in such haste that they did not take time to prepare for the journey, but left in "working clothes from their places of business."[2] The Washington Artillery and National Light Infantry were reported as being "entirely unarmed."[3] Only the Ringgold Light Artillery and Logan Guards were fully armed. Amounting to thirty-four men, the latter carried Springfield rifle muskets, but these were without powder or ammunition. Only one man carried a box of percussion caps, which he distributed among his comrades. Hence, with muskets capped and carried half cocked at "support arms," the Baltimore "mob" was fooled into thinking the arms were loaded, and were held at bay as all five companies passed through that city.[4] The arrival of these troops caused great rejoicing in the capital and gained for them the title "the First Defenders." These companies subsequently entered three months' service as part of the 25th Pennsylvania Infantry.[5]

The volunteers from the mid-Atlantic states (Pennsylvania, New York, New Jersey, Delaware, Maryland, and the District of Columbia) that followed the First Defenders and rallied around the flag in defense of the Union in 1861 wore uniforms varying greatly in quality and durability. The colorful Zouave influence of French military fashion was particularly well represented within the ranks both of Pennsylvania and New York troops. At least seven regiments and companies wearing Zouave-style uniforms were formed within the "Keystone State," including the Philadelphia Zouave Corps, Baxter's Fire Zouaves, and the Keystone Zouaves. A further eleven Zouave regiments, such as Duryee's Zouaves and D'Epineuil Zouaves, were recruited in the "Empire State." Regiments wearing French-style chasseur uniforms, like the 62nd and 83rd Pennsylvania and the 17th New York—also known as the Westchester Chasseurs—were also prevalent in both states.

The use of "shoddy" cloth and poorly made footwear was rife in several mid-Atlantic states, particularly in Pennsylvania and New York. A major swindle took place in Pennsylvania during April and May 1861, in which thousands of volunteers received coats, pants, caps, and shoes that literally fell apart within a matter of weeks, if not days. New York volunteers fared little better, with vast amounts of "shoddy" clothing being supplied by Brooks Brothers of New York City. The three-month men who joined the ranks of the 1st Delaware Infantry during June 1861 suffered a similar experience, with uniform clothing that quickly fell apart. In comparison, the volunteers from New Jersey and the District of Columbia seem to have been clothed more adequately from the outset, as were the loyal volunteers of Maryland.

A shortage of "army blue" cloth led to whole regiments being uniformed in gray, which was a popular color for militia in the North before the war. In New York, the state militia regulations of 1858 prescribed a gray uniform. Due to a shortage of dark-blue cloth, at least twelve New York regiments were clothed in gray as a result of the contract with Brooks Brothers in April 1861. This led to fatal and costly incidents of "friendly fire" at Big Bethel, First Bull Run, and Ball's Bluff. It was not until August 1861 that the federal army made the first effort to standardize dark blue as the color of uniform for its troops. On August 21, Gen. George Brinton McClellan, commanding the Military Division of the Potomac, issued orders forbidding "the purchase of gray uniforms," which he called, "the rebels' color."[6] Quartermaster Gen. Montgomery C. Meigs consolidated the situation in November 1861 by inviting proposals from contractors to provide uniforms for much of the Union army, stating categorically, "Light or dark blue cloths preferred, and light greys will not be considered,"[7] and by the end of the year most of the Union army wore "Army Blue."[8]

ACKNOWLEDGMENTS

The author is very grateful to numerous individuals and institutions for providing images and sharing knowledge and information that made this study possible. As with the first volume in this series, Michael J. McAfee, curator of uniforms at the US Military Academy, New York, provided valuable advice and numerous images from his extensive collection. Peter Harrington, curator at the Anne S. K. Brown Military Collection, gave generously of his services during my examination of the Frederick Todd Collection at the John Hay Library, Brown University, Rhode Island, during 2010. To Robert Biondi, senior editor at Schiffer Publishing, I owe a great debt of gratitude for his patience and encouragement during the long period of time this project was in various stages of preparation. To Daniel Miller, I am further indebted for so generously sharing images and advice from his collection of Zouave imagery. Thanks also to Courtney T. Burns, chief curator of New York State Military Museum, Saratoga Springs, New York; Randy L. Goss, coordinator of accessioning and Processing / photo archivist / preservation officer, Delaware Public Archives; Carol Johnson, curator of photography, Library of Congress, Prints and Photographs Division, Washington, DC; David Kuzma, Special Collections and University Archives, Rutgers University Libraries, New Brunswick, New Jersey; Sarah Wilson LeCount, collections manager, Rochester Museum & Science Center, Rochester, New York; Marlea Leljedal, Photocopy and Scanning Services, United States Army Heritage and Education Center at Carlisle (USAHEC), Pennsylvania; Barbara Miller, information resource specialist II, Delaware Public Archives; Ronn Palm, the Ronn Palm Museum Collection, Gettysburg, Pennsylvania; Kay Peterson, National Museum of American History, Smithsonian Institute, Washington, DC; Ed Richi, curator of printed media, the Delaware Historical Society; Harry Ridgeway, the Civil War Relicman; Michael D. Sherbon, associate archivist, Pennsylvania State Archives, Harrisburg, Pennsylvania; Elizabeth Sikorski, Rochester Museum & Science Center, Rochester, New York; Sam and Wes Small of the Horse Soldier at Gettysburg, Pennsylvania; and including Joseph Bilby, Gil Barrett, Seward R. Osborne, Don Troiani, Dennis Schurr, Alan Thrower, Martin Schoenfeld, Paul Mehney, Bryan Watson, Daniel J. Binder, Paul Russinoff, and Dr. Michael R. Cunningham.

Ron Field, *2018*

Yes we'll rally round the flag, boys,
we'll rally once again,
Shouting the battle cry of freedom,
We will rally from the hillside,
we'll gather from the plain,
Shouting the battle cry of freedom!

CHAPTER 1:

PENNSYLVANIA

Wearing a uniform based on that of the Zouaves of the Imperial Guard of France, the Philadelphia Zouaves, commanded by Capt. Edmund Baudin, parade past Independence Hall in 1860. Complete with *vivandière*, this company enlisted for three months' service in the 18th Pennsylvania during April 1861. *Colored lithograph by P. S. Duval & Son, Philadelphia; author's collection*

Fourteen regiments of militia were requested from the Commonwealth of Pennsylvania for three months' federal service. Those who were accepted consisted of the eight Philadelphia regiments, while the separate volunteer militia companies throughout the state were ordered to report to Camp Curtin, half a mile west of the state capital, Harrisburg; Camp Slifer, near Chambersburg; Camp Wayne, in West Chester; Camp Scott, in York; and Camp Wilkins, near Pittsburgh. Because the authorities were uncertain of the condition of these troops, which amounted to over 400 companies, permission was granted for the raising of new regiments. As a result, a total of twenty-five three-month regiments were actually organized, and Governor Andrew Curtin was finally induced to accept them all. In addition, there remained enough unorganized companies sufficient to form a further thirty Pennsylvania regiments if needed. About half the active Volunteer Militia in the state was absorbed into the twenty-five regiments accepted, which were organized between April 16 and May 27, 1861. The Philadelphia regiments consisted of the 17th through

The Cadwalader Grays formed part of the 1st Regiment Artillery, First Division, Pennsylvania Militia, prior to the war. When this regiment served as infantry for three months in 1861, as the 17th Pennsylvania, the Cadwalader Grays became Companies H and K. This unidentified enlisted man wears the prewar full dress of the Cadwalader Grays. His black felt shako has a distinctive plate containing part of the state coat of arms within a wreath, underneath which is a ribbon inscribed "FIRST ARTILY." Above this is a small die-struck brass pompon ornament bearing crossed cannon superimposed on a flaming bomb device and red pompon. His gray jacket is trimmed with blind buttonholes on collar and cuffs and has brass shoulder scales attached. Matching pants have double seam stripes. His white shoulder belt has a rectangular plate with what appears to be a bust of George Washington. *Carte de visite, Michael J. McAfee collection*

24th Infantry, while those organized throughout the state were the 1st through 16th and 25th Infantry.

A report in the *Centre Democrat* of Bellafonte, Pennsylvania, described the raw state of many Pennsylvanians rallying around the flag at Camp Curtin toward the end of April 1861:

> The appearance of some of these volunteers, as they enter the city, strongly speaks to the heart of the object that has brought them here. They come clothed in the coarsest fabrics, and that scantily enough in some cases. Under their arms they carry a pair of new brogans anticipating, as it were, the demand that may be made upon their feet in marching, before they get thr'o; while in their hands they sling an old leather bag, containing a change of raiment or an extra shirt or two. At the side of some of them, strapped to their waists, dangle old swords, which, perhaps, were wielded by their forefathers in the first great struggle for American liberty, while others carry old muskets, of a half a century ago make, on their shoulders, all of them seemingly determined to use what means have been provided them, to the best of their ability. And then of the pistols, the Colt's revolvers and other weapons, thrust into their pockets, at the last moment, by parents and friends.[1]

This cap was worn by a member of the Cadwalader Grays, a company of the 1st Regiment Artillery, First Division, Pennsylvania Militia. The gilt die-struck brass cap plate displays the shield portion of the Pennsylvania coat of arms adopted in 1809, enclosed within a wreath bearing a "ribbon" with the abbreviated designation "FIRST ARTILY." Devices in three sections of the shield show a sailing ship, a plow, and three sheaves of wheat, representing the commerce of the state. The smaller plate attached above bears a flaming grenade, over which are crossed cannon—also seen on the buttons fastening the chin strap—indicating the branch of service. This cap is minus the black woolen pompon worn by the Cadwalader Grays. *National Museum of American History, Kenneth E. Behring Center: Accession no. 223708*

Col. Francis E. Patterson wears an example of the drab felt hats presented by the "patriotic citizens" of Philadelphia to the 17th Pennsylvania (three months, 1st Regiment Artillery, First Division, Pennsylvania Militia) on June 6, 1861, after which his regiment was nicknamed the "Quaker Regiment." The crossed-cannon insignia attached to the front of its crown echoes the 1st Artillery militia designation of his command. His coarsely made five-button coat is indicative of the poor-quality uniforms worn by many three-month volunteers from Pennsylvania. *Anne S. K. Brown Military Collection, Brown University*

In contrast, a number of three-month regiments—and individual companies within regiments, plus reserves and home guards—wore distinctive full dress or fatigue uniforms when they joined the ranks in April 1861. Serving as infantry and designated the 17th Pennsylvania, the 1st Artillery Regiment, First Division, Pennsylvania Militia, was commanded by Col. Francis E. Patterson and included the National Artillery, Cadwalader Grays, Philadelphia City Grays, and Washington Grays. When this regiment left Philadelphia for the federal capital on May 8, 1861, the *Press* reported that most of the men had "their hair shaved close," and two companies wore "gray overcoats." Regarding equipage, their "blankets were rolled up and buckled to the top of their knapsacks," and they carried "full cartridge boxes."[2] The 17th Pennsylvania became known as "the Quaker Regiment," after being gifted drab felt hats by the "patriotic citizens" of Philadelphia on June 6, while encamped on Kalorama Heights near Washington, DC. After campaigning along the banks of the Potomac, this regiment returned home on July 25 to be mustered out, on which occasion the *Inquirer* observed:

> The men were covered with dust and their clothing seemed considerably worn. They carried their grey overcoats on their knapsacks, and the new Kossuth regulation hat, which each man wore, gave to the men an appearance which contrasted strongly with others that have come home with the flat caps that were given by Uncle Sam to all his sons. These hats were presented to Col. Patterson's Regiment by gentlemen of this city, who, as a personal appreciation, sent them to the boys when they were encamped at Washington.[3]

One of the first Pennsylvania Zouave units (the Philadelphia Zouave Corps) was mainly recruited among the French population of that city. Commanded by Capt. Edmund Baudin, they were attached to the 1st Regiment of Infantry, First Brigade, First Division, Pennsylvania Militia, during April 1860.[4] Also containing companies such as the State Fencibles, Washington Blues, and Garde Lafayette, this regiment entered three months' service as the 18th Pennsylvania Infantry. On the occasion of their inspection in 1860, the Zouave Corps wore a uniform based on that of the Zouaves of the Imperial Guard of France, which the *Philadelphia Press* stated consisted of "a red Turkish cap, bound round with a roll of white muslin resembling a turban; a blue vest fitting close to the body with a yellow stripe down the centre, from the neck to the waist." Over this was worn "a loose blue cloth jacket with arabesque yellow worsted trimmings and red cuffs." Trousers were of "red cloth, and wide, with plaited folds, reaching down below the knee," where they were "'tucked' up." Below this, each man wore "a set of leather leggings reaching to the ankle, with white over-gaiters over the shoes." The neck was described as "perfectly bare with no sign of a shirt. Each man wore his hair cropped short and his moustaches turned up at the corners." The officers wore "blue frock coats, red caps with gold trimmings, and satin vests."[5] During August of the same year, the *Philadelphia Inquirer* stated that when "off duty," the Zouaves wore "a light fatigue cap, red, and with yellow tassel. A small cartridge box dangles from a black belt, and their trousers are ornamented with yellow trimmings."[6]

On the occasion of their first public parade, the Philadelphia Zouave Corps was accompanied by "a genuine female 'vivandiere,' equipped *a la* Daughter of the Regiment," who was later in May 1861 reported dressed in "Turco costume."[7] Following the arrival of the 18th Pennsylvania (three months) near Baltimore, Maryland, in 1861, this *vivandière* visited the 8th Massachusetts at Camp Essex on June 11, of which occasion a Massachusetts volunteer commented:

> We had a lioness in camp yesterday: a vivandiere of Pennsylvania Zouaves. Dressed in the appropriate uniform of her regiment with her ***baril de liqueur*** slung jauntily from her shoulder, she attracted great attention on the field and received the ***devoirs*** of nearly the entire regiment. Being of French Canadian extraction, with snapping black eyes that indicated the temper of the tigress rather than a leonine magnanimity, wearing a sword of no trifling dimensions, and being a married woman, into the bargain, —she was treated with all due deference."[8]

During a visit to New York City in celebration of the birthday of the Marquis de La Fayette in August 1861, a small delegation of the Philadelphia Zouave Corps was accompanied by "the cantinere [*sic*], Madam Pequin," who wore "a dark blue frock coat, with yellow trimmings, red pants, and Zouave gaiters."[9]

Incorporated into the Pennsylvania militia in 1856 as the battalion-sized "Infantry Corps, National Guards of Philadelphia," the National Guards was expanded into a regiment by 1860 and wore for full dress a gray tailcoat trimmed with black and gold and a black "National Guard"-pattern cap with brass plate marked "2" and "National Guard," plus black pompon, although there was some variation between companies regarding trim color according to photographic evidence. During February 1861, this battalion paraded in Harrisburg for the anniversary of George Washington's birthday, wearing "fatigue dress, black hat and red cockade."[10] Commanded by Mexican War veteran Peter Lyle, the National Guard formed the 19th Pennsylvania three-month volunteers in April 1861. Clothed in what was inaccurately described as "the regular United States service uniform"—which was later reported to be an inferior-quality gray roundabout and pants—they left for Baltimore on April 27, 1861.[11] As late as July 19, the 19th Pennsylvania paraded in that city "still clad in the miserable dirty grey, old pantaloons and roundabouts."[12]

Organized as a regiment of eight companies in 1860, the National Guards of Philadelphia had adopted a new uniform in February 1859, consisting of a gray tailcoat trimmed with black and gold, black dress cap with brass plate marked "2," and a black pompon. By December 1860, this had been changed to include a red pompon. Photographed in 1861, this first sergeant holds a small book with the letter "C" on its cover, possibly indicating he was 1st Sgt. B/C. J. Burr Jr., Co. C, National Guards of Philadelphia, who was listed when the unit paraded as a regiment for the first time in December 1860. His white waist buff leather belt is fastened with a round, two-piece plate of unknown pattern and a shoulder belt with "eagle plate." He is armed with what appears to be an M1850 foot officer's sword, plus an altered M1822 musket. In April 1861, the National Guard enlisted for three months as the 19th Pennsylvania and wore a service dress consisting of gray roundabout and matching pants. *Copy print of a crystalograph, Anne S. K. Brown Military Collection, Brown University*

This unidentified enlisted man of the Sarsfield Rifles, Pennsylvania militia, wears an unusual coat with high standing collar, shoulder straps, and "hunting shirt" style, with two-inch-long fringe around the skirts. His 1851-pattern dress cap has a red-tinted fountain plume, 1858-pattern hat "eagle" plate, and brass letters "S R." He holds an M1841 rifle, and his accouterments consist of an 1839-pattern Rifleman's powder flask and pouch and a buff leather waist belt fastened by a small 1839-pattern "US" oval plate. Originally organized in 1858, the Philadelphia Rifle Battalion expanded into the German Rifle Regiment, or 21st Pennsylvania Volunteer Infantry (Philadelphia Rifles), for three months' service under Col. John F. Ballier in April 1861. Upon reenlistment, the Sarsfield Rifles became part of the 98th Pennsylvania Infantry. *Sixth-plate tintype with "Melainotype Plate for Neff's Pat 19 Feb 56" stamp, author's collection*

When the 18th and 19th Pennsylvania occupied Fort McHenry under Maj. Gen. George Cadwalader on May 14, 1861, a correspondent of the *Baltimore American and Commercial Advertiser* commented that companies such as the Philadelphia Zouaves and Garde Lafayette were "thoroughly equipped with the United States uniforms and accoutrements. . . . All of the Companies left their usual uniforms—some of which are costly and beautiful—in Philadelphia." On parade several days later, these volunteers wore "army overcoats," while the officers appeared in "their regular uniforms, with fatigue caps."[13]

The Scott Legion was formed as an independent company-sized organization by "the surviving officers and soldiers of the Mexican War" by 1855. Elements of this unit appeared in uniform "similar to that worn by them in Mexico" for the dedication of a monument of the Scott Legion on April 18 of that year.[14] When they adopted a new uniform in June 1858, this was described as "a sky-blue roundabout and pants, and blue cloth cap. Medal on the right breast."[15] Enlisted for three months as the 20th Pennsylvania in April 1861, the Scott Legion received their "new uniform, and were armed with new muskets" by May 18, 1861.[16] When it left Philadelphia for Camp Curtin on May 29, 1861, the legion was reported by *The Press* to be wearing "the old regulation uniform, consisting of

Promoted brigadier general of the 1st Brigade, 18th Division, Pennsylvania Militia, prior to the war, James Scott Negley took command of the three-month volunteers being raised in the Western Department of Pennsylvania and forwarded them to Harrisburg during April/May 1861. He next commanded the 5th Brigade, 2nd Division, Army of Pennsylvania, and served under Patterson in Maryland and Virginia until July 20, 1861, following which he continued as a brigade commander of three-year troops in the Army of the Ohio. He wears a militia uniform with heavily trimmed plastron front, epaulets, and buff-colored waist sash. His plumed cocked hat, or chapeau, rests on the table by his side. *Michael J. McAfee collection*

light-blue cloth roundabouts and pantaloons, and dark-blue cloth fatigue caps. Each man was furnished with a Havelock, and in their haversacks were stored three days' rations."[17] Earlier, on May 17, the same journal had commented, "In their new sky-blue suits, the Legion had a soldierly and gallant appearance. The blue blouses of other regiments have a sorry look beside these old time suits, which went marching on the backs of Northern volunteers through Mexico."[18] Officers wore "handsome dark blue uniforms … made at the Brown Stone Clothing Hall of Rockhill & Wilson" when this regiment went into camp at Suffolk Park on May 24, 1861.[19] (Rockhill & Wilson became the principal maker of uniforms in Philadelphia.) On June 17, 1861, *The Press* reported that the firm appeared:

> to be the leading house for the manufacturing of military clothing. In the upper stories they have some twenty cutters employed and about seven hundred hands are constantly engaged in making up the work. Over three thousand coats were made up by this firm in ten days, for the State, besides full suits for several companies of Home Guards [see below], and for officers of the army and navy.

Mustered out on August 6, 1861, the Scott Legion reorganized for three years as the 68th Pennsylvania.[20]

Composed of the Jackson Rifles, Lafayette Rifles, Pennsylvania Rifles, and Washington Rifles, the Philadelphia Rifle Battalion expanded into the German Rifle Regiment (or 21st Pennsylvania) for three months' service in 1861. When this regiment assembled on April 25, *The Press* reported, "But few of the men had uniforms, and none but the officers were armed. The men are a hardy set, and look as if they could stand a fierce fight without flinching. Many of them have already been engaged in hard service in Europe."[21] Upon the return of the 21st Pennsylvania to Philadelphia after the short campaign in Maryland and Virginia with Maj. Gen. Robert Patterson's Army of Pennsylvania, the same journal stated, "The blue uniforms of the men are in fine preservation, and many of them appear sufficiently stout to last three months longer."[22]

The Artillery Battalion, Third Brigade, First Division, Pennsylvania Militia, was expanded into a regiment on February 22, 1861, and became the 23rd

This partially colorized *carte de visite* depicts an unidentified early war militiaman photographed in Blossburg, Tioga County, Pennsylvania. He wears a gray jacket with red facings and matching pants with red seam stripes, and his headgear consists of an 1851-pattern dress cap with round red worsted pompom and 1858-pattern infantry-enlisted cap insignia. *Carte de visite with back mark "G. Osborne / Photographer / Blossburg, / PA."; author's collection*

Pennsylvania on April 21, 1861, with the Continental Guards forming Companies A and E.[23] Upon formation at the beginning of 1851, the Continental Guards adopted a Revolutionary War–style uniform composed of "blue hunting shirts, faced with yellow, cocked hat, with buck's tail, yellow breeches, top boots, white neckerchief, and ruffle shirt, all in conformity with the fashion of the 'times that tried men's souls.'" When this regiment left for Perryville, Maryland, on April 27, 1861, they were described as "uniformed and armed, but were not supplied with cartridge boxes or haversacks."[24]

As the only volunteer cavalry organization accepted under the first ninety-day call, the wealthy First Troop Philadelphia City Cavalry, or City Troop,

First organized in 1774 as the Light Horse of the City of Philadelphia, the First Troop Philadelphia City Troop was one of the first patriotic military organizations established during the American Revolution and today is the oldest continuously serving unit in the US military. Both these militiamen wear the full-dress summer uniform of the Philadelphia City Cavalry, consisting of a dark-blue coatee with red collar with silver lace trim and three rows of white metal ball buttons connected by silver lace cord; silver lace wings; scarlet and white belt; white breeches; and high patent leather boots. Placed on the table in both images is the unit's elaborate headgear, which consisted of a patent leather helmet trimmed with white metal and large bearskin crest. Both men wear the white shoulder belt, supporting a black leather pouch containing nine cartridges, and hold sabers patterned after the 1833 Dragoon model specially purchased for the unit. Both John W. Grigg (left) and John Fossitt (right) were wealthy Philadelphia merchants who served in the unit prior to the Civil War. Grigg enlisted for three months' service in James's Independent Company, Pennsylvania Cavalry (Philadelphia City Cavalry), in 1861. *Cartes de visite, Anne S. K. Brown Military Collection, Brown University*

provided their own service uniforms, plus horses and equipment, which cost between $300 and $500 per man. The former was reported as being "in accordance with the regulation pattern" and consisted of a US dragoon jacket, plain blue forage cap, sky-blue trousers, and dark-blue overcoat. Upon their return from three months' service, the City Troop wore "the regulation blue blouse, light blue pants, and brogans," which were observed in stark contrast with "the white breeches, high boots, and showy uniform coats" of those "old members" of the unit who turned out to escort them.[25]

Wearing their "rich dress uniform of deep black," the Black Hussars of Philadelphia formed part of the escort when Col. Robert Anderson—of Fort Sumter fame—visited the city on May 13, 1861. However, the Hussars were refused financial help from the city councils and failed to enlist, since they could not afford to mount, clothe, or equip themselves.[26] On July 12, 1861, the *Inquirer* reported that the Philadelphia Merchant Troop wore "red uniforms and peculiar round caps" that presented "quite a British appearance." A month earlier, the pro-Unionist *Baltimore Clipper* of Maryland had commented that "the Scotch features of their uniform" looked "very well."[27] This company was attached to the 3rd Cavalry (60th Pennsylvania)—also known as Young's Kentucky Regiment of Light Cavalry—as Co. A. The first volunteer cavalry regiment of the Union army, this unit was assembled in Washington, DC, and served with the Army of the Potomac until 1864.

The Independent Rangers, or McMullin's Rangers, commanded by Capt. William McMullin, were largely recruited among "the rough and tumble Moyamensing Hose Company, of Philadelphia." Organized as a group of 100 picked men as "rangers and scouts," this unit received uniforms from the state during May 1861 that proved to be "badly stitched." As a result, they privately procured their own clothing, including boots, in Philadelphia. On the basis of a *Harper's Weekly* engraving published on July 20, 1861, this consisted of a roundabout, or jacket, and matching pants with broad, light-colored seam stripes, plus chasseur-pattern caps. According to a report in the *Inquirer*, the pants of "wool cassimere" were "treble stitched along the inseams" for service in the saddle.[28] Another Philadelphia newspaper reported that Capt. McMullin wore "the United States regulation uniform."[29]

Organized as an independent militia in Philadelphia for home defense during April 1861, the Reserve Brigade, consisting of four regiments of infantry and one squadron of cavalry, purchased its own uniforms, while US arms and accoutrements were provided through the friendship of its officers with Secretary of War Simon Cameron, a native Pennsylvanian. The 1st Regiment, also known as the Gray Reserves, were described as "looking like a 'regiment of Quakers'" because they wore "a slouch hat, turned up at one side, fastened with the arms of the State, a long gray coat, fitting closely at the waist, and hanging down loosely, nearly to the knees, and gray trousers."

Organized to serve as mounted riflemen and serving as a special bodyguard to Gen. Robert Patterson during their three-month service, the Independent Rangers, or McMullin's Rangers, were illustrated near Hagerstown, Maryland, in *Harper's Weekly* of July 20, 1861, wearing chasseur-pattern fatigue caps, jackets, and pants with wide seam stripes, and armed with the "patent Minnie muskets." *Author's collection*

Capt. George W. Wood commanded Co. G, 1st Regiment, Reserve Brigade (Grey Reserves). At left he wears an example of the black-felt 1858 uniform, or "Hardee" hat, with insignia consisting of a gold bullion horn embroidered on a black velvet patch with brass numeral "1" inset. His double-breasted overcoat is not of the federal pattern. At right he was photographed in the plain gray full-dress frock and matching pants worn by officers of his regiment. The significance of the medal or decoration on his chest is not known. *Cartes de visite by J. Cremer & Co. of Philadelphia, Michael J. McAfee collection*

This waist belt plate is of the type worn by the "Grey Reserves" and depicts the state seal of Pennsylvania—which consists of two horses over a coat of arms with symbolism of agriculture and commerce—and "RB" below, representing the Reserve Brigade of Philadelphia. *The Civil War Relicman*

Parading through Philadelphia on May 27, 1861, this regiment wore a fatigue dress consisting of a "light grey coat, pants and cap, without any ornament excepting the brass buttons, and a black band around the cap." Without arms on this occasion, they eventually received smooth-bore percussion muskets from the US arsenal at Frankford. Known as the Blue Reserves, the second regiment wore "blue single-breasted frock coats and pants, and blue caps."[30] The 3rd Regiment was also clothed in gray, as was the six-company infantry battalion of the 4th Regiment, which was uniformed in "Bullock's Cadet cloth," described by the *Philadelphia Inquirer* as "a very handsome grey."[31] The remainder of the 4th Regiment consisted of a four-company Zouave battalion, of which Co. A was the Gymnast Zouaves and Co. B the Ellsworth Zouave Corps.[32] According to an *Inquirer* report, the uniform for the Zouave battalion was to be "a blue Zouave jacket, light blue vest, trimmed with red, blue pants, the shape of which will be peg-topped, with a red stripe down the side."[33]

First formed during April 1861 as a "Corps of Gymnasts" at the Gymnasium on Arch Street, in Philadelphia, owned by Louis Hildebrand, the original Gymnast Zouaves proposed wearing "the improved Zouave costume, the jacket and pants being of blue cloth, trimmed with red, with vest of the same cloth, trimmed with stripes of white, and ornamented in front with a row of gilt buttons, Zouave boots, and a blue sash with crimson border." Expanded into what was also known as the Gymnast Zouave Battalion once they were attached to the 4th Regiment, Reserve

Known only as "Andrew Hayley," this unidentified Pennsylvanian wears a state-seal belt plate, and his uniform matches a contemporaneous description of the fatigue dress of the 1st Regiment, Reserve Brigade, a.k.a. "Grey Reserves." *Carte de visite, Michael J. McAfee collection*

This unidentified private wears the full dress of the 1st Regiment, Reserve Brigade, a.k.a. the "Grey Reserves," consisting of a plain gray nine-button frock with shoulder straps and plain gray pants. He holds a "Hardee" hat with federal-pattern insignia, and his waist belt plate displays the Pennsylvania state seal. His long arm is an altered Model 1816 musket. *Carte de visite by J. Cremer & Co. of Philadelphia, Michael J. McAfee collection*

Based on a photograph taken at the studio of Jones & Brother, on Arch Street, Philadelphia, this lithograph shows the officers and noncommissioned officers (NCOs) of the Gymnast Zouaves. Organized and trained by Louis Hildebrand at his gymnasium on the same street during April 1861, the Gymnast Zouaves had expanded into a battalion by July of that year and entered federal service as part of the 23rd Pennsylvania Volunteers. The NCOs are dressed in a Zouave uniform adopted by their unit by July 1861, while the officers wear red chasseur-pattern caps with their dark-blue coats and pants. *Anne S. K. Brown Military Collection, Brown University*

These two enlisted men wear the Zouave uniform adopted by the Gymnast Zouaves Battalion by July 1861, consisting of "a dark blue jacket, trimmed with red, light blue vest, dark blue peg-topped pants with red stripe, and leggings." Caps were "dark blue, with a light blue crown piece." The brass letter "A" attached to their cap fronts indicates that they belonged to Co. A of the militia Zouave battalion. This image is partially identified in pencil on the reverse as "M. F. & Pap Beirn." *Carte de visite, Daniel J. Miller collection*

Brigade, by July, their uniform was confirmed as consisting of "a dark blue jacket, trimmed with red, light blue vest, dark blue peg-topped pants with red stripe, and leggings." Their caps were "dark blue, with a light blue crown piece." This unit later formed the basis for the three-year 23rd Pennsylvania, also known as Birney's Zouaves (see below).[34]

Moves to establish a home guard in Philadelphia began on April 19, 1861, when Mayor Alexander Henry appointed Col. Augustus J. Pleasanton as "Commander of the Home Guard of the city of Philadelphia."[35] Companies forming these auxiliary regiments initially wore makeshift uniforms of various cut and color. For example, before joining the 2nd Regiment, Infantry of the Line, as Co. G, the Tenth Ward Home Guard, under Capt. E. H. Grant, wore "a red shirt, trimmed with black, and grey pants and coat."[36] On April 22, Col. Pleasanton published General Order No. 3, which stated, "The Uniform for the HOME GUARD will consist of a single-breasted light or cadet gray frock coat, with standing collar, and buttons of the arm to which the regiment may belong; pantaloons of the same material; cap of army pattern, of drab color, with a rosette of the National Colors, Red, White, and Blue." These uniforms were to be "habitually worn, so that on the occasion of an alarm the officers and men" could "repair at once to

Identified as a member of the Philadelphia Home Guard by his belt plate, bearing the letters "PHG," this Pennsylvanian NCO appears to be wearing a blue coat and pants, which might indicate that his company either chose to wear that color or could not acquire the gray cloth prescribed by General Order No. 3 on April 2, 1861. His chasseur-pattern cap has a dark band. A prewar militia dress tailcoat, complete with brass shoulder scales and cartridge box, is draped across the photographer's prop, against which rests a Model 1842 rifle musket with fixed bayonet. A militia-pattern NCO's sword with Roman helmet pommel and pearl grip is suspended from his waist belt. *Carte de visite, Michael J. McAfee collection*

Based on the federal pattern of 1839, and made and purchased locally in Philadelphia, this oval waist belt plate was produced for the Philadelphia Home Guard in 1861. A cartridge box plate was issued struck from the same die. *The Civil War Relicman*

their armories, without stopping to change their clothes." Referred to as "Special Military Organizations," those companies of Home Guards that wished to "select their own Uniforms" were allowed to do so. Two days later, Pleasanton advised that due to a shortage of Cadet Gray, "any other shade of gray" would be acceptable as long as it was "sufficient for a whole regiment."[37]

Influenced by the 1860 drill tour of Elmer Ellsworth's United States Zouave Cadets and the advent of the Philadelphia Zouave Corps, other Zouave companies proliferated in Pennsylvania. Formed during August 1860, the United States Zouave Cadets of Pittsburgh adopted a uniform "similar to the Chicago company" commanded by Ellsworth.[38] This company enlisted for three months service as Co. I, 12th Pennsylvania, in April 1861 and reenlisted for three years during September 1861 as Co. M of the expanded 23rd Pennsylvania (Birney's Zouaves; see below). Another company recruited in Pittsburgh during 1860, the First Pennsylvania Zouaves, commanded by Capt. Joseph Gerard, probably wore a full French Zouave uniform. When they took part in the anniversary parade celebrating George Washington's birthday on February 22, 1861, they were mentioned as wearing "wide unmentionables, which seemed to provoke a smile from every quarter."[39] This company enlisted for three months as Co. F, 7th Pennsylvania, and later served as Co. K, 61st Pennsylvania.

Several Pennsylvania companies existed that were called the United States Zouaves. Commanded by

An NCO of the Mænnerchor Rifles—a Philadelphia Home Guard unit designated Co. A, 1st Battalion, 1st Regiment Rifles—Sgt. J. Saches wears a gray uniform probably based on that prescribed for the Home Guards on April 22, 1861. His waist belt plate bears the Pennsylvania state arms. Commanded by Mexican War veteran Capt. John A. Koltes, this company was formed by members of the Mænnerchor Vocal Society, which was composed of the German citizens of Philadelphia. *Carte de visite, Michael J. McAfee collection*

Capt. George Seigrist, the United States Zouaves of Pittsburgh became Co. K, 5th Pennsylvania (three months). Another unit by the same name, also known as the Pittsburgh Zouaves and commanded by Capt. John P. Glass, arrived in Philadelphia on June 23, 1861, en route for New York, where they were mustered in as Co. A, 74th New York (Fifth Excelsior), of Daniel E. Sickles's brigade. According to *The Press*, "A portion of them were uniformed, in red pantaloons and blue blouse. The majority, however, were dressed as citizens."[40]

The Johnstown Zouave Cadets were organized in Cambria County, Pennsylvania, during August 1860[41] and, according to the *Pennsylvania Daily Telegraph*, took part in the parade at Harrisburg on February 22, wearing "red pants, blue coats [&] red cap." On the same occasion, the *Daily Patriot and Union* commented that they wore a dress uniform "similar to the Chicago Zouaves," and their drill was described as being "not far behind them."[42] When this company enlisted for three months' service as Co. A, 3rd Pennsylvania, during April, a member of the Logan Rifle Rangers (Co. E) of that regiment wrote from Camp Scott, in York, "We are not wholly uniformed yet, but have received our shoes, underclothes and blouses. Of course we have our company uniforms, and some of them (the Johnstone Zouaves [*sic*] for instance) are noticeably pretty."[43] The Johnstown Zouave Cadets reenlisted "for the war" as Co. A, 54th Pennsylvania, during August/September 1861.

These two enlisted men of the Ellsworth Zouaves, organized at York, Pennsylvania, on May 10, 1861, wear examples of the second uniform acquired by their company. Similar to that worn by the 5th New York Volunteers, or Duryee's Zouaves, this included a blue jacket with red trim, red pantaloons, and blue waist sash edged and trimmed with light blue. However, there were differences in that worn by the Ellsworth Zouaves, such as the way the jacket was fastened with a hook and eye some distance from the neck, and the yellow tassel on their red fezzes, rather than the dark-blue ones worn by Duryee's Zouaves. Also note the puckering of the trim around the *tombeau* on the jacket worn by the man at right. They both hold Austrian rifle muskets. *Sixth-plate tintype, Daniel J. Miller collection*

Nineteen-year-old private Evan Thomas wears the uniform of the Johnstown Zouave Cadets, of Cambria County, who enlisted for three months' service in April 1861 as Co. A, 3rd Pennsylvania Infantry. Similar to that worn by the Chicago Zouave Cadets in 1860, this consisted of a red cap with light-colored band, blue jacket edged around the front with a double row of red tape and ball buttons, red pants, and brown leathers gaiters. *Ca. 1900 copy of 1861 image, Daniel J. Miller collection*

The First City Zouaves were originally formed under Captain D. B. Randolph Keim in Harrisburg on April 15, 1861, as the Harrisburg Rifles. On June 1, they were redesignated the First City Zouaves and adopted a uniform described as "similar in style to that of the New York Fire Zouaves," which consisted of "a State regulation cap with red cord around the top and brass frontispiece containing the letter Z, blue jackets trimmed with yellow, red shirt with blue stripe in the centre, bluish gray pants, white leggins, red sash, [&] regulation belt with brass plate marked U.S."[44] This company enlisted for nine months in August 1862 as Co. A, 127th Pennsylvania.

The Ellsworth Zouaves began recruiting in York County, Pennsylvania, on May 10, 1861, and enlisted for three years as Co. B, 50th Pennsylvania. Named for Elmer Ellsworth—the martyred commander of the

Photographed at Lancaster, Pennsylvania, this Zouave of an unidentified company wears a rarely seen stocking cap, rather than the more usual fez worn by Zouave units. He proudly holds a Model 1817 common rifle converted to percussion. *Carte de visite, Michael J. McAfee collection*

Recruited in Erie, Crawford, and Warren Counties, Pennsylvania, the Erie Regiment was provided by their local women with semi-Zouave uniforms of light-blue flannel that quickly wore out during their three months' service. The yellow shirt that accompanied the uniform appears very dark on this enlisted man. Note the letters "ER" in the wreath on his cap front. His belt is fastened with an 1851-pattern enlisted "eagle" plate. *Sixth-plate ambrotype, Daniel J. Miller collection*

11th New York Volunteers (1st New York Fire Zouaves) who was shot dead after pulling down a Confederate flag in Alexandria, Virginia, on May 24, 1861—the Ellsworth Zouaves at first acquired a suit of "blue worsted goods" described as "close fitting."[45] Toward the end of June 1861, they obtained a new uniform consisting of "a suit of blue army cloth tastefully trimmed with scarlet cloth, after the style of those worn by the Solferino Zouaves, in the Crimean War."[46] According to photographic evidence, this consisted of a full Zouave uniform similar to that worn by the 5th New York, or Duryee's Zouaves.

Organized at Gettysburg during April/May 1861, the Gettysburg Zouaves wore a "Grey uniform, neatly trimmed with black" when they paraded later in the year. On the basis of photographic evidence, this also included chasseur-style caps and white canvas gaiters. On the same occasion, the Scott Zouaves, of Abbottstown, had "red pants, white stripe, and neat grey roundabout," and the Fairfield Zouaves wore a "red roundabout-dark pants" that were "Regular uniform grey-Zouave style."[47]

The Erie Regiment—also known as McLane's Regiment after its commander, Col. John W. McLane—acquired hastily made semi-Zouave uniforms at the start of its three-months' service. Organized within four days at Camp Wayne, in the eastern part of Erie, this regiment left for Pittsburgh on April 29, being the first to reach Camp Wilkins, established on the fairground near that city as the rendezvous for volunteers from the western part of the state. Made by local women before their departure from home, their uniforms were made from blue flannel cloth acquired from the tailoring establishment of John Gensheimer of Erie. A member of the regiment stated at the time, "It was determined that the regiment should be uniformed in some shape before leaving for the scene of action. The needle and the sewing machine were kept busy night and day, and before the day of our departure nearly all the companies were clad in a handsome uniform consisting of a blue jacket and pants and a shirt of yellow flannel. This suit was a sort of compromise between the Zouave and the regular uniform, and, though not durable, it was one of the most singular and picturesque that we have seen during the war."[48] These uniforms did not stand the test of time. On July 2, 1861, the *Pennsylvania Daily Telegraph* reported, "The Erie regiment which has been in camp at Pittsburgh for some time, disbanded the other day, and most of the men went home ragged and barefooted. The regiment is to be reorganized immediately, and put into service for three years, or the war," as the 83rd Pennsylvania Infantry, which was one of several regiments to receive a French-style chasseur uniform (see below).[49]

Vivandières were present in several other Pennsylvania commands besides the Philadelphia Zouave Corps. As they marched into camp at Suffolk Park on May 25, the 21st Pennsylvania, or German Rifle Regiment, was accompanied by several *vivandières* who, according to the *Inquirer*, wore "short tri-colored skirts" and "quaint, turned up beavers upon their heads." Of the same occasion *The Press* added, "Both were dressed alike, in short skirts, in 'Child of the Regiment' style. Their dresses were red, white, and blue, and they wore semi military beavers on their heads."[50] This regiment subsequently joined Maj. Gen. Robert Patterson's command operating on the upper Potomac.[51] When the 27th Pennsylvania arrived at Washington, DC, it was accompanied by five *vivandières* dressed in "short blue skirts, red bodice, and walking hats."[52]

As a makeshift uniform, Garibaldian-style red shirts were also popular among Pennsylvania volunteers. Formed by the Hydraulian Fire Company of Pottsville, in Schuylkill County, the Union Guards (Co. I), 16th Pennsylvania, made "a splendid appearance in their Garibaldi uniforms of Red shirts and Blue pants" when they left for Harrisburg on April 24, 1861.[53] During the following month, Co. B of the Home Guards, recruited at Altoona, Pennsylvania, chose as their uniform a "black glazed Zouave cap, red shirt with blue collar, and black pants."[54] Also of Altoona, the Logan Rifle Rangers adopted an undress uniform during the summer of 1860 that the local press reported as consisting of "light oil cloth caps instead of their heavy dress parade caps, and red shirts instead of their dress frock coats."[55] Attracting much attention when they arrived in Harrisburg on April 29, 1861, the Wyoming Artillerists, of Luzerne County, wore "red shirts, cap and gray pantaloons, with dark stripe."[56]

The Kane Rifles, consisting of 350 "rugged backwoodsmen" from northwestern Pennsylvania, commanded by Col. Thomas L. Kane, arrived in Harrisburg on May 2, 1861, clad in "red shirts trimmed with white and blue." Actually composed of the McKean County Rifles, Elk County Rifles, and Cameron County Rifles, these volunteers were also distinguished by a deer tail attached to their hats and caps. According to their regimental history, an enlisted man of the McKean County Rifles noticed a deer's hide hanging outside a butcher shop opposite the court house at Smethport, where Kane had his headquarters. Crossing the street, he pulled out a knife, cut off the tail, and stuck it in his cap. Upon the man's return to headquarters, Kane noticed the appendage on his headgear and announced that the force he was recruiting should be known as "Bucktails."[57]

An account of the arrival of this unit at Camp Curtin described their hats and caps as being "each surmounted with a fox tail [*sic*], emblematic of their back woods home. They bore in the ranks an immense pair of buck-horns, which attracted much attention, and elicited numerous cheers. Each of the men brought with them their own rifles, with whose use they are familiar, and with which, if the service permitted, they could do terrible execution against an enemy."[58] On June 18, 1861, the Kane Rifles would form the nucleus of the 13th Reserves, which were also variously designated the 42nd Pennsylvania, the 1st Pennsylvania Rifles, or simply the "Bucktails" (see below).

Enlisting as Co. D, 42nd Pennsylvania (13th Reserves), the Raftsmen's Guards of Curwensville, in Warren County, Pennsylvania, wore "a handsome blue uniform" when they descended the Allegheny River to Pittsburgh in "large skiffs, rowed by six men each," on May 24, 1861.[59] After their arrival at Camp Curtin, Cpl. H. J. Ramsdell Jr., of Tioga Invincibles (Co. H), 5th Reserves, observed that the Raftsmen's Guards' "suits are uniform, cap, shirt, belt and pants, and were furnished by their commissioned officers."[60] Mustered-in as Co. K of the same regiment, each man in the Raftsmen's Rangers was presented with "a good flannel military shirt" on their way to Harrisburg.[61]

A company of Philadelphia Scots raised a "Scotch Rifle Company" that eventually enlisted as Co. K, 28th Pennsylvania. It has not been confirmed whether or not they ever donned "the Macgregor plaid and Glengarry bonnet" they proposed to wear toward the end of May 1861.[62]

To prepare their troops for war service, the commonwealth set about clothing its volunteers. With the reorganization of the Pennsylvania State Military Establishment on April 12, 1861, Reuben C. Hale was appointed quartermaster general with the rank of major, and his office was established in "the east room of the Farmers' and Merchants' Bank Building."[63] Challenged with the task of finding uniforms for the flood of volunteers enlisting for three months' service, Hale had done nothing by April 20 other than to requisition the federal government for clothing stored at the nearby Schuylkill Arsenal, only to be informed that "the state would be required to furnish its own uniforms."[64] As a result, Governor Andrew G. Curtin sent state agent Robert L. Martin with Capt. George Gibson, formerly of the US arsenal, to Philadelphia to provide "at once for uniforms for ten thousand Pennsylvania troops." By April 23, Martin had established a "uniform manufactory" at the Girard House, a recently vacated hotel off Market Street in that city.[65] From this establishment, each volunteer was to receive "One cap, one overcoat, one

The uniforms worn by these enlisted men of the City Guard, of Pittsburgh, who enlisted as Co. K, 12th Pennsylvania Infantry, are examples of the shoddy clothing worn by the three-month volunteers in April/May 1861. Standing at far right, private Samuel B. M. Young would return to service as a commissioned captain of the 4th Pennsylvania Cavalry and rose to the rank of brigadier general of volunteers by 1865. After the war, he became first president of the Army War College at Carlisle and first chief of staff of the US Army. *S. B. M. Young collection, USAHEC*

pair shoes, one blue army blouse, one pair pants, two merino shirts, two pair canton flannel drawers, two pair woollen stockings."[66]

Within four days, about 23,000 garments had been produced by thirty cutters and 525 females employed in sewing at the Girard House factory, with the help of several thousand at home workers. Overseeing the work was Philadelphia tailor Samuel S. Kelly.

A reporter from *The Press* visiting that establishment observed:

> Several hundred suits of clothing have been finished at the Girard House. One thousand pairs of drawers were laid out in the dining-room yesterday, with almost as many coats. The old billiard room is tenanted by thirty cutters, and all the sitting and sleeping chambers are filled with sewing ladies. Fair hands and plump feet guide the sewing machines, and some faces that have graced the drawing-rooms of wealth and fashion moved down the aisles with hands laden with soldier clothes. Strict order is enforced through the house; all work is done expeditiously, quietly, and carefully, and communications are made in the most laconic terms and answered correspondingly.[67]

By April 30, 1861, the *Inquirer* stated, "Most of the volunteers who are about starting South have been furnished with the new regulation garments . . . and they were seen in every direction in the streets." By the end of the month, the same journal commented, "The State order for 10,000 suits of clothing, is rapidly approaching completion. . . . Some of the garments are entirely finished, and most of the hands are now busy on sack coats and overcoats."[68] The *Inquirer* further commented that the uniforms being made were "neat, serviceable, becoming, and exceedingly comfortable. Blue sack coats loose and easy to the form; blue pantaloons cut large and freer grey flannel shirts, open at the neck, and fatigue caps," which contrasted "favorably with the tight padded coats, leather stocks and hats, shakos, &c., of other times."[69] On May 10, the *Inquirer* reported, "At the State establishment in the Girard House, the order for 10,000 suits of clothes, equipments, &c, is about being closed." A few days later work ceased, since nearly the whole of the requisition had been completed.[70]

Regarding the provision of uniforms for the remaining 15,000 Pennsylvania volunteers gathering at other military encampments throughout the state, the quartermaster general's office at Harrisburg next adopted the contract system and advertised on May 1, 1861, for "15,000 Great Coats. 15,000 Army Blouses, Indigo Blue or Cadet Grey. 15,000 Pairs Trousers. 15,000 Undress Caps. 30,000 Flannel or Knit Woolen Shirts. 30,000 Pairs Canton Flannel Drawers. 30,000 Pairs Woolen Stockings. 15,000 Pairs Bootees," all of which had to be "army pattern, and conform strictly to the regulation of the United States army, in quality of material and finish."[71] By May 21, 1861, contracts had been issued for "Overcoats, Blouses and Pantaloons" to clothiers and hatters in Philadelphia. Firms such as Rockhill & Wilson and Charles Harkness made overcoats and pants. Straus & Goldman also produced blouses. Caps were made by Sullender & Pascall, Bartalott & Blynn, and Charles Hallowell.[72] Two days later, further contracts were advertised for "12,000 Pairs brown linen trousers, undress," plus same numbers of army blankets, metallic letters and numbers, and 500 sergeant's sashes.[73]

Meanwhile, thousands of Pennsylvania volunteers had yet to be uniformed.

On departure from Philadelphia for Washington, DC, on April 30, 1861, a civilian observed hundreds of men in "a large tent . . . in very poor conditions with scarcely clothing, some without shoes, some without shirts . . . they had left home in haste and had not mustered into the Service."[74] The 5th Pennsylvania arrived at Washington in citizen's clothing on April 27 and were described in the *Evening Star* as "real flat-footed raw militia, having no uniforms, but all equipped with Government equipments."[75] Having been promised their "outfit" at Harrisburg, this regiment sent a special messenger to Philadelphia six days later to "hurry them up." As a result of the lack of uniforms, these volunteers were compelled "to keep themselves cooped up in their quarters all day long," because they were "ashamed to parade the streets with their 'old clothes' on," while the other regiments were "luxuriating in grand dress parades on Pennsylvania avenue and quiet strolls" around the "beautiful city."[76] When the 6th Pennsylvania passed through Philadelphia from Schuylkill County on April 28, 1861, *The Press* reported, "Few of the soldiers

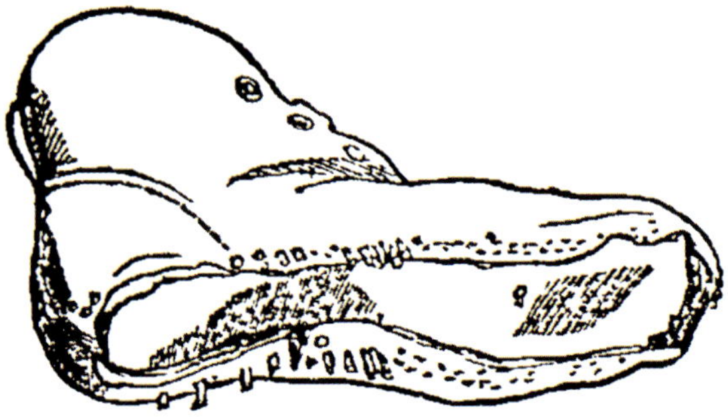

Titled "Pair of Pantaloons after Four Days' Wear at Camp Scott" and "A White-Pine Sole Army Shoe, after Three Days' Wear," these engravings were published in the *Philadelphia Inquirer* on May 21, 1861, to expose the "barefaced robbery" of the military suppliers providing clothing and footwear for the troops at Camp Scott, near York, Pennsylvania. They were possibly originally published in the *National Guard*, a camp newspaper published by the 19th Pennsylvania (three months), the ranks of which contained not only "printers and literary men, but skilled designers and engravers." *Author's collection*

wore full uniforms. Some had checked shirts, and some flannel shirts; others no shirts, but only a jacket buttoned to the throat to hide their nakedness."[77]

Observing future elements of the 13th Reserves, one man wrote from Camp Curtin, at Harrisburg, regarding the lack of uniforms, "Quite a number of them flourish bucktail plumes." Seeing "German rifle companies" at the same encampment, another man wrote that "in nine cases out of ten their uniforms are the color of boiled spinach, and how I wish you could only see the stunning hats some of them wear."[78] Elsewhere, a letter dated May 6, written from Camp Wayne, near West Chester, stated, "But few of the troops are uniformed. The State has furnished a rifle or musket for each soldier but their clothing has not yet been furnished. Nor have they cartridge boxes, belts, or ammunition. Each man carries a coarse blanket, a tin cup, and a haversack, provided by the authorities. The haversack is more properly a 'satchel' made of canvas. . . . They all expect their uniforms in a few days, together with a supply of ammunition."[79] Two days later, a "Volunteer" at Camp Scott reported, "Some of the men's clothes, citizen's dress, are fast wearing out, and no indication of them being supplied with a uniform, although it has been promised to them frequently by some of the officers."[80]

At the federal capital, the 5th Pennsylvania finally received "a complete outfit of clothing" from Philadelphia on May 7, 1861, which was quickly found to be unsatisfactory. Eight days later, a member of the Minersville Artillerists (Co. E) wrote that they would be "fit objects to be placed in corn fields as scare-crows . . . on the morning after the uniforms were distributed, several men of the Regiment went out in rear of our quarters to see a company of regulars [of the 3rd Artillery] drilling at their guns; after their dismissal from drill they commenced teasing our men, calling them Hostlers, Horse Jockeys, Boot Blacks &c. . . . Our men cannot pass through the streets but what they are hooted at by the boys, and the troops of other states."[81]

The volunteers at Camp Slifer, near Chambersburg, were in receipt of some of the inferior contract clothing by May 9, 1861; the *Philadelphia Inquirer* reported that all the companies composing the 7th, 8th, and 10th Pennsylvania had received their "blouse, pants and grey shirts" but had not as yet been provided with "undershirts and socks, or, with the exception of one company, with overcoats." On May 28, musician Henry H. Fortney of the Burns Infantry (Co. I), 7th Pennsylvania, wrote, "We received, yesterday, our overcoats, a very fine article, much better than any other clothing we have yet received."[82] Following Patterson's advance into Virginia on July 1, 1861, the 10th Pennsylvania, as part of the 3rd Brigade, Second Division, eventually received replacement uniforms. According to Bates's short history of this regiment, "During the night, a small train of wagons arrived from Hagerstown, with clothing for the Tenth regiment, which was greatly needed, the uniforms of many of the men being badly tattered. They were sometimes taunted by the well-dressed soldiers for their shabby appearance; but beneath their rags they carried hearts as stout and brave as any who kept step to the music of the Union."[83]

The 2nd Pennsylvania—one of the regiments at Camp Scott—received their uniforms by May 14, 1861, which according to a letter published in the *Columbia Spy* consisted of a "blue blouse (coarse in material and make), gray trousers, blue cap and gray overcoat." A member of the Shawnee Guards (Co. F) of this regiment, the letter writer continued:

> We are also furnished with brogans, undershirts, drawers, socks and blankets. By some mysterious dispensation the uniforms falling to the share of our company all appear to be cut to two sizes and the shoes made over two lasts—they either fit John Zell or Sergeant [John] Peart. Of caps we have secured the same judicious and convenient variety. Quartermaster [J. J.] Gault rejoiced in a head covering capacious enough to accommodate his head and beard to the neck, with a couple of inches of room all around. On last Saturday he paid a visit to Columbia in the rain. When he returned to camp his cap was a rather tight fit. Our 'awkward squad' met and debated the question: 'Did the Quartermaster's cap shrink, or did the Quartermaster's head swell!' We have received our belts, cartridge boxes and canteens, but no knapsacks. We only await these to be ready to move, completely equipped and ready for work.[84]

Correspondence from a member of the Independent Blues (Co. E), 2nd Pennsylvania, also confirmed receipt of ill-fitting clothing, stating, "I am just trying on my pants. Oh what a fit!—I must have sixteen inches, more or less, taken off below, and five or six inches around the 'bread-basket.' A word in regard to our shoes, if we are allowed to call them such. My usual No. is 6, but I got No. 10. Of course that leaves enough leather to set up a small tannery." By May 20, the Independent Blues were also in receipt of flannel shirts "trimmed with black," which were "intended to be worn as a uniform," courtesy of the ladies of Gettysburg.[85] The whole of the 2nd Pennsylvania received replacement pants on June 22, 1861, which occasioned a member of the Blues to write, "Today Uncle Samuel presented our Regiment with a new pair of so-called trowsers for each man. The only difference between these and the first is, that these are 'heaven's blue and indigo dye,' whilst the others are a sort of grey. I have employed a tailor to operate on mine, who is trying to reduce them to proper shape."[86] Writing about "the miserable army clothing" during the same period, a volunteer in the Bellafonte Fencibles (Co. H), 2nd Pennsylvania, stated, "Fortunately for us, we secured a good quality of heavy shoes; these, with the red flannel shirts so kindly sent us by the ladies at home, comprise the only serviceable and comfortable article of clothing which the men have; many of the pantaloons and blouses are already worn through and bid fair to be ready to be replaced by new ones before the end of the month."[87]

Complaints about the poor quality of the received uniform clothing became more widespread. At Washington, a member of the 1st Rhode Island, encamped nearby, observed on May 12, 1861, "One of the Pennsylvania regiments received their uniforms this week. They make considerable complaint about them, and from the appearance of those I have seen on the street they are hardly what was necessary."[88] In a letter dated May 18, a man in the 5th Pennsylvania wrote, "Many of the coats and pants rip after a few days wear. They were all made in Philadelphia, and as the whole contract appears to have been given to that end of the State, I am surprised the makers did not become expert in sewing, after so much experience."[89] Two days later, an unknown officer in the same regiment complained, "The overcoats which reached here yesterday for the Fifth, were of nine different colors and shades of color. Col. [R. P.] McDowell very properly refused to receive them. They are made up of remnants of cloth. His men walking guard these damp chill nights, need good overcoats, but they are without them."[90] Unusually, the 11th Pennsylvania at Camp Curtin received "blue roundabouts, or jockeys," with their "gray pants, blue cap, and dyed blue overcoats." The latter was considered "of very inferior manufacture and quality… more cotton than anything else," and subject to fading by "rain or the rays of the sun."[91]

At Camp Scott, a soldier wrote on May 13, "This morning we received the first installment of our equipment in the shape of shoes and pantaloons; the latter we very much need, as those we brought from Pittsburgh were not half made and now more than half worn out, and containing to each pair enough grease to make a kettle of soap. When our other fixings will be handed over, it is impossible to say."[92] Writing from the same place, an enlisted man of the 12th Pennsylvania reported on May 25, 1861:

> Of the clothing furnished us lately . . . Our blouses are of every shade, dark and light blue, dark and light gray—they are the only serviceable articles of clothing we have received, and they are dear at a dollar and a half. I would not give a farmer's 'wamus' for two of them." Regarding the pants, the informant stated they "gave way the first time I stooped, the waist or body band going up with the suspenders, the seat and legs dropping down.[93]

Visiting the Quartermaster's Department of the brigade commanded by Brig. Gen. George C. Wynkoop at Camp Scott, William White Harding, editor of the *Philadelphia Inquirer*, stated, "I was shown a pile of pantaloons (eighty-five pairs), some of which had been worn eight or ten days, others three or four, some one day, and some only two hours, and others, still, which had only been brief on, and yet there was not a single one of these pairs that was not wholly worthless. In a word, the material was so rotten that the slightest tension would tear it." Footwear was equally as poorly made, with soles made from "pine sharings"; the heels were reported to have fallen off "one hour from the time they were first put on the men's feet."[94]

Some inferior headgear also appears to have been produced, since on May 30, 1861, the *Philadelphia Inquirer* published advice from a "merchant of Baltimore City" stating:

> the caps furnished the soldiers of the First Regiment of Infantry was scarcely a hue of their original color. The blue has entirely deserted them, and they now have the foxy red appearance which common blue cloth colored with logwood assumes after a few days exposure to wind and rain. These caps cost a fair round price. The same gentleman stated that to him it appeared that the only article of clothing worn by that regiment, which appeared to be fit for a soldier's use, were the shirts. These, you will remember, were, generally speaking, either furnished by the soldiers themselves, or their friends.[95]

It was not until toward the end of May 1861 that the poor state of clothing being issued to some

Pvt. Frederick Klinefelter enlisted for three months in the York Voltigeurs (Co. H), 16th Pennsylvania Infantry, in April 1861, while a senior undergraduate at Pennsylvania College in Gettysburg. In 1863, he was commissioned as a captain of Co. A, 26th Pennsylvania Emergency Militia Regiment. Photographed during his three months' service in 1861, he wears a state-issue uniform consisting of a fatigue sack coat and light-blue kersey trousers. His fatigue cap has the company letter "H" attached, and his overcoat is a variation of the federal contract pattern, since it has two additional small buttons on the collar. His cartridge box strap and waist belt are unusual, in that they appear to have been made of woven cloth, which may be indicative of a shortage of leather for Pennsylvania three-month volunteers in 1861. *Sixth-plate tintype, Paul Russinoff collection*

This unidentified Pennsylvanian volunteer was photographed in Philadelphia in 1861 and wears an unusual uniform consisting of a fatigue sack coat with six-button front and dark-colored pants with a narrow seam stripe. He holds a fatigue cap with a brass company letter "A" attached to its top. *Author's collection*

Pennsylvania troops came to the attention of Gov. Curtin, who immediately dispatched Benjamin Haywood and Jacob Fry Jr. to Washington to investigate the condition of the Pennsylvania regiments there. Col. R. Biddle Roberts, aid to Gov. Curtin, arrived around the same time. By May 28, Haywood and Fry reported that the 25th Pennsylvania, quartered at the arsenal, were "not badly off, having United States uniforms." However, the 4th and 5th Pennsylvania were found to be "suffering greatly." According to a letter from Pvt. J. F. Holahan of the Eagle Guards (Co. H), 4th Pennsylvania, his company had by May 11, 1861, received "grey pants, Kentucky Jean blouse, clumsy shoes, the whole surmounted by a blue cap."[96] A further account published in the *Philadelphia Inquirer* several weeks later advised that these regiments had blouses and pants of "all colors, and made of damaged goods of inferior quality, mostly of 'shoddy' and some of 'Kentucky jean.'" Their blankets were "of the quality of ice blankets, not fit for horses." Their shoes were "of wretched material," and many men were "almost barefoot."[97]

Visiting the camp of the Pennsylvania volunteers in Baltimore on June 10, 1861, an *Inquirer* correspondent noted that many wore "heavy cloth overcoats, closely buttoned, in the warmest days, in order to hide gaping rents in their other garments."[98] Observing the 19th Pennsylvania nine days later, he stated, "Quite a number of facetious fellows belonging to the different companies, by way of practically demonstrating the swindle practiced upon them, had immense red patches conspicuously displayed on portions of their garments. When drawn up in line these scarlet appendages looked remarkably funny, and told more forcibly than language how shamefully those exhibiting them had been cheated." This report added that a supply of new uniforms had just "come to hand for this regiment."[99]

During their investigations, Haywood and Fry established that a contract had been issued by Charles M. "Bucky" Neal—a Philadelphia lawyer and "Special Agent" of Gov. Curtin—to a group of Pittsburgh businessmen called Frowenfeld & Morganstern for $22,385 worth of uniforms to be made from cloth purchased from Slade & Lee, of Philadelphia.[100] As a result, Frowenfeld and Morganstern, plus Neal, were indicted for fraud in furnishing inferior clothing to the commonwealth on June 16, 1861.[101] Preliminary proceedings were held on July 2, and the case against them finally came before criminal court in Pittsburgh on April 2, 1862, on which occasion Morganstern & Brothers and A. & A. Frowenfeld were "ready and anxious to have their case disposed of." Because Emanuel and Maurice Frowenfeld, plus "Bucky" Neal, were absent and "supposed to be in Europe," Judge Thomas Mellon stated that "the parties who had fled to avoid a trial should be presumed dishonest." Morganstern & Brothers and A. & A. Frowenfeld were acquitted, both parties being adjudged to have "borne up manfully under a tremendous pressure of public opinion."[102]

Meanwhile, by May 23, 1861, the quartermaster general's office at Harrisburg had issued further contracts to reclothe the Pennsylvania three-month volunteers. E. A. Green and Straus and Goldman were to supply "Indigo blue flannel blouses." G. W.

Colladay & Co., Johnson & Co., and Wilson & Co. were to produce "Blue Army Cloth Trousers," while "Blue Cloth Caps, Army Regulation" were to be made by Bartalott & Blynn, Sullender & Pascall, and C. Hallowell. "Light Blue Army Cloth Overcoats" were to be produced by John Cummings and Thomas Webster Jr.[103] As a result of "Special Order, No. 1," issued four days later, Quartermaster General Hale issued clothing "as per requisition dated 23d May last" to the 4th and 5th Pennsylvania, since they were "in actual service and in great need of proper clothing."[104] Better uniforms must have been received by mid-June, since on the fifteenth of that month, the 5th Pennsylvania was inspected at Alexandria, Virginia, and the *Philadelphia Inquirer* reported on "the changed appearance of the Pennsylvania Fifth," stating it was difficult to believe they were "the same men who were formerly designated as the 'Ragged Fifth.'"[105] On June 16, a member of the Eagle Guards (J. F. H.) (Co. H), 4th Pennsylvania, encamped outside Washington, DC, wrote, "The old 'uniforms' furnished us by the State in the first instance have been replaced by others of a substantial nature, together with cartouche-boxes, knapsacks, provision sacks, canteens, &c."[106]

Recruited for three years' service during early June 1861, the 28th Pennsylvania was originally uniformed in gray and armed with the Enfield rifle musket complete with saber bayonet, all of which was paid for by its commander, Col. John W. Geary, who was ex-mayor of San Francisco and ex-governor of Kansas Territory. Because he holds the correct long arm, this gray-clad volunteer is tentatively identified as an enlisted man of the 28th regiment. *Carte de visite, Michael J. McAfee collection*

Having enlisted in the Scott Rifles at Duncansville, Blair County, Pennsylvania, Private Christian Malone poses for the camera in gray jacket and trousers. Commanded by Capt. Thomas Holland, the Scott Rifles were mustered-in as Co. H, 14th Pennsylvania (three months) on April 24, 1861. Malone proudly holds a Model 1861 rifle musket. *Carte de visite, Michael J. McAfee collection*

This detail from a *carte de visite* in the "Illustrations of Camp Life" series produced by Matthew Brady's studio at Washington, DC, shows enlisted men of the Quaker City Guards (Co. B), 4th Reserves (33rd Pennsylvania Volunteers). Recruited throughout Philadelphia County, they wear the plain light-blue jacket and pants referred to as "full dress" received by the Pennsylvania Reserve Corps during July 1861. Note the waist belt loop on the jacket worn by the man second from left. He and several others also wear canvas leggings. *Carte de visite detail, Michael J. McAfee collection*

The president issued his first call for three-year volunteers on May 3, 1861, and required 42,034 men, amounting to forty regiments. Although the allotted share for Pennsylvania was ten regiments, the Keystone State had already exceeded this, and the general government was reluctant to accept any more. Nonetheless, four additional Pennsylvania regiments were accepted during this period. Originally known as the "Jackson Regiment," the 29th Pennsylvania, commanded by Col. John K. Murphy, was uniformed in "grey pants, trimmed with black, grey jackets, and the regular volunteer cap, made of the same material."[107] Besides being issued "the regular United States blue uniform," the 28th Pennsylvania also received "a service dress of grey," including "a nine-button jacket, or roundabout," and every man was presented with "a havelock, a gift of the ladies of Philadelphia."[108] Known as the Washington Brigade, both the 26th and 27th Pennsylvania were referred to as being "blue-bloused and gray-shirted" before departure from the city.[109]

Determined to utilize its remaining undesignated volunteers, Pennsylvania decided to act on its own and raised a new state force called the "Reserve Volunteer Corps of the Commonwealth," or, more commonly, the "Pennsylvania Reserve Corps." Constituted on May 15, 1861, this consisted of thirteen regiments of infantry, one of cavalry, and one of artillery, with an aggregate of 15,856 officers and men. The law creating the Reserve Corps stipulated that it would be subject at all times to a call by the general government, and this came during the alarm following the Union disaster at Bull Run on July 21, 1861. All fifteen regiments were mustered in for three years and passed out of state control, being given a general state, as well as reserve designation. Hence, the 1st Reserves became the 30th Pennsylvania Volunteers through 13th Reserves, which were designated 42nd Pennsylvania.

Visiting Camp Wayne, at West Chester, Pennsylvania, on June 7, 1861, a correspondent of the *Philadelphia Inquirer* noted that several of the companies soon to be mustered in as part of the 1st Reserves (30th Pennsylvania) had arrived already

Another Brady image from the "Illustrations of Camp Life" series, this cabinet card shows two more volunteers of the 4th Reserves (33rd Pennsylvania Volunteers) wearing "full dress" composed of plain light-blue jacket and pants. They also wear white cotton dress gloves and are armed with Model 1842 smoothbore muskets. The man at right wears knee-high canvas gaiters, which appear to have been part of the dress uniform. *Cabinet card, Michael J. McAfee collection*

uniformed. The Carlisle Light Infantry (Co. H) wore "United States uniforms . . . bought by private subscription." The Brandywine Guards (Co. A) wore "a new uniform of blue cloth" acquired by the same means. The Phoenix Artillery (Co. G) also had "the regular service uniform," while the other companies awaited their outfit.[110] The Adams Infantry (Co. K), from Gettysburg, had received "havelocks and drilling jackets," courtesy of "the ladies of Adams county."[111] According to a company history, the 1st Reserves was partly uniformed on July 1, 1861, with "white duck pants and flannel shirts, furnished by the state, and a fancy grey Jacket, sent from home while Caps and Overcoats, were issued by the government; arms and accoutrements were also distributed." A newspaper report confirmed that this clothing was distributed among the troops at Camp Wayne on July 2.[112]

The 2nd through 4th Reserves (31st through 33rd Pennsylvania) were assembled at Camp Washington, on the fairgrounds at Easton, Pennsylvania, from where a volunteer in the 2nd Reserves reported on June 23, "As yet we are devoid of uniforms. . . . Should this continue much longer, most of the clothing of the poor fellows will become tattered and torn." At Camp Curtin, Harrisburg, a member of the Cookman Rangers (Co. K), 5th Reserves (34th Pennsylvania), wrote six days later, "Our boys look ragged; many of them are not fit to be seen out of camp. We do not know when they will get their pants from the State." Most of the troops at Camp Washington received some "new clothing" consisting of a pair of "good linen or duck pantaloons" on July 2, 1861.[113] The 5th Reserves were in receipt of their new uniforms by July 4, 1861, while at Camp Mason and Dixon in Pennsylvania, a few miles from the Maryland state line. A letter from the Cookman Rangers (Co. K) stated:

> These consist of two suits, one—full dress —of light blue army cloth and trousers—we will receive the jacket in a day or so—the other is a blue blouse similar to those worn by the three month men, but of better material, and a pair of first rate brown duck trowsers. This clothing is all of good quality, and in marked contrast to the shoddy rags put off on the first organized regiments now in active service. Of course there is the usual difficulty as to fit, most of the trousers being calculated for Tom Wilson's mode of wearing them – with a drawing-string round the neck, and pocket holes for the arms.[114]

The 1st Reserves had also received "two suits of clothes" by July 12, 1861.[115] The 7th Reserves (36th Pennsylvania) had received their "new summer uniform" by the same date.[116] Leaving Camp Curtin on July 12, the 6th Reserves (35th Pennsylvania) had received "overcoats, blouses, dress and fatigue pants, forage caps, shoes and stockings – all of the army pattern."[117] According to Pvt. Charles B. Brockway of the Iron Guards (Co. A) of this regiment, the overcoats were of "light blue cloth" and cost about $15 each.[118]

The mustering-in of the Reserve Corps was followed by a steady demand for more troops for three years' service, and by the end of 1861 the total number of three-month and three-year infantry regiments raised in Pennsylvania amounted to 108,

This unidentified corporal of the 23rd Pennsylvania Volunteers, or Birney's Zouaves, wears an example of the "dark blue army cloth" Zouave uniform ordered from Rockhill & Wilson by the Schuylkill Arsenal during fall 1861. Although originally intended to be similar to that of the Gymnast Zouaves, the uniform of Birney's Zouaves was more elaborately trimmed, including "trefoils" on the jacket front and triple seam stripes on chasseur-pattern trousers, while headgear consisted of a red fez, rather than a dark-blue cap. This corporal also wears a plain shirt underneath his dark-blue vest and has a Bowie knife with horn grip, plus a Colt Pocket revolver tucked into his waist belt. *Carte de visite–size tintype, Daniel J. Miller collection*

Made from dark-blue wool ornamented with loosely woven red yarn, this jacket and vest was worn in 1861 by a first sergeant of the 23rd Pennsylvania Volunteers, also known as Birney's Zouaves, after the regimental commander, Col. David Bell Birney. *West Point Museum, acc. no. 10,259*

while thirteen cavalry regiments and two artillery regiments had been formed, plus various reserve and home guard regiments. Many of these units wore a variety of uniforms.

The Gymnast Zouaves Battalion, 4th Regiment, Philadelphia Home Guards, enlisted in the 23rd Pennsylvania Volunteers—also known as Birney's Zouaves—during August, becoming Companies B and K of that regiment. At that time Quartermaster Gen. Meigs issued a special order authorizing Col. David Bell Birney to uniform his regiment in "the peculiar uniform of the Gymnast Zouaves," which was contracted by the Schuylkill Arsenal to Rockhill & Wilson of Philadelphia.[119] In September, recruits were promised "a good suit of dark-blue army cloth Zouave uniform" that was more elaborately trimmed than that of the Gymnast Zouaves.[120] This began to wear out after six months and was replaced by federal-issue dress and undress clothing. According to the regimental history, this was "very trying to the men of the Twenty-third regiment," since the cost of all three uniforms was deducted "from the accounts of those who had overdrawn their clothing allowance."[121] The 23rd Pennsylvania was expanded to 1,500 men during September 1861 with additional companies, including the United States Zouave Cadets, of Pittsburgh, under Capt. George W. Tanner, which became Co. M.[122] These extra companies were reassigned in February 1862, although Co. M was disbanded and distributed among the other ten companies.[123]

Originally known as the Second Regiment, Scott Legion, and designated the 33rd Pennsylvania, the regiment commanded by Mexican War veteran Samuel W. Black was redesignated the 62nd Pennsylvania by November 1861, after the 4th Reserves took precedence as the 33rd Regiment. In early August 1861, Black requested the same style of uniform as supplied to the first Scott Legion. The army contracted with the firm of George W. Colladay in Philadelphia, and by August 31, 1861, an initial delivery of 247 pairs of sky-blue trousers and 449 sky-blue jackets were

Commanded by Capt. John J. Carberry, the Jackson Zouaves were recruited in Philadelphia and enlisted as Co. I, 32nd Pennsylvania Volunteers—also known as the Lincoln Legion—during December 1861. This regiment was redesignated the 99th Pennsylvania and in 1862 garrisoned the chain of forts forming the southern defenses of the federal capital, with the Jackson Zouaves manning Fort Ricketts. This unidentified enlisted man wears the elaborately trimmed dark-blue jacket with looped yellow braid that distinguished his company. *Sixth-plate ambrotype, Daniel J. Miller collection*

received. According to Maj. Jacob B. Sweitzer, the 33rd Pennsylvania received its uniforms on September 3, 1861, which consisted of "a pair of sky-blue pantaloons and a neat roundabout or jacket of the same color and material, and a dark blue cap besides a good serviceable overcoat, shoes, underclothing etc. Companies L [Chambers Zouaves] and M wore a dark blue blouse which distinguished them from the others as the flanking companies or skirmishers for the regiment."[124] As one of five best-drilled regiments in the division of Gen. Fitz-John Porter, Army of the Potomac, the 62nd Pennsylvania received French chasseur uniforms in place of their sky-blue dress during January 1862 (see below).

Several other Pennsylvania regiments recruited during July 1861 received gray uniforms. Known as the "Chippewa Guards Regiment," the 81st Pennsylvania was uniformed in "cadet grey cloth, trimmed with black." The 99th Pennsylvania, or "Keystone Regiment," received "two suits of clothing, one of heavy material, and the other of light stuff suitable for extreme warm weather." This was also made of "cadet grey, trimmed with a black stripe on the outer seams of the pants; jacket with belt supporters, and shoulder straps trimmed with the same color."[125]

Four three-year Pennsylvania regiments were created from the California Brigade, organized for three years' service by Edward D. Baker, a former resident of California and US senator from Oregon. Initially recruited as the "California Regiment" in Philadelphia and New York City during April/May 1861, this unit was expanded into a brigade consisting of the 2nd through 5th California during October 1861. However, the recruitment of these regiments in Philadelphia prompted Gov. Curtin to complain that Baker was hindering Pennsylvania's efforts to complete her quota of volunteers. As a result, Baker's brigade was officially designated as Pennsylvania Volunteers, becoming the 71st, 69th, 72nd, and 106th Pennsylvania. Following Baker's death at Ball's Bluff, Virginia, on October 21, 1861, these regiments permanently shed their "California" association and became known as the "Philadelphia Brigade," being the only organization of its kind to be recruited in a single city of the North.[126]

The 71st Pennsylvania was organized mainly from the original "California Regiment." While still encamped at Fort Schuyler, near Westchester, New York, this unit was uniformed in gray suits possibly confiscated by the New York police in April 1861, when about to be shipped south to clothe a Confederate regiment. According to a letter published in the *Philadelphia Inquirer* dated May 30, 1861, this consisted of "cadet grey roundabout and pants, trimmed with red, and light blue overcoats," described as "not such flimsy as has been heretofore furnished to the volunteers."[127] A fuller description of this outfit was provided by Pvt. George Beidelman (Co. C), who wrote to his father from Fortress Monroe on July 26, 1861, stating:

> Our uniform is dark gray jacket, cap, and pants – trimmed with red cord. Our overcoats are very superior, made of light blue pilot cloth. In addition to our regular uniforms, we were furnished with a pair of good flannel shirts each, and two pairs of stockings; also good shoes, and a pair of overalls, to keep our pants

nice; also good blankets, besides my India Rubber [blanket], which, though heavy to carry keeps me very comfortable.[128]

By the beginning of 1862, this regiment wore Union blue.

The basis for the 69th Pennsylvania was the Irish American 2nd Regiment, Second Brigade, First Division, Pennsylvania Militia, from which the 24th Pennsylvania—also known as "the Irish Brigade"—was formed for three months' service in April 1861. Commanded by Welsh-born Col. Joshua T. Owen, this unit served under Maj. Gen. Robert Patterson on the upper Potomac and in the Shenandoah valley but saw little action. Like many other three-month regiments, it was poorly uniformed. According to the regimental history, when its men returned home in July, they marched through the streets of Philadelphia "wearing their overcoats in a hot, sweltering sun, their modesty preferring to suffer from the oppressive heat rather than submit to the exposure from insufficient clothing."[129]

Reorganized for three years' service as the "Second California," Owen's Irish regiment was mustered-in by Col. Baker as the 69th Pennsylvania on August 19, 1861. On August 31, it received 500 "uniforms, Minnie muskets, and accoutrements" for the five companies thus far recruited, the former including "a dark blue roundabout, trimmed in green."[130] On September 9, the *Philadelphia Press* reported, "The men . . . have their uniforms which are in marked contrast to that given them when away on three-months [*sic*] service. The pants are of light blue cloth; the jackets of dark-blue cloth, trimmed with green."[131] Recruited as an "Independent Zouave Company" during September/October 1861, the Reville Zouaves, also known as the Baker Guard Zouaves, became Co. K, 69th Pennsylvania. Commanded by Capt. William Davis, who had previously served as a lieutenant in the largely Irish 69th New York State Militia, they also received "uniforms, of light and dark blue, trimmed with green." By mid-October, a "Second Company of Independent Zouaves," which was probably the Tiger Zouaves, commanded by Capt. James F. Anderson, had been attached to the regiment as Co. I and were "in active service under Col. Baker, being within a few miles of Harper's Ferry," being "employed on scouting parties."[132]

At least one company of the 69th Pennsylvania may have acquired Zouave uniforms before the rest of the regiment and thereby influenced what the whole regiment wore. Note the rows of ball buttons reminiscent of the jacket worn by the Chicago Zouave Cadets. With his leg balanced across his knee, he shows off his high white canvas gaiters. *Sixth-plate ambrotype, Daniel J. Miller collection*

According to photographic evidence, the uniform worn by the Reville Zouaves was of semi-Zouave style. Although after the French Zouave pattern, the jacket had rounded edges and a low-standing collar. Cuffs were slit but not buttoned or hooked. A double row of green tape was sewn on the edges of the jacket front, and around the collar and cuffs. Probably influenced by the original United States Zouave Cadets, the front edges of this garment were also ornamented with ball buttons, as were the cuffs. Their dark-blue chasseur-pattern forage cap was trimmed with green braid around top and band. Their sky-blue vest had a single row of nine buttons down its front. Pants were also sky blue and tucked into high white canvas gaiters.

With ranks swelled during July/August 1861 by returning three-month volunteers, plus recruits from the fire companies of Philadelphia, Col. DeWitt Clinton Baxter's "Third California"—reorganized as the 72nd Pennsylvania, or "Philadelphia Fire Zouaves"—acquired their uniform from Rockhill &

During April 1861, DeWitt Clinton Baxter became lieutenant colonel of the 19th Pennsylvania Volunteers, but when that three-month enlistment expired, he organized and led the "Third California Regiment," which reorganized as the 72nd Pennsylvania Volunteers, or "Baxter's Fire Zouaves" (Pennsylvania Fire Zouaves). Photographed in an officer's version of the red-trimmed Zouave jacket worn by his regiment, his vest is a lighter blue with red-trimmed placket front. Trousers are sky blue with red double seam stripe, and shoes are of civilian pattern of black-and-white patent leather. He cradles a model 1850 foot officer sword. *MOLLUS-Mass Civil War Photograph Collection, USAHEC*

Photographed sometime after enlistment in Philadelphia on October 25, 1861, in Co. G, 72nd Pennsylvania (Baxter's Zouaves), German-born private Jacob Snyder holds a Liège-made Saxon rifle musket with distinctive double-strapped center band. He has a Remington revolver tucked in his waist belt. His dark-blue wool Zouave-style jacket is trimmed with red grosgrain tape and has sixteen brass ball buttons either side, plus two more adorning each cuff. His elaborately trimmed light-blue shirt is fastened by white mother-of-pearl buttons. Synder transferred to the 183rd Pennsylvania on July 19, 1864. *Cabinet card copy of original tintype or ambrotype, Michael J. McAfee collection*

Wilson, who by September 1861 were considered to be one of the "principal contractors" of the city.[133] This consisted of a dark-blue chasseur-pattern cap trimmed with red cord; dark-blue Zouave jacket embellished with brass ball buttons, of the same pattern as worn within the 69th Pennsylvania, but with red trim; lighter-blue pullover shirt with placket front fastened by eight mother-of-pearl buttons, on either side of which ran looped red trim; and sky-blue trousers with narrow red seam stripes, plus white canvas gaiters. In his *History of the Philadelphia Brigade*, Charles H. Banes was most critical of this uniform. He stated that the jacket had "rows of bright bell buttons, only one of which was for use—that next the throat." He added ruefully that it was "well adapted to keep the throat warm in summer, and to expose the vital parts of the body to the blasts of winter, and by the utter absence of any convenient location for pockets it deprived the men of a safe hiding-place for many a little luxury, while it furnished nothing to carry extra ammunition." Also, when worn "at night or on the skirmish line," the white leggings were "dangerously conspicuous, and gave poor compensation for their only advantage—the protection of the feet from the dust while on the march." The shirt was "of some bright color, not unfrequently [*sic*] having the letter of the company embroidered on the bosom."[134]

By October 1861, a *vivandière* named Virginia Hall was attached to the 72nd Pennsylvania. She wore a uniform consisting of "a blue Zouave shirt, trimmed with same colored braid, a Zouave jacket of the same color, and similarly ornamented, a tunic shirt, dark pants, Zouave light leather gaiters, extending from the knee down, a liberty cap with a red band, a blue top, a green sash and hospital steward's chevron. She wears a short sword and small revolver attached to her belt."[135]

The basis for the "Fifth California" was the 1st Regiment, 3rd Brigade, First Division, PM—or "Philadelphia Light Guard"—which served for three months as the 22nd Pennsylvania and, as part of the Philadelphia Brigade, became the 106th Pennsylvania. As far as can be ascertained, this regiment wore dark-blue uniforms.

The 76th Pennsylvania, also known as the "Keystone Zouaves," was "a regiment of light infantry" recruited through August/September 1861 and organized at Camp Cameron on October 18, 1861. Composed of previously independent companies such as the Lawrence Zouaves, Sharon Zouaves, and Curtin Zouaves, it was led by Col. John M. Power, who originally commanded the Johnstown Zouave Cadets and was lt. col. of the 3rd Pennsylvania (three months). Although preenlistment uniforms were probably worn by some of the companies that joined the Keystone Zouaves, the whole unit appears to have been uniformed by September, since on the fourth of that month, a report in the *Philadelphia Inquirer* advised that this was made of "handsome army cloth" and consisted of a "dark blue cap and jacket, light blue pantaloons, and leather leggings, all in the Zouave style."[136] About three weeks later, a recruit

The photographer's colorist has carefully picked out the red trim on the jacket and vest—or overshirt—of this unidentified enlisted man of the 72nd Pennsylvania, or Baxter's Zouaves. In this case, the eight buttons on the vest are ball buttons of the same pattern as that on the jacket. *Sixth-plate tintype, Daniel J. Miller collection*

This unidentified enlisted man wears the first uniform of the 76th Pennsylvania, or "Keystone Zouaves," which included a Zouave jacket with a broad band of trim around opening edges and cuffs and loose Zouave pantaloons. His plain pullover shirt with placket front has a large patch breast pocket. Headgear consists of a tasseled fez. He holds an 1853-pattern Enfield rifled musket with fixed-socket bayonet. *Sixth-plate ambrotype, Daniel J. Miller collection*

Also wearing the same early-war uniform of the 76th Pennsylvania, Private William Wambaugh enlisted on October 26, 1861, in Co. H of that regiment, which was recruited in Luzerne County, Pennsylvania. Wambaugh was captured at Fort Wagner, Morris Island, South Carolina, on July 11, 1863. After being paroled, he was mustered out at Raleigh, North Carolina, on July 18, 1865. *Michael J. McAfee collection*

pseudonym "Keystone" wrote from Camp Cameron, stating, "All the men in the Zouave Regiment are now uniformed."[137] On the basis of scant photographic evidence, this seems to have included a rather plain blue Zouave jacket with broad, light-colored facings around the edges and cuffs, underneath which was worn a plain pullover shirt with placket front fastened by three or four small buttons. Headgear appears to have been a mixture of forage caps and tasseled fezzes, and sky-blue pants varied in style and cut. At the beginning of February 1862, a letter from a member of the regiment in Beaufort, South Carolina, mentioned that the 76th Pennsylvania was "dressed in the French uniforms that the government has recently imported, and are decidedly neat."[138]

Upon departure from Philadelphia for the front on October 12, 1861, the 95th Pennsylvania, or "Gosline Pennsylvania Zouaves," commanded by Col. John M. Gosline, was reported "clad in neat blue uniforms, trimmed in red, presenting a soldier-like as well as handsome appearance, their garments all having been cut by measurement for the wearers; consequently, there was not an awkward fitting garment in the whole regiment."[139] Earlier, during recruitment, this dress had been reported as "entirely blue, with gaiters, and the ordinary kepi cap."[140] Describing the appearance of the 95th Pennsylvania after the war, a member of Co. A recalled:

> The regimental uniform was of the zouave pattern, and differed but little from other zouave organizations—Birney's and Baxter's—then forming in the city. It was manufactured by the firm of Rockhill & Wilson and consisted of the best material, heavy marine cloth. The jacket, which was of the sacque pattern, was

This unidentified enlisted man of Co. D, 95th Pennsylvania (Gosline's Zouaves), wears the quasi-Zouave uniform of his regiment, complete with elaborately braided vest. He holds an Austrian Lorenz rifle and has a rarely seen double-ended "Anti-Garotter" straight-bladed knife with one blade tucked in his belt and the other unfolded in a handle with a small cross guard at either end. *Michael J. McAfee collection*

Pvt. John L. Perkins enlisted in 1861 and was mustered into service on September 24, 1861, as a member of Co. D, 95th Pennsylvania. Perkins served with the regiment until December 29, 1862, when he was discharged from service for physical disability. His jacket is well preserved and is an excellent example of part of the first uniform issued to his regiment, this one being most likely of Rockhill & Wilson origin. It has a three-piece body with four-piece lining made of a heavy twill material. There is a pocket in the left breast between the padding and jacket body. The sixteen buttons on each lapel, and two on each cuff, are dome pattern, and 5/8 in. in diameter. *West Point Museum, acc. no. 18,072*

> open, and rounded at the waist, and trimmed with broad and narrow scarlet braid. Down each side was a row of brass buttons, adding greatly to its beauty and finish. The pants were of full length, not so wide as the regular "Zouave Petticoat," but just wide enough to harmonize with the pleated waist, in broad folds. The over shirt was of Navy flannel, with silver-plated buttons, corresponding with those on the jacket, but several sizes smaller. The cap was the McClellan style, braided with narrow scarlet braid. A pair of leather leggings nearly reaching the knees finished the uniform, which, upon the whole, was very neat and attractive.[141]

Several companies of this regiment established their rendezvous above the establishment of clothiers Rockhill & Wilson at 603 and 605 Chestnut, Philadelphia, and this firm produced most of its outfit after an initial order with the Schuylkill Arsenal could not be completed.

The Collis Zouaves, or *Zouaves d'Afrique*, were recruited by Charles H. T. Collis, ex-sergeant major of the 18th Pennsylvania (three months), who was requested by "several old soldiers" to form an independent company of infantry to be "drilled as Voltigeurs in the French army" and "uniformed similarly to the Zouaves D'Afrique."[142] As originally organized, the Collis Zouaves contained volunteers who had seen action in "the Crimean, Italian, and other recent campaigns."[143] Recruitment began on July 25, and this unit was accepted by the War Department on August 15, at which time US quartermaster gen. Montgomery C. Meigs issued orders that it should be uniformed in "the French Zouave costume." After serving as a "protective force," or bodyguard, for Maj. Gen. Nathaniel P. Banks in the Shenandoah valley, Collis's Zouaves

Recruited by Charles H. T. Collis, an ex-sergeant major of the 18th Pennsylvania (three months), Collis' Zouaves initially served as a bodyguard for Maj. Gen. Nathaniel P. Banks in the Shenandoah valley and were expanded into a Zouave regiment designated the 114th Pennsylvania in 1862. This unidentified Zouave wears full dress, complete with a white turban wrapped around his fez. His dark-blue jacket has the distinctive light-blue cuffs with red trefoil trim and a large, red *tombeau* either side at the front. His dark-blue pullover vest was also trimmed red. His waist sash was sky blue, and pantaloons were red and tucked into white canvas leggings. *Carte de visite by Sachs & Walker / 732 Chestnut St. / corner of 8th / Philadelphia, Daniel J. Miller collection*

were expanded into a Zouave regiment designated the 114th Pennsylvania in 1862.

On August 2, 1861, the *Philadelphia Inquirer* reported that the Zouaves d'Afrique had established a recruiting station in "a tent in the Custom House yard," and that "About twenty recruits passed up Chestnut street . . . presenting a curious yet inspiring sight in their red breeches and citizens' coats."[144] Several days later, the same journal stated that this Zouave company would be "costumed in the French style, with full red pantaloons, and red fez cap."[145] In his history of the 114th Pennsylvania, musician Frank Rauscher wrote, "The uniform adopted for the regiment was precisely like that of the original company—red pants, Zouave jacket, white leggings, blue sash around the waist, and white turban."[146]

On the basis of surviving clothing and photographic evidence, the dark-blue jacket was edged with red and had sky-blue pointed cuffs also piped with red trim. Under this was a dark-blue pullover vest with three or four buttons hidden by a flap edged in red. The red fez was piped at the bottom with thin yellow lace and had a yellow tassel. This was surmounted by a white turban usually worn on guard duty, but probably not during combat. The waist sash was sky blue. Red pantaloons were trimmed with yellow lace and tucked into tan leather greaves, or *jambières*, worn over white canvas leggings.

This unidentified private of the 83rd Pennsylvania Infantry wears one of the chasseur uniforms imported from France in 1861. The dark-blue jacket with white metal buttons was trimmed with yellow braid, and the epaulets were green worsted. Pantaloons were medium blue with tan leather greaves over white canvas leggings. His black leather cap appears to be minus a brass plate at front but is surmounted by a black cock's-feather plume. He has standard accoutrements and holds a Model 1861 rifle musket. When the 83rd Regiment left for the Peninsula in spring 1862, these French uniforms were packed up and stored in a warehouse in Georgetown, DC. *Michael J. McAfee collection*

This chasseur jacket, pants, and dress cap belonged to Robert N. Martin, who enlisted on August 9, 1861, as an orderly sergeant in Co. M, 62nd Pennsylvania Volunteers. He was promoted to first lieutenant on May 1, 1864. The jacket of dark-blue woolen broadcloth is piped with yellow trim and has the original yellow and green cloth epaulets attached to the shoulders. Eight of the original pewter buttons remain on the front, with two smaller ones at each cuff, and another smaller one securing a belt loop at the left side. Four more buttons and two small, yellow-wool-embroidered "bugles" ornament the coattails. The quilted white canvas lining is marked in ink with the name "R N Martin" and also has some miscellaneous French manufacturer's markings. The pants are made from medium-blue wool with very full legs, and they are pleated around the waistband and gathered at the lower cuffs, which are closed by a small tin button. Two hip pockets were inserted in the outer seam, and a watch pocket was sewn in the waist. A narrow belt adjusts the waist at the back. The Model 1860 cap of stiff black leather has attached the metal rosette and elaborate plate with spread eagle and coat of arms surmounting a wreath of oak and laurel with hunting horn inset. *Courtesy of the Horse Soldier, Gettysburg, Pennsylvania*

Buttons attached to the chasseur uniforms were white metal, one piece, and convex, with an American eagle, over which were arched thirteen five-pointed stars. Supplied by Henry et Antione Cordier, the back mark simply stated "PARIS." *The Civil War Relicman*

Sgt. Scott C. McDowell, Co. G, 62nd Pennsylvania Infantry, wears an example of the 10,000 chasseur uniforms acquired by the federal Quartermaster Department from M. Alexis Godillot, of Paris, France, on August 9, 1861. The narrow yellow braid on his full-dress, dark-blue chasseur jacket is not evident due to the photographic process, although his sergeant's stripes and epaulets have been colorized. Also known as a *bonnet de police*, his regimental fatigue headgear consisting of a dark-blue pointed and tasseled cap sits on the table by his side. *Sixth-plate tintype, Ronn Palm Museum Collection Gettysburg*

On August 9, 1861, the federal Quartermaster Department ordered from M. Alexis Godillot of Paris, France, 10,000 complete suits of 1860 pattern *chasseurs a pied* (light infantry uniforms), with the intention of eventually clothing the entire Union army in this manner. Upon receipt, these uniforms were issued as a first step to the five best-drilled regiments as noted by Maj. Gen. George McClellan, during a review of the division of Gen. Fitz-John Porter, Army of the Potomac, at Bailey's Cross Roads, Virginia, on November 9, 1861,[147] being awarded to the 62nd and 83rd Pennsylvania, plus the 18th Massachusetts and 49th and 72nd New York. According to the regimental history of the 83rd Pennsylvania, "The uniform was that of the Chasseur de Vincennes, consisting of a shako, two jaunty, tasteful suits, dress and fatigue, with cloak, two pairs of shoes, two pairs of white gloves, two night-caps, gaiters, sac le petite

Louis Fagan was a twenty-year-old clerk from Philadelphia when he enlisted as a three-month volunteer in the 17th Pennsylvania Infantry, being mustered into Co. A on April 18, 1861. He served in this capacity until honorably mustered out on August 2, 1861. He then enrolled in the Anderson Troop—originally established as a headquarters guard for the hero of Fort Sumter, Brig. Gen. Robert Anderson—and was mustered-in on November 20, 1861. He served with this unit until nominated and commissioned as a second lieutenant in the US Marine Corps on June 14, 1862. His Pascal-pattern havelock hat is embellished with a small circular patch with the letters "RA," a large die-struck brass crossed sabers insignia, a black ostrich-feather plume, and a worsted hat cord, which was probably red to match the trim on his jacket. *Carte de visite by W. L. Germon, Philadelphia; Michael J. McAfee collection*

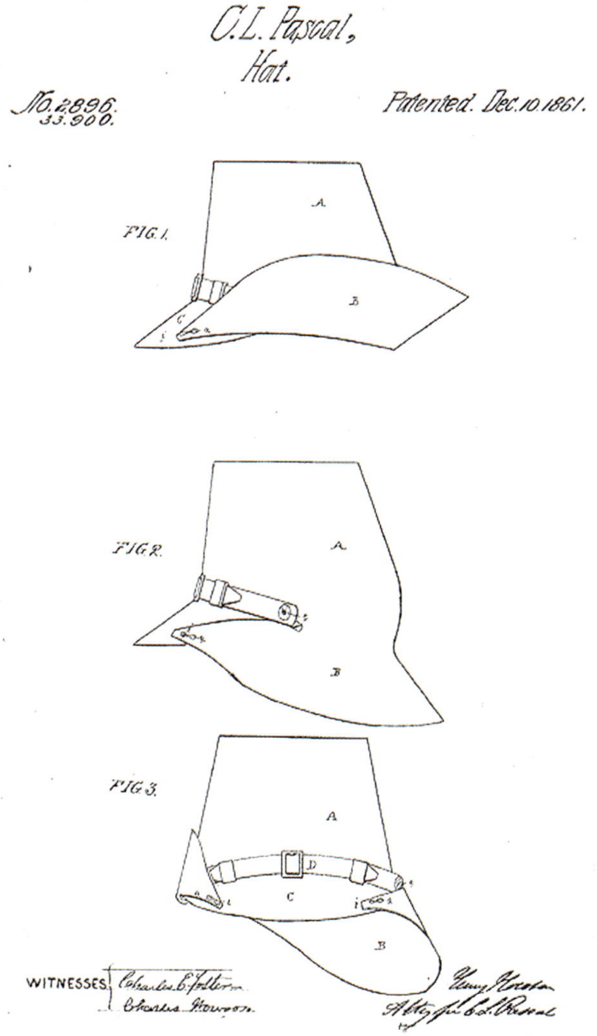

Figure 1 of the drawings accompanying Charles Lacroix Pascal's application to patent his "improved military hat" shows what he termed the "flap," or cape (B), turned up. The pointed front end of the flap was secured to the top of the visor by a small brass catch, which is shield shaped on a surviving example of a Pascal hat held by the Cumberland County Historical Society at Carlisle, Pennsylvania. In figure 2, the flap is turned down, forming what Pascal described as "a brim equivalent to an ordinary Havelock" by unfastening the buttons and refastening them once the operation was completed. This view also shows that this type of hat was seamless. To conform to General Order No. 4 of February 1861, which required that the brims of 1858-pattern dress or Hardee hats of all officers and mounted enlisted men should be looped up on the right, while that of foot soldiers should be looped up on the left, Pascal stated of his hat, "When it is desirous to distinguish one arm of the service from another, one side of the flap may be elevated and the other lowered. Thus, the infantry may have the left side of the flap turned up and the right side turned down, while the cavalry may have the flap reversed, the right side being turned up and the left down, as seen in Fig. 3." *United States Patent Office*

Although cut in the style of a government-issue cavalry jacket, the faded red trim around the front and bottom edge, plus cuffs, of this jacket worn by the Anderson Troop is nonregulation. *Historical Imagebank, CWu6ds*

[haversack], containing five brushes for various purposes. Needle case, with combs, thread, spool, cloak pin, and various other conveniences."[148] The full dress uniform consisted of a dark-blue chasseur jacket with yellow braid, white metal buttons, and yellow worsted epaulets; medium-blue pantaloons with tan leather greaves and white leggings; and black leather cap with brass plate and black cock's-feather plume. The fatigue headgear consisted of a *bonnet de police*, or dark-blue pointed and tasseled cap. These European uniforms proved generally too small for the typical American soldier and were discarded when McClellan finally began offensive operations against the Confederate army encamped nearby around Centerville and Manassas, Virginia, on March 10, 1862.

According to Pascal's description of his havelock hat, officers' caps could be "distinguished by cords and tassels, plumes, or other ornaments." The hat displayed by this officer, possibly either of the 2nd or 6th Pennsylvania Cavalry, has an oval patch containing an embroidered wreath and letters "US," a light-colored (probably yellow) hat cord, and ostrich feather plume. *Carte de visite by J. E. McClees of Philadelphia, Michael J. McAfee collection*

A graduate of the US Military Academy and late a captain of artillery in the Regular Army, Richard H. Rush, of Philadelphia, received authority from the War Department to recruit a volunteer regiment of "Philadelphia Light Cavalry" for three years' service on July 27, 1861. Although the 6th Pennsylvania Cavalry (Rush's Lancers) was supplied with clothing from the US depot in Philadelphia, it received headgear consisting of an unusual havelock hat made by hatters Sullender & Pascal, of Philadelphia. The example worn by Rush has the brim turned up and is embellished by a black ostrich-feather plume and an embroidered 1858-pattern crossed-sabers hat insignia on a black-felt background. *MOLLUS-Mass Civil War Photograph Collection, Vol. 51, p. L2517, USAHEC*

Havelock hats patented by master hatter Charles Lacroix Pascal and produced by Sullender & Pascal of Philadelphia were worn by the 2nd, 6th, and 15th Pennsylvania Cavalry. The 1861–62 Quartermaster's Contract Book in the Pennsylvania State Archives indicates that these hats were purchased "fully trimmed and mounted" for $4.60 each. The first known contract for this Havelock hat was completed in November 1861 and consisted of 100 pieces for an independent cavalry command called the Anderson Body Guard or Anderson Troop, which was originally intended to serve as a headquarters guard for Brig. Gen. Robert Anderson, hero of Fort Sumter. However,

Charles H. Masland was an eighteen-year-old stocking weaver when he enlisted in Co. E, 6th Pennsylvania Cavalry (Rush's Lancers), on September 17, 1861. His Sullender & Pascal–patent hat rests on the table with an 1858-pattern crossed-sabers insignia and company letter attached to its front. He holds a US Model 1840 dragoon saber and metal scabbard. *Cumberland County Historical Society, USAHEC*

Anderson was succeeded by Brig. Gen. Don Carlos Buell before the unit could report for duty, but the name was retained. Elements of Anderson Troop would later form part of the 15th Pennsylvania Cavalry during summer 1862. Actually composed of "163 picked men," the Anderson Body Guard was quartered at Carlisle Barracks when they received their complete uniform of "dark blue cloth, trimmed with red, blue overcoats, and black felt hats with the initial letters R. A. and a brass on the front."[149]

Recruited as the Philadelphia Light Cavalry, the 6th Pennsylvania Cavalry—also known as Rush's Lancers—paraded in the same type of headgear on December 10, 1861, on which occasion the *Philadelphia Press* reported, "Their hats were of felt, with the brim turned up and fastened with a brazen cockade."[150] The rest of the uniform issued to this regiment consisted of a "dark blue jacket and cap, and sky blue pants, all trimmed with yellow braid."[151] According to Pascal's description on application for a patent, his hat was suitable for dress or fatigue purposes. Its crown was "of a shape somewhat similar to that known as the fatigue-cap," with shade, or visor, plus strap and buckle in front. A flap, or cape, could be folded down to protect the neck, with a unique brass catch that "locked" it either in the up or down position. Pascal also indicated that when it was "desirous to distinguish one arm of the service from another, one side of the flap may be elevated and the other lowered. Thus the infantry may have the left side of the flap turned up and the right side turned down, while the cavalry may have the flap reversed, the right side being turned up and the left down."[152] This arrangement for headgear complied with General Order No. 4, issued by the US Army in February 1861.

Although this unit was to be armed with "the sabre and large sized revolver," Gen. George McClellan requested that it be supplied with lances described as "simply rods of stout wood, perhaps eight feet long, pointed with a short dart or spear-head, in shape like a bayonet of the old time that had been cut off midway. Upon each lance-pole a red flag was fastened, bearing the letter of the company."[153]

Pennsylvania Order of Battle, 1861

Pennsylvania numbered all regiments in sequence, regardless of branch of service. Hence, the 59th Regiment was also known as the 2nd Cavalry, etc.

Pennsylvania Militia (PM) ("Three-months' Service")

First Defenders—a provisional force of five volunteer militia companies who were the first to reach Washington, DC (see 25th Regiment).

1st Troop, Philadelphia City Cavalry

Philadelphia Merchant Troop (later Co. A, 60th Regiment or 3rd Cavalry)

1st Regiment

2nd Regiment

3rd Regiment

4th Regiment

5th Regiment

6th Regiment

7th Regiment

8th Regiment

9th Regiment

10th Regiment

11th Regiment

12th Regiment

13th Regiment

14th Regiment

15th Regiment

16th Regiment

17th Regiment (1st Artillery Regiment or Quaker Regiment)

18th Regiment

19th Regiment (National Guards)

20th Regiment (Scott Legion)

21st Regiment (German Rifle Regiment)

22nd Regiment

23rd Regiment (Philadelphia City Guard—later Birney's Zouaves)

24th Regiment (Irish Brigade)

25th Regiment (formed around First Defenders)

Philadelphia Reserve Brigade

1st Regiment (Gray Reserves)

2nd Regiment (Blue Reserves)

3rd Regiment (2nd Gray Reserves)

4th Regiment (included Zouave Battalion)

Philadelphia Home Guard Brigade

1st Infantry

2nd Regiment

3rd Regiment

Volunteers

26th Regiment (originally 1st Regiment, Washington Guards)

27th Regiment (originally 2nd Regiment, Washington Guards)

28th Regiment (Goldstream Regiment)

29th Regiment (Jackson Infantry)

30th Regiment (1st Regiment Reserve Corps)

31st Regiment (2nd Regiment Reserve Corps)

32nd Regiment (3rd Regiment Reserve Corps)

33rd Regiment (4th Regiment Reserve Corps)

34th Regiment (5th Regiment Reserve Corps)

35th Regiment (6th Regiment Reserve Corps)

36th Regiment (7th Regiment Reserve Corps)

37th Regiment (8th Regiment Reserve Corps)

38th Regiment (9th Regiment Reserve Corps)

39th Regiment (10th Regiment Reserve Corps)

40th Regiment (11th Regiment Reserve Corps)

41st Regiment (12th Regiment Reserve Corps)

42nd Regiment (13th Regiment Reserve Corps) (Bucktails or 1st PA Rifles)

43rd Regiment (14th Regiment Reserve Corps—1st Light Artillery)

44th Regiment (15th Regiment Reserve Corps—later 1st Cavalry)

45th Regiment

46th Regiment

47th Regiment

48th Regiment

49th Regiment

50th Regiment

51st Regiment

52nd Regiment

53rd Regiment

54th Regiment

55th Regiment

56th Regiment

57th Regiment

58th Regiment

59th Regiment (2nd Cavalry)

60th Regiment (3rd Cavalry)

61st Regiment

62nd Regiment

63rd Regiment

64th Regiment (4th Cavalry)

65th Regiment (5th Cavalry or Cameron Dragoons)

66th Regiment

67th Regiment

68th Regiment (2nd Regiment, Scott Legion)

69th Regiment (Second California)

70th Regiment (6th Cavalry or Rush's Lancers)

71st Regiment (California Regiment)

72nd Regiment (Baxter's Philadelphia Fire Zouaves)

73rd Regiment (Pennsylvania Legion)

74th Regiment (1st German Regiment)

75th Regiment (2nd German Regiment)

76th Regiment (Keystone Zouaves)

77th Regiment

78th Regiment

79th Regiment

80th Regiment (7th Cavalry)

81st Regiment (Chippewa Guards Regiment)

82nd Regiment

83rd Regiment

84th Regiment

85th Regiment

86th Regiment

87th Regiment (Thomas A. Scott Regiment)

88th Regiment (Cameron Light Guards)

89th Regiment (8th Cavalry)

90th Regiment

91st Regiment

92nd Regiment (9th Cavalry)

93rd Regiment (Lebanon Regiment)

94th Regiment (failed to complete organization)

95th Regiment (Gosline's Zouaves or Pennsylvania Zouaves)

96th Regiment (1st Artillery Regiment or Quaker Regiment)

97th Regiment

98th Regiment

99th Regiment (Lincoln Legion)

100th Regiment (Roundheads)

101st Regiment

102nd Regiment

103rd Regiment

104th Regiment (Ringgold Regiment)

105th Regiment (Wild Cat Regiment)

106th Regiment

108th Regiment (11th Cavalry)

109th Regiment (Curtin Light Guards)

110th Regiment

111th Regiment

112th Regiment (2nd Heavy Artillery)

113th Regiment (12th Cavalry)

Squadron of Irish Dragoons

Collis Zouaves (Zouaves d'Afrique)

CHAPTER 2:
NEW YORK

This detail from a stereoscopic view by E. & H. T. Anthony shows the 7th New York State Militia, or National Guard, wearing summer full dress while at "Camp Scott," near Dorf, on Staten Island, in July 1860. This consisted of a gray coat trimmed with black tape on collar, cuffs, and chest; 1851-pattern dress cap with white pompon; white worsted epaulets; and white cotton pants. An officer stands third in front on the left, while several bandsmen in dark-blue coats with scarlet plastrons and trimmings are seen at right. *Detail from stereoview, author's collection*

The Empire State provided eleven militia regiments totaling 8,450 men in response to the president's call on April 15, 1861. These consisted of the 5th through 8th, 12th, 13th, 28th, 69th, and 71st regiments from New York and Brooklyn; the 20th from Kingston; and the 25th from Albany. All of these units left the state for Washington, DC; Annapolis, Maryland; or Fortress Monroe, Virginia, between April 19 and 27, 1861. Some of these regiments wore elements of full dress, fatigue dress, or both that conformed to Special Orders No. 187 issued from the State Adjutant's Office at Albany in 1857, the detail of which was stipulated in *General Regulations for the Military Forces of the State of New York*, published during the following year. Essentially the uniform adopted by the US Army in 1854, this consisted of a full dress composed of a dark-blue frock coat and sky-blue pants with dark-blue 1854-pattern cap. Branch service trim used on collar and cuffs was scarlet for heavy and light artillery, sky blue for infantry, emerald green for riflemen, and orange for cavalry. For fatigue wear, heavy artillery, infantry, and riflemen were prescribed cadet-gray jackets with "polka style skirt" extending about five inches below the waist, nine-button front,

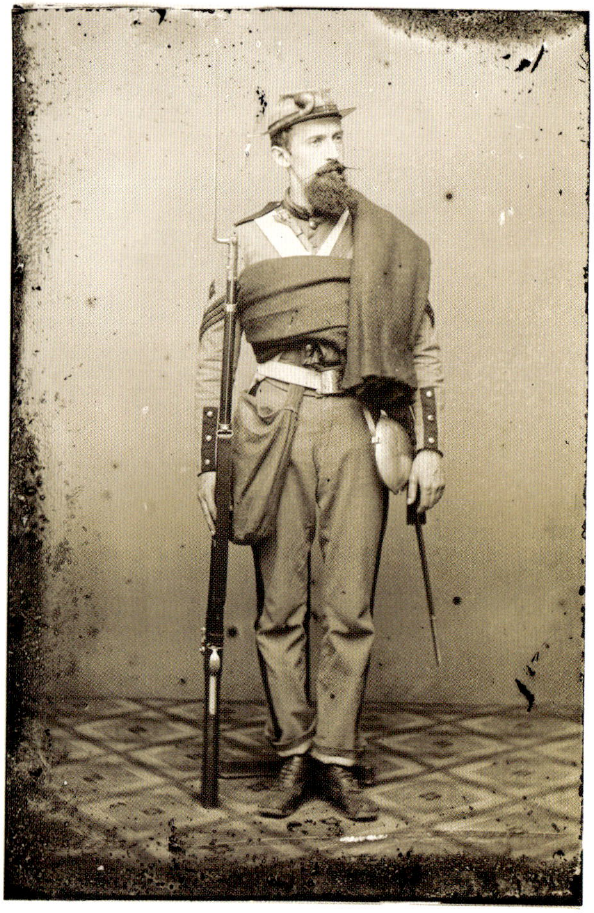

Tentatively identified as 1st Sgt. F. Cozzens, Sixth Company, 7th NYSM, this volunteer wears the fatigue dress of his regiment and is also equipped for campaign life. His blanket is wrapped around his body in unorthodox style, and his cloth haversack and 1858-pattern canteen are suspended from straps over his shoulders. His chasseur-pattern fatigue cap has a black band and is quartered with narrow black cord. His jacket has black trim around the collar, solid-black shoulder straps, and black cloth strips with three small buttons on the cuffs. His first sergeant's stripes and lozenge are also of black cloth, and rank is also indicated via a red wool waist sash mostly concealed under his blanket. His wool trousers, with black seam stripes, are turned up, revealing a cotton lining and showing his lace-up bootees. His white buff leather waist belt has a brass plate bearing the monogram "NG" above the company number "SIXTH." He holds an M1855 rifle musket with fixed bayonet. An essential piece of campaign equipment is the pipe tucked into the elastic chinstrap on his cap. *Library of Congress LC-DIG-cwpb-05291*

Commanded by 1st Lt. Henry A. Cragin, the Ninth Company, also designated the "First Troop, National Guard," 7th NYSM, consisted of only twenty-five men when it arrived in Washington on April 25, 1861. One of these men was Charles Deborah White, who joined the regiment as a private on January 14, 1860. Regarding further service, White was listed as "dropped May 12, 1862," but it is uncertain whether he resigned, transferred to another regiment, or was dismissed from the 7th NYSM for failing to report for duty. A small Union flag pin attached to the breast of his jacket has been painted over to make it more distinct. *Dr. Michael R. Cunningham collection*

and black facings on collar and cuffs, plus shoulder straps "corded or edged" with black. Light artillery and cavalry could wear dark-blue jackets of the same pattern trimmed on collar and cuffs with scarlet or orange, respectively. Fatigue headgear for heavy artillery, infantry, and riflemen was cadet gray, while that for light artillery and cavalry was dark blue. [1]

Composed mainly of members of the German population of New York, the 5th New York State Militia (NYSM), or Jefferson Guard, commanded by Col. Christian Schwarzwaelder, was originally organized as heavy artillery but was classed as light infantry by 1861; hence its full dress had "scarlet facings and trimmings." The rest of this was composed of a "dark blue frock coat, with one row of State regulation buttons, . . . trowsers of light mixed blue gray cloth, with a welt of scarlet cloth on the outer seam; cap, as prescribed by general regulations—blue bodies, with black enamelled patent leather; long scarlet pompon, chinstrap of gilt scales; metal gilt frontispiece of arms of the State impaling those of the United States, with motto and crest of the State."

The officers'-quality waist belt worn by Charles White and his fellow troopers was designed to carry a saber, and remains of attached saber straps can be seen on the underside of the belt. The Allegheny-pattern cap box with shield-shaped front has the soldier's initials "CDW" carved under the flap. The carbine cartridge box with brass script NG insignia was designed for only one vertical layer of cartridges, similar to federal-issue carbine boxes with a wooden block. This one had a tinned iron liner with a center divider, allowing it to hold two packages of ten Sharps, or comparable ammunition. *Dr. Michael R. Cunningham collection*

Made of gray wool jean, the cadet-gray fatigue cap worn by Charles C. White was made by military importers and suppliers James S. Smith & Sons, whose manufactory was at 15 Dutch Street in New York City. This firm had supplied NYSM insignia in 1858. Note the now-faded black cord that quartered the cap top and encircled its top. The 7th Regiment had elastic chinstraps on their caps, rather than the customary leather chinstrap, although the former is now missing off that worn by White. *Dr. Michael R. Cunningham collection*

The three-month volunteers of the 5th NYSM were reported in the *New York Herald* to be wearing "dark gray pants, dark blue coats [or jackets] and caps, and army overcoats" when it sailed for Fortress Monroe on April 27.[2] Also originally artillery but serving as infantry, the 6th NYSM, or Governor's Guard, under Col. Joseph C. Pinckney, left for Washington, DC, on April 21, wearing "the dress cap and pompon, the uniform frock coat and overcoat, and pants." Fatigue jackets of probable 1858 pattern were packed in knapsacks.[3] In a parade on the occasion of the visit of the Prince of Wales to the US during the previous October, the dress uniform of the 6th NYSM was described as "very plain, blue trimmed with red," and "not so striking in appearance," but "one that will stand service."[4]

Departing New York on April 19, the elite 7th NYSM, or National Guard, was mustered into service for only thirty days on arrival at the federal capital a

Photographed at Arlington Heights, Virginia, on July 16, 1861—two hours before the 8th NYSM set out on the First Bull Run Campaign—this camp scene shows seven enlisted men wearing plain gray over shirts of various patterns issued to their regiment by the state Quartermaster Department. Trousers are also plain gray. The man holding the axe wears the regimental fatigue uniform with solid-black facings on the collar and shoulder straps and cuffs on his jacket, as well as a broad black seam stripe on his pants. The breast plate on the man at right shows the head of George Washington set within a wreath. In the foreground stands a stack of M1842 rifled muskets, from which hangs a pattern 1842 cartridge box. *Carte de visite, Michael J. McAfee collection*

This unidentified enlisted man wears the prewar full dress uniform of the 12th NYSM, consisting of a dark-blue, double-breasted frock coat with 1854-pattern shoulder scales, sky-blue pants with white seam stripes, and dark-blue, 1851-pattern dress cap with white pompon. Note the numeral "12" within the wreath on his cap front. *Ninth-plate ambrotype, Michael J. McAfee collection*

week later. This regiment wore "full fatigue dress," which was described in the *Evening Star* of Washington, DC, as a "gray uniform, with black trimmings," plus "gray cap and long blue army overcoat." According to this report, each man carried a knapsack, on the top of which was rolled a heavy blanket and in which was conveyed "under clothing, an extra pair of boots or shoes, a knife, fork, spoon, tin cup, plate, with body belt and cap pouch." All were provided on starting out for the capital with "one day's rations, and twenty rounds of [Minié] ball cartridges were dealt to each man at the armory . . . to be used during the journey if necessary." The fifty-four-man Engineer Corps were armed with "rifles and sabre bayonets"; the twenty-five-man Cavalry Troop, with "pistols and heavy swords"; and the eight companies of infantry, with M1855 rifle muskets. In anticipation of hostility from the prosecessionist element during their passage through Baltimore, almost every man had "a revolver, carried in a pouch in the front of his belt," while some also had "heavy dirks and knives, for hand-to-hand fighting." The musicians and servants were likewise armed with revolvers.[5]

During their stay in the capital, by May 7 the 7th NYSM had received over 1,000 white-linen havelocks from "the ladies of New York" of "the British pattern, so famous in India and the Crimea, worn also by the French at Solferino," plus a supply of "loose, dark gray, knit worsted jackets" called "Aspinwalls" after their donor, retired businessman William H. Aspinwall. The Havelock and "Aspinwall" made a marked change in the appearance of the regiment; as one militiaman wrote, "No more tight-bodied dress-coats; no more pretty white cross-belts to hamper us down; no more heavy, stiff caps; no more fashionable pantaloons. Give us a little time after we get home—if we do get there—and we will show you a serviceable, neat, and inexpensive uniform."[6]

Also unidentified, this man wears an example of the chasseur uniform received by the 12th NYSM in May 1861. The coat was dark-blue trimmed with white cord piping, "light, greyish blue" pantaloons, "bright blue" cap trimmed with white, and russet leather leggings. *Carte de visite, Daniel J. Miller collection*

Reported to be uniformed "the same as the New York Seventh" on arrival at Washington, DC, on May 18, 1861, the 8th NYSM, or Washington Grays, in fact wore a cadet-gray fatigue uniform similar to that of the 7th NYSM, although black collar, cuff, and cap trim differed. This regiment also received 1,000 gray "overshirts" and 1,000 pairs of plain gray trousers via the New York State Quartermaster Department before their departure for the Manassas Campaign.[7]

The nucleus of the 12th NYSM, or Independence Guard, consisting of "400 men of the regular Regiment," arrived in the federal capital on April 28, 1861, wearing the uniform adopted by the regiment in 1857, which consisted of "a dark blue frock coat, trimmed with light blue; blue pantaloons, with a white stripe; and the army regulation cap." During October 1860, this had been more fully described as being composed of "dark blue frock coats, faced with light blue cloth and white cord; pants of indigo blue cloth, with wide white stripes on the sides; blue bodied French infantry caps, with patent leather tops, frontispiece of a very tasteful design, with the numerical designation of the regiment in the centre; on the top of their caps the troops wear a neat white wool pompon; their equipments are made of black enamelled leather, superbly ornamented with gilt insignia."

This regiment was accompanied by a twenty-one-strong "drum corps in full Zouave uniform" when it arrived at Washington, DC. On the departure of this unit from New York six days earlier, the *Herald* reported that its "regular members . . . wore their usual uniform and felt hats, with fatigue cap slung, and many were provided with revolvers, in addition to their muskets. The volunteers [or new recruits] also wore felt hats and were furnished with blankets." In addition, each man "bore on his breast a satin badge of red, white and blue, with figures '12' printed upon it."[8]

The 12th NYSM had contracted to have a new regimental uniform made during mid-April, which was received on May 9, 1861, after their arrival in Washington. The *Herald* commented that it was "styled the *Chasseur d'Affrique* [*sic*], is something like the Zouave costume, and will also be provided for the volunteers, as well as for the regular members of the regiment."[9] According to the *Washington Evening Star*, it consisted of a "bright blue fatigue cap trimmed with white cord, short chasseur coat with slashed skirt, the material being of dark blue set off at the seams with white cord." The pants were "wide Zouave of light greyish blue, made to buckle around the ankle under high Zouave leggings."[10] The *National Republican* of the same city added that its dress was composed of "a light-blue cap, with dark-blue band; a short skirted coat, with a slit in each side, trimmed with white; full light-blue pantaloons, trimmed with white, the bottoms being gathered in and encased in buff leggings."[11]

Originally in the 23rd N.Y.S.M., the National Grays transferred to the 12th NYSM as Co. I in 1860. Also known as the "Howitzer Company," this unit was photographed at Camp Anderson in May 1861. Most wear the chasseur uniform received by the 12th NYSM on May 9, 1861. Some men have havelock caps, and a few wear felt hats. The twenty-one drummers in the regiment wore a Zouave uniform. One of these sits at front right playing cards with comrades, while another stands in the back row, center left. Note the six-pounder howitzer at either end of the gathering. *National Archives, 111-B-4513*

Organized in Brooklyn, the old members of the 13th NYSM, or National Grays, wore the fatigue uniform detailed in their "Bill of Dress" adopted in 1857, when they departed for the federal capital on April 23, 1861. This consisted of a fatigue jacket of "cadet mixed grey cloth, the same color and shade as used at West Point," with black mohair binding around the collar, shoulder straps, and cuff patches. Trousers were also gray, with 1.5-inch-wide black seam stripes. Gray caps had a black band and a "gilt block number 13," above which was pinned the company letter. Overcoats were sky blue.[12]

Lacking uniforms or equipment, about 450 new recruits were left behind but finally joined the 13th NYSM on May 12, while it was performing guard duty near Annapolis, Maryland. On the same occasion the regiment received a new outfit, following which a correspondent of the *New York Morning Express* wrote, "They are entirely different from the old uniforms. The overcoats are a light grey, while the pants are a dark satinet with a blue stripe down the side. Their hats are not much on the military order, being broad brimmed felt."[13]

Formed by the Victory Fire Engine Company from Williamsburg, in the Eastern District of Brooklyn, Co. F of the 13th NYSM initially wore their firemen's uniform, consisting of "felt hats, black fire coats, drab pants and red shirts." The firemen may have acquired their own

Patriotic organizations such as the Ladies Relief Committee, of New York City, flooded the volunteer army with havelock cap covers and havelock caps in 1861. The linen havelock cap worn by Pvt. Elias A. Brown, who enlisted in Co. K, 90th New York Infantry, at Brooklyn, New York, on November 17, 1861, has a removable pasteboard crown and leather brim. Havelock caps were described in the *New York Morning Express* of May 1, 1861, as being "something like a military fatigue cap, with a linen peak, and a sort of curtain hanging down behind." Advising that soldiers' ears and neck were becoming "blistered by the sun," T. D'Oremieulx, chairman of correspondence and supplies at Albany, provided Mayor George H. Thacher with "a havelock pattern" and recommended that they be made of "either heavy dark linen or mixed flannel and cotton." Toward the end of the year, this form of headgear was judged to be largely useless, since the armies in the field grew used to exposure to the elements. *Dr. Michael R. Cunningham collection*

This unidentified corporal of the 13th NYSM wears the "Cadet mixed gray cloth"-trimmed black fatigue uniform of his regiment. His waist belt and sword frog are of black "enameled leather," with polished brass plate bearing the company letter "B" "engraved and lacquered" with "National" above and "Greys" below. Note the "Union Cockade" pinned to his breast. Described as consisting of "a tri-color, containing a medallion head of Washington, with red, white and blue streamers, containing the words 'Constitution' and 'Union,'" A. W. Spies & Co., of 187 Broadway, had "nearly 150 girls constantly employed to supply the demand" for these patriotic emblems during May 1861. *Carte de visite, Michael J. McAfee collection*

uniforms, since on May 15 the *Express* added, "The Victory Engine Company boys, of the 13th Regiment, have just had their uniforms sent on. - They are a light grey satinet, but, as the saying is, the clothes fit them too much; some of the pants are much too long, and some of the coats are large enough for Daddy Lambert. The firemen appear altogether out of their element in them."[14] The only action seen by the 13th NYSM was the capture of a Confederate-held armory in Easton, Maryland, on May 18, which surrendered without a fight, although one New Yorker was supposedly killed.

Also organized in Brooklyn, the 28th NYSM, commanded by Col. Michael Bennett and composed mainly of Germans, spent most of their three-month term of enlistment in the Washington defenses and was guarding the bridge at Georgetown during the battle on July 21, 1861. Having been made a rifle regiment in 1859, this unit wore a full dress of "dark blue and green." On their return to New York the evening of July 28, the *Herald* reported that the "men

Having hosted Elmer Ellsworth's United States Zouave Cadets during their visit to Brooklyn in July 1860, the 13th NYSM was impressed by their appearance, and Co. B of the regiment subsequently adopted a Zouave uniform. Mustering into federal service in April 1861 as a private in the 13th Regiment, NYSM, George W. Scott wears the Zouave uniform adopted by Co. B. This consisted of a light-blue jacket with white cord piping and red pointed cuffs edged with two 1/2-inch strips of yellow lace. Trim on the chest was also yellow lace enclosing a white *tombeau*, or loop, leading into a trefoil. The vest was blue with yellow trim, and the fez and pantaloons were red. His belt plate bears the company letter "B," plus "National Greys," and his waist belt supports a nonregulation-pattern cap pouch. *Carte de visite, courtesy of the Anne S. K. Brown Military Collection, Brown University*

This unidentified member of Co. D, 69th NYSM, wears the undress uniform in which prewar members of his regiment went to war during April 1861. This consisted of the frock worn for full dress minus red worsted epaulets, and dark-blue caps bearing the brass letter and numerals signifying company and regimental designation. Because the 69th NYSM was nominally an artillery unit, the coat was trimmed with scarlet cord around collar and cuffs and had solid-red shoulder straps, while their sky-blue trousers had narrow scarlet seam stripes. *Carte de visite, Michael J. McAfee collection*

Photographed in spring 1861, Meagher wears a uniform patterned on that adopted by the Phoenix Zouaves, which was in turn based on that worn by "the Zouaves of Inkerman," a small theatrical group of French veterans of the Crimean War who toured the major US cities demonstrating Zouave military drill during 1861. The Phoenix Zouaves were originally attached to the "First Regiment of the Phoenix Brigade," which was described in Meagher's memoirs as "the Military portion of the Fenian Brotherhood" of New York. When Meagher organized the Second Regiment of the Phoenix Brigade in 1861, the Zouaves transferred to that organization. During the rush to arms with the outbreak of civil war, many officers and men of the Phoenix Brigade enlisted in the 69th NYSM, the ranks of which were solidly Irish. When a vacancy occurred for a Co. K in the ranks of that regiment, Meagher quickly recruited a company called the Irish Zouaves to complete that unit. Commissioned a brigadier general February 3, 1862, Meagher went on to command the Irish Brigade, First Division, II Corps, Army of the Potomac, and served at Second Bull Run, Antietam, and Fredericksburg in 1862 and at Chancellorsville in 1863. Following the decimation of his brigade at the latter action he resigned his commission but later commanded a provisional division under Gen William T. Sherman in 1864–65, following which he finally resigned on May 15, 1865. *Massachusetts Commandery, Military Order of the Loyal Legion of the United States (MASS-MOLLUS), acc # RG98s, USAHEC*

looked exceedingly well by the light of the street lamps, in their gray [fatigue] uniforms, which were not so much soiled as those of the men who had been in actual conflict." These uniforms were similar to the undress of the 7th NYSM, although headgear consisted of black felt hats.[15]

Another artillery regiment serving as infantry—the 69th NYSM, or National Cadets—wore for fatigue purposes in April 1861 their New York State–pattern full dress uniform adjusted for fatigue purposes. This

In camp at Georgetown, DC, Capt. Thomas Francis Meagher (1823–67) sits among the Irish Zouaves (Co. K), 69th NYSM, after their arrival to join the regiment toward the end of May 1861. The Zouaves wore dark-blue caps with brass numeral "69" at front, blue jackets and vests trimmed with red, blue-gray straight-legged trousers, and green waist sashes. *Michael J. McAfee collection*

consisted of a dark-blue frock coat with scarlet trim around collar, cuffs, and shoulder straps—but minus full-dress epaulets—and sky-blue trousers with 1/8-inch-wide scarlet seam stripes. Their headgear consisted of a non-state-regulation dark-blue forage cap. Recruits unable to acquire this uniform complete appear to have been supplied with flannel shirts and dark-blue, state-pattern light artillery fatigue jackets with scarlet trim on collar, cuffs, and shoulder straps.

Joining the 69th NYSM as Co. K on May 23, 1861, the Irish Zouaves, also known as the Thomas Francis Meagher Zouaves, were reported by a *New York Herald* correspondent to be wearing "a loose navy blue jacket fringed with red, and pantaloons of a bluish gray, with caps *a la* Sixty-ninth regiment."[16] On arrival in Washington, DC, they were further described as being uniformed in "a dark-blue Zouave jacket, gray Zouave pants, all trimmed with red, and blue Zouave cap."[17] The only company in the 69th NYSM to wear a Zouave uniform, the Irish Zouaves were disbanded when the three-month period of service of the regiment expired.

Although recruits for the 69th NYSM were to be furnished with "as much of the uniform as could be obtained upon such short notice,"[18] nothing appears to have been received until May 19, 1861, when Pvt. John Cogan, Co. C, wrote from the regimental encampment at Georgetown, DC, "We all have our uniforms—they are very neat and look good; but the material is none of the best in the world—blue frock coat, blue pants, shoes, fatigue cap each, with two red flannel shirts, two pair of drawers, two pair of socks, cartridge box, cap box, bayonet sheath and body belt, with knapsack and haversack. We also have a very good thing to keep off the sun from our heads; it is a white hood, a present from Mrs. Judge Daly, of New York, with the haversacks, to the regiment: the balance of our uniform is from the State of New York."[19]

Suffering in the summer heat, another man in this regiment wrote from Fort Corcoran on June 3, 1861, "Will you beg the Defence Committee to send on to us light suits of flannel and straw hats for the men? The havelocks sent by Mrs. Judge Daly, and the many patriotic ladies who assisted her, have been of great—infinite—service; but we want straw hats, for the regulation caps under the havelocks are too heavy."[20] After weeks of hard labor digging trenches and throwing up earthworks, the clothing issued at

Photographed ca. 1857–61, this unidentified enlisted man of the 71st NYSM, or American Guard, wears the full dress uniform of his regiment, consisting of a dark-blue frock coat with sky-blue collar and cuffs trimmed with black cord and gold lace and a "National Guard"-style cap topped with white wool pompon. Not shown in this image is a small, embroidered infantry horn attached to the back of his collar. The stamped-brass ornament on the cap front shows the seal of New York City and has only the numeral "71" underneath, as opposed to the sunburst plate with numerals seen on other surviving images of members of this regiment. His white buff leather waist belt is fastened by an oval "SNY" plate, and his breast plate is plain brass. The lack of cap pouch on this belt may indicate that he was still armed with a flintlock musket, or that he carried his percussion caps in a coat pocket. His black epaulets with brass crescents are a leftover from the uniform of the American Rifles, from which his regiment emerged in 1852. He also wears white cotton dress pants. *Quarter-plate ambrotype, author's collection*

Posing with a rigid knapsack painted with the regimental number "71," complete with tin ration container attached, and with a blanket roll on top, this enlisted man of the 71st NYSM also wears full dress minus white shoulder belts. Placed atop the pedestal, his dress cap has a sunburst plate at its front. *Carte de visite, Michael J. McAfee collection*

Georgetown had become tattered and torn, and according to another letter written on July 3, "many of the coats have disappeared altogether."[21]

According to Capt. Meagher, as the regiment left their entrenchments at Fort Corcoran and advanced toward Manassas on July 16, 1861, the Engineer Corps led the way, "uniformed in a reddish grey flannel blouse."[22] After the battle on July 21, the *Irish American Weekly* reported that "the men of the Sixty-ninth stripped to the skin, except their pants, and pitched into the fight regardless of fatigue or personal safety."[23] Following this regiment's return to New York City on July 26, 1861, the *Atlas and Argus* of Albany observed that "Every imaginable uniform was worn by the men, as they had picked up off the field of Manassas the garments that the combatants had thrown away. Red and green and blue; Southern as well as Northern garb; weapons of every regiment; Zouave caps and regulation felts; turbans, straw hats, civilian's dresses, as well as militia men's clothes."[24]

George W. Wade enlisted in Co. C, 71st NYSM, or American Guard, on April 20, 1861. He was mustered out of US service on August 10, 1861. He wears the fatigue suit worn by members of his regiment on arrival in Washington, DC, on April 26, 1861, consisting of a dark-blue jacket, blue pants with black stripe and gold trim, and blue fatigue caps. His white buff shoulder belts support a cartridge box and bayonet scabbard. *Carte de visite, Michael J. McAfee collection*

Formed among the American-born citizens of New York City in the early 1850s, the 71st NYSM, or American Guard, wore a full dress composed of dark-blue frock coat with sky-blue collar and cuffs trimmed with black cord and gold lace, sky-blue trousers with black seam stripes edged in gold, and "National Guard"-style caps topped with white wool pompon. On April 20, 1861, this regiment was ordered to report to its "several armories" for departure for Washington, DC, dressed in "full fatigue, with fatigue cap," which was described as consisting of "dark blue suits trimmed with black and gold, and blue overcoats." This was further reported on arrival of the regiment in Washington, DC, as being composed of a "dark blue coat, blue pants with black stripe and gilt borders, and blue fatigue cap."[25] The reported uniform does not match the description of the prewar fatigue dress of this regiment, which consisted of a dark-blue jacket with light-blue shoulder straps and dark-blue forage cap. It is possible that Col. Abraham S. Vosburgh preferred his command to wear elements of dress uniform on arrival in Washington. Indeed, the *Star* advised that its uniform was to be "slightly changed in some particular now since their arrival," and this may refer to sky-blue pants received for fatigue wear. Some of the 71st NYSM complained about these "uniform pantaloons," which were privately purchased at $10 a pair from "the clothing merchants of Broadway." They thought "new pants ought to last from the New York to Washington," yet found them "ripping and giving away in all directions." On April 27, the *Evening Star* commented, "Hundreds of the men were this morning trying to make arrangements to get out on leave, in order to hunt up our city tailors, with a view to repairing damages."[26] About 300 recruits with the 71st NYSM lacked a uniform and were "dressed as taste and fancy dictated," presenting "a most motley appearance. Some were armed with old, rusty muskets, and one with only a hachet."[27] According to the regimental

An unidentified young militiaman of the 20th NYSM, or Ulster Guard—with female companion—proudly holds his "National Guard"-pattern cap on his lap. His heavily tinted shoulder scales are partially anchored in place by white worsted bridle straps. *Quarter-plate ambrotype, Seward R. Osborne collection*

history, when the 71st NYSM marched out of the Navy Yard at Washington to join Burnside's brigade prior to the Battle of Bull Run on July 16, 1861, its coats had been exchanged for "a gray blouse."[28]

By August 1861, and following the end of their first three-month period of service, nothing remained of the dress of the 71st NYSM but "the coat and shako, and these were not considered in keeping with the service conditions existing." The regiment therefore wore their fatigue dress consisting of "army (light) blue trousers, the dark blue jacket previously worn as fatigue, with white belts and fatigue cap."[29]

Based on state regulations, the full dress uniform of the 20th NYSM, or Ulster Guard, had distinctive insignia, buttons, and shoulder straps, plus a "National Guard"-style shako with sunburst plate encircling the numeral "20." Toward the end of April, new recruits for this regiment were given their first vestiges of fatigue uniform when "each man was provided with a soft, light colored Kossuth hat, and a leather collar [or stock] about two inches high."[30] On April 29, the *Commercial Advertiser* reported more fully that this consisted of a "blue coat, blue pantaloons and a white wide-awake round hat; the letters of the company printed thereon in black." After arrival at Annapolis Junction on May 8, 1861, the Ulster Guard was described as consisting of "countrymen from the interior counties of the State" and wore "a blue-black

The "National Guard"-pattern cap worn by the 20th NYSM had a dark-blue cloth body with enameled leather top and binding and white worsted pompon. A gilt star-ray plate with "ULSTER GUARD" on its inner rim had the brass numeral "20" inset. Above this was a heptagon-shaped plate displaying an ornate shield bearing the New York coat of arms, consisting of a rising sun and a ribbon bearing the motto "EXCELSIOR" surmounted by a hand, the whole of which was surrounded by the regimental motto "THIS HAND FOR OUR COUNTRY." *Seward R. Osborne collection*

frock coat, grey pants, and a dull white felt hat, now so discoloured that it would pass for brown, upon which is pencilled in charcoal, 'Twentieth regiment.'" On July 21, the *Baltimore Clipper* advised that the "drab felt hats" worn by the 20th NYSM were being "changed for caps."[31] All the fatigue clothing for this regiment was obtained via private subscription, "the Ulster County Banks providing $10,000 for that object."[32]

Also organized at Albany, the 500-strong 25th NYSM wore a uniform adopted in February 1861, which consisted of gray frock coats trimmed with red and medium-blue pants with white seam stripes, plus blue forage caps. For the first time attached to the New York State Militia, the Albany Burgess Corps was mustered-in on April 23 and joined the ranks of the 25th NYSM, being designated Co. R. This wealthy unit took with it to Washington "two full uniforms [including dark-blue frock coats], a knapsack, canteen, sword, revolver, musket, eating utensils, and the necessary camp equipage." Their dress uniform consisted of a "bear-skin cap, red coat, elaborately trimmed and faced with gold, white pants, [&] dark belts."[33] Each company member also received a "pair of over-shirts" for fatigue wear. New recruits were without uniforms when the 25th NYSM departed for Washington on April 22, 1861.[34] Probably referring to some of these men, on May 3, 1861, Capt. John Gray, commanding the Worth Guard (Co. C), wrote from Washington, "The only thing we lack is uniforms and clothing."[35]

Reporting on the condition of the 25th NYSM after its arrival in Washington, a correspondent of the *Atlas and Argus* commented:

> Our troops . . . need summer clothing. The weather there has suddenly turned to midsummer heat. The men of the 25th Regiment sleep in their stiff heavy uniforms, for they have no change of apparel.—What they need is a light suit of wool—pantaloons and firemen's shirt. Summer suits would be a luxury but this light woolen costume is a necessity. There is danger of great sickness in the crowded quarters; and in a campaign like this, fever is more fatal than artillery. One third of the money spent in flags, would pay for this outfit.[36]

In response, the Committee of the Common Council, in New York City, contracted with Davis, Craft & Wilson, of 465 Broadway, Albany, for 875 pairs of pants and the same number of "first quality knit jacket shirts" to be delivered by June 1, 1861.[37] Although this clothing was received by June 3, it appears not to have been immediately issued, since the regiment was heavily involved in felling trees for building fortifications, and according to 1st Sgt. William T. Wooley, Albany Republican Artillery (Co. A), it would have been quickly ruined by hard labor.[38] On return to Albany on July 28, 1861, the 25th NYSM was reported in the *New York Herald* as looking "tough and well, but much dilapidated as to clothing." The *Atlas and Argus* commented on "the dingy color of their uniforms" but also mentioned the "jaunty red, skull caps" worn by the Worth Guard (Co. C) of the regiment.[39]

By May 1861, New York City had been drained of much if its militia force, and their absence caused considerable concern among propertied interests, who felt defenseless in the face of a possible Southern invasion. As a result, a home guard called the Union Grays was organized on May 13, 1861. Although largely made up of employees of the businesses that sponsored the regiment, several unattached militia companies, such as the Federal Chasseurs—originally commanded by Noah "Pony" Farnham, who afterward became colonel of the 11th New York (First Fire Zouaves)—and the City Cadets, formed by members of the prestigious "White Ball Club," also helped fill its ranks. The uniform acquired by the Union Grays by May 21—which were also nicknamed the "Strawberry Grays"—was described in their regimental history as consisting of "a single-breasted frock coat, cut in the French style, with the skirt reaching to the knee, made of gray cloth, with red collar and cuffs, trimmed with white piping. The

Photographed sometime during April to August 1861, Drummers William Vallet and Joseph S. Schepmoes, Co. B, 20th NYSM, were distinguished by the letters "D" and "C" for Drum Corps, plus the numerals "20" and company letter "B" on their cap fronts. Fourteen-year-old Vallet also wears a plastron front on his jacket, which was probably light blue. A narrow leather belt around his waist supports a small, holstered revolver or pistol. Schepmoes was the thirteen-year-old son of a farmer resident in Gardiner, Ulster County, New York. Because George Vallet, the twenty-five-year-old brother of William, was listed as "daguerrean artist" in the 1860 census, with a studio at 72 North Front Street, Kingston, New York, it is possible that this image was taken by him. *Cabinet card from ambrotype, Seward R. Osborne collection*

The Union Grays, or 22nd New York National Guard, wore a gray frock coat with red collar and cuffs trimmed at the edges with white lace. Trousers were also gray, with red seam stripes edged with white. The gray chasseur-pattern cap had a red band at its base and was trimmed and quartered with white cord. The regimental number was attached to the cap front, with company letters on the belt plate. These three enlisted men of Co. G are identified on the reverse of this imperial-size, hand-colored salt print as brothers Augustus Lord Hyde, Frederick Erastus Hyde, and Edwin Francis Hyde. The latter two served in the field for three months with this regiment in 1862, and the former did likewise in 1863. *Salt print, Michael J. McAfee collection*

trousers were of gray, with a red stripe edged with white piping down the sides; the cap was a gray kepi, with red band and top, each edged with white piping. Yellow leathern leggins were afterwards adopted." Arms consisted of Enfield rifles with sword bayonet. The Union Grays were accepted into the militia system on September 17, 1861, being designated the 22nd Regiment, National Guard of the State of New York.[40]

On April 16, 1861, the New York legislature passed a bill providing for the enrolment of 30,000 "volunteer militia" to take the place of the three-month troops and to serve for two years. As a result, Gov. Edwin D. Morgan ordered the establishment of thirty-eight new regiments, which were numbered in a new series commencing with the "1st," and whose designation was changed from militia to volunteers. The authorization of these new regiments presented the state with major clothing problems. Being informed that the general government would attempt to equip but could not uniform these regiments, New York created a military board that rapidly set about procuring clothing, plus much of the equipage as well. The main part of the uniform established by the state for its troops on April 22 was described as "a jacket of dark army blue cloth, cut to flow from the waist and to fall about four inches below the belt. The coat to be buttoned with eight buttons . . . a low standing collar . . . buttons to be those of the State militia." The trousers and overcoat were briefly described as "light army blue," with the former "cut full in the leg and large around the foot." The overcoat was to be "of the pattern worn by the United States infantry." Headgear consisted of "a fatigue cap of dark blue, with a water-proof cover, to be made with a cape which will fall to the shoulder. The cover to be buttoned at the visor, and furnished with strings, so that it may be tied under the chin." The state button was also used on the overcoat and cap.[41]

On April 25, a contract was duly awarded by military board treasurer Philip Dorsheimer to Brooks Brothers of New York City to supply 12,000 jackets, trousers, and overcoats. The original cost of this uniform was estimated at $26, but Brooks Brothers' bid of $19.50 was accepted. Meanwhile, J. G. Cotrell & Son and J. H. McDonald Jr., both of Albany, were contracted to provide the caps at $12 a dozen. Murphy & Childs, of New York City, were contracted to provide the same at $11.40 per dozen. This headgear

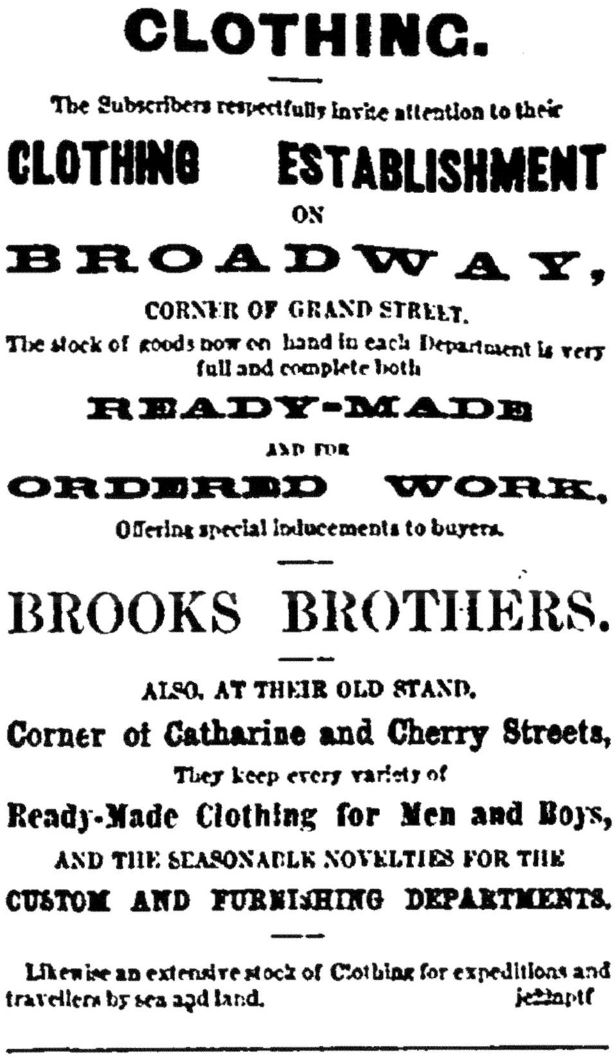

Founded in New York City during 1818, by 1861 the clothing firm of Brooks Brothers was owned by brothers Elisha, Daniel, Edward, and John Brooks. With a contract issued on April 25, 1861, from New York State to supply dark-blue uniforms for the New York volunteers, Brooks Brothers found there was a shortage of blue cloth and resorted to using gray cloth largely produced from pressed rags called "shoddy," which tended to fall apart in the rain and was the subject of ridicule from regiments from other states. Following an investigation, the State Military Board withheld payment and the firm was required to replace these inferior uniforms with ones of better-quality dark-blue cloth via another contract issued on May 23, 1861. *New York Evening Post, author's collection*

was later fitted with brass letters and numerals. The contract for shoes was awarded to Woolverton & Co., of Albany, and Wood, Willard & Prentice, of Troy—both of which were to supply 6,000 of "good stout cowhide Brogans, lined, at $1.25 a pair." The above was sufficient to outfit sixteen of the seventeen new regiments the state planned to establish first, or all seventeen regiments if understrength.[42]

There were several significant details regarding the cut and trim of the uniform that were not included in the general description above. The jacket had shoulder straps, a belt loop on the left side, and a breast pocket. Details varied, depending on the maker. For example, the pocket could be on the right or left breast. Known as a welt or slit pocket, this feature was made by cutting the jacket front open and sewing additional pieces into it. Trim on the edges of the jacket collar, shoulder straps, and belt loop also varied widely both in size and color. Some was true welting, which was formed into a tube and sewn between the edges of the collar and straps. Other trim simply consisted of colored cord sewn to the edges. With at least one regiment, the shoulder straps had solid facing color. Finally, a varied number of buttons were attached to the rear of the nonfunctional cuffs. The jacket was meant to extend four inches below the waist, but many were made considerably shorter.

Soon after going into production, Brooks Brothers discovered that the normal sources of army blue cloth required for the jackets were exhausted. Hence it was necessary to renegotiate the contract to allow the substitution of another type of material. Philip Dorsheimer published his account of events in the Buffalo newspapers in late May 1861:

> I found Inspector-Gen. [William A.] Jackson at the Astor House, who informed me that the City had been searched, and that army cloth was not in market, but that goods of another description had been submitted to him and other military gentlemen in New-York, which were as near what was wanted as could be got, and quite satisfactory. A sample of the goods was furnished and a contract was drawn up by the Judge Advocate, who also examined the goods. . . . Before signing the contract, I personally inquired of eight or ten of the first merchant tailors in New York, who all told me that the army cloth could not be got. The sample was sent to Albany and submitted to the Board, with the contract, and with a full explanation of all circumstances, and the contract was confirmed.[43]

Much of the cloth available to Dorsheimer on this occasion was gray, not blue. Because the NYSM regulations of 1858 had already prescribed a gray nine-button jacket, and gray was a popular color for militia in the North, permission was granted for its use. Of the jackets subsequently made from it and supplied by Brooks Brothers, 7,300 were made of a gray "cadet mixed satinet" woven with a cotton warp and woolen weft and had a deceptive satin-like surface. A further 2,600 were of "dark blue kersey"—rough, coarse wool that was usually ribbed and, prior to this date, was used chiefly for enlisted men's trousers and overcoats. The remaining 2,100 were of a very inferior "dark blue felt." Regarding trousers, 7,200 pairs were produced using gray "cadet mixed satinet," 2,400 were "dark blue kersey," and 2,400 were light-blue, all-wool "army kersey." Of overcoats, 4,400 were gray "cadet doeskin," which was a smooth, close-woven, woolen cloth; 4,000 were of "brown mixed" wool; 1,600 were of dark-blue "petersham" wool; and 2,000 were "mixed kersey."[44]

A *New York Times* correspondent visiting Brooks Brothers on May 9, 1861, described the scene as the company fulfilled its order:

> [O]ver 50 men were engaged receiving, cutting and distributing the cloth, and 5,000 hands were busy sewing, pressing, folding and packing for delivery. In a brief space of time garments were ready by the thousands. Yesterday, however, was the principal delivery day, and . . . the contract, we are assured, will be filled and delivered before the specified time. The uniforms are neat and serviceable, and reflect credit upon both contracting parties. Besides the very large number of boxes sent off during the day yesterday, full uniforms for three regiments were sent to Albany last evening. A visit to the Brooks' establishment would astonish the uninitiated, and perfectly bewilder and confound our "Southern brethren." There are four floors, 200 feet by 100, and a basement of the same size for packing, in which nimble clerks and lusty porters are counting and tugging away all day long. Should the Government resolve to depend upon the private enterprise of the New-York City merchants, such as the Brooks', instead of upon "red tape," it would certainly find a gratifying difference in the time in which troops well furnished, could be brought into the field.[45]

Before the completion of the Brooks Brothers' order, the military board was advised that "a portion of the clothing had been made from improper and unfit material." A committee was appointed to investigate the matter, which included Lt. Gov. Robert Campbell and State Engineer and Surveyor Van R. Richmond. This body found that the gray uniforms supplied, particularly those sent to the Elmira depot, were entirely unsatisfactory, having been made of low-grade yarn obtained by tearing to shreds woolen rags, with some new wool added to make it look like a superior article. This produced a worthless fabric known as "shoddy." Many accounts of this cloth survive in the contemporaneous press. On May 27, 1861, the *Rochester Union Advertiser* described it as "a rusty gray satinet material composed of cotton and 'shotty' with a sprinkling of dog's hair and bristles."[46] Three days later, the *Syracuse Daily Courier and Union* stated:

> The overcoat is of some coarse material—cotton and wool—resembling felted goods, but not as durable or firm in texture. Its color is a blueish grey. . . . The jacket and trowsers are made of a sort of satinet. The material is "shoddy" and cotton, and in color, the stuff is a dark, dirty gray, of three or four shades! All the garments are cut and made in the most slip-shod and disgraceful manner, and nobody expects they will last more than two months. . . . The caps are of dark blue cloth—or were to be, we understand, but, in fact, many of them are black. They are made of as coarse cloth as could be found.[47]

The military board later reported that "the greater part of the 7,300 gray jackets and the greater part of the [7,200] gray trousers . . . were in fact of inferior cloth . . . tender and unfit for use, so much decayed that such uniforms when manufactured from the same piece of gray cloth would present several different colors or shades of color. All of the gray uniforms were badly cut, badly sewed and made up and the buttons used upon all the jackets were of a poor quality and not properly sewed upon such garments. A large number of overcoats . . . were made of cloth which was unfit for use and inferior to the samples."[48]

As a consequence, the board directed the state comptroller to withhold the payment of $80,000 to Brooks Brothers until the contract had been properly completed. In response, the company made rapid restitution of these defects and was awarded subsequent contracts for more-substantial "regular army standard weight" blue uniforms during the following months. Similar problems were revealed with the manufacture of caps. Part of the cap contract was awarded to Murphy & Childs, of New York, who sublet to I. & L. J. Phillips, of the same city, at $7 per dozen, which drew complaints from the "Capmakers' Association."[49]

Despite widespread dissatisfaction with poor-quality clothing, the delivery of gray uniforms had already begun, being received in the New York City area first. While quartered at Staten Island, the 1st New York, or Scandinavian Volunteers, commanded by Col. William H. Allen, received a quarter of its uniforms on May 11, 1861, and the remainder four days later. This was described in the *New York Times* as "a loose-fitting costume, and the color is a serviceable dark grey." The following day the *Tribune* commented that it was "a plain ordinary gray military suit" with "a capacious, dusty-colored surtout [overcoat]." About two weeks later, the *Herald* added that this regiment wore "a gray polka jacket [faced with blue], United States service style, gray pants, and heavy gray coat."[50]

Organized among the German population of New York City, the 7th New York Volunteers, or "Steuben Volunteers," were described as "mostly all picked men, nine-tenths of them . . . veterans, having been engaged in European wars or participated in the revolutions of 1848." The ill-fitting uniform received by this regiment by May 11 included "drab pants, overcoats, and glazed military fatigue caps." Visiting their quarters, a correspondent of the *New York Herald* reported:

> [E]very other suit is found to be three or four inches too large for the tallest man in the ranks. A tailoring establishment has been organized, by taking men from the ranks who are of that profession, and the uniforms are re-fitted on the spot. A sewing machine has been added, to aid in hurrying the completion of the outfit. By making the uniforms so large, a great deal of material is wasted, but the contractors are determined to give enough for the money. In another portion of the room, where the tailors

are at work, a number of men are engaged in making caps, and a corps of shoemakers is about to be organized, to attend to the mending of shoes for the regiment.[51]

In the Troy area, the 2nd New York Volunteers, or Troy Regiment, under Col. Joseph B. Carr, was issued their first vestiges of military apparel at Camp Willard on May 2, when they received "fez caps" made by hatter K. W. Boughton, described as "'Zouave' in style and very jaunty, forming, even without any other portion of the uniform, a very valuable distinguishing mark for the volunteers."[52] Although this regiment expected to be clothed in blue, it received ill-fitting cadet-gray uniforms on May 17, of which occasion a report published in the *Troy Daily Whig* stated, "The soldiers were engaged in putting on their neat, serviceable uniforms, in which they look very finely. The change for the better caused by gray in place of Joseph's coats of many colors, is most marked. The soldiers all seemed pleased with the order to go, and forgot even the inconvenience occasioned by Brooks & Brothers having made all their clothes on a scale suited to a regiment of giants."[53] Arriving in New York City on May 19, the 2nd New York was described as wearing a "dark gray chasseur jacket, pants, and overcoat, with a blue regulation cap."[54]

According to a postwar account by Col. Carr, this clothing was of "the vilest 'shoddy'" and deteriorated rapidly. While serving at Fortress Monroe, Virginia, the regiment appeared on parade at Camp Hamilton "with blankets wrapped around them to conceal a lack of proper garments, and sometimes stood sentinel with naked feet, and almost naked bodies."[55] When a party of 116 men returned home on July 10, having been discharged for medical reasons, the *Daily Whig* commented, "Candor compels us to state that the returned volunteers presented a somewhat melancholy spectacle. To be sure their 'shoddy' uniforms—worn out at that and never very handsome or well fitting when new, were not the style of garments to add to their physique. They looked tired, and were evidently 'glad to get home.'"[56] Another report in the same journal added that the uniforms were "wretchedly made;—their knapsacks have been condemned;—many of the men are entirely without shoes;—and nearly all of them without shirts."[57]

When the 28th New York, or Scott Life Guard / Niagara Rifles, was organized at Albany, the *New York Herald* reported on May 31, 1861, that "two-thirds of their uniforms, with the exception of their pantaloons," were rotten and that "the shoes are States [*sic*] Prison ones."[58] On arrival at Washington, DC, this regiment wore "gray jackets and pantaloons, much like the Seventh Regiment, but of a deeper color," plus "the low crowned Turner hat." They were armed with "the rifled Minie musket." A report in the *Evening Star* of Washington, DC, added that "every man is provided with knapsack and cooking utensils for field duty, the officers bearing the same burden equally and cheerfully with the soldiers."[59]

Gray uniforms began to reach the Elmira depot on May 17, but distribution was delayed due to lack of funds to pay freight costs.[60] Also known as the Onondaga Regiment or Independence Guard, the 12th New York received theirs on May 20, 1861, consisting of "pants and roundabouts, or jackets, of dark gray satinet, gray woolen overcoats, blue fatigue caps, furnished with oil-cloth covers and capes, to be used in rainy weather." The correspondence in the *Syracuse Daily Standard* of May 25 added, "The garments are nearly all too large for the men."[61] Several days after receipt of this uniform, several members of Co. E on furlough visited friends in Syracuse, on which occasion the *Daily Courier and Union* stated that they wore "a gray overcoat with military buttons, round jacket of the same material and blue pants with narrow white stripe down the seams."[62] During the same period, the *Daily Standard* published a report by one of the editors of the *Rochester Evening Express* after his visit to the camp of the 12th New York at Elmira that stated, "They were dressed in their new uniforms, and looked very '*rich*, not gaudy.' At first sight, I thought I beheld a large parcel of boys, enveloped in their fathers' clothes; and intermingled with these, were a quantity of unmistakable *men*, who had donned their childhood apparel. But as a whole, there appeared to have been a great waste of cloth at the country's expense."[63] On June 24, Cpl. Abiah P. Mabine, Co. E, wrote from Camp Onondaga, on East Capitol Hill, Washington, stating:

> The uniforms we have are nothing but Satinet bags; if I live to come home, and can manage to keep one of these garments together, I will show you a specimen of what they are. I am ashamed to go up to the city with my uniform on, so when I go, I borrow a suit from one of the

boys who seemed to have the presentiment of the manner in which the poor soldier was to be swindled, and therefore brought his home suit with him.[64]

The 13th New York, or Rochester Regiment, was issued uniforms at Elmira on May 22, 1861, which according to the *Utica Morning Herald* consisted of "grey jackets and pants, trimmed with light blue, and dark blue fatigue caps," plus "heavy grey overcoats."[65] A jacket attributed to Sgt. William Brownell, Rochester Light Guard (Zouaves, Co. A), 13th New York—which survives today in the collection of the Rochester Museum and Science Center—indicates that the trim was medium blue.[66] The jackets issued to this regiment were described as "wretched" in a report on the activities of the military board published on June 4, 1861.[67] A letter to the *Rochester Evening Express* from Arlington Heights, Virginia, dated June 5, 1861, from a lieutenant of Co. A stated, "Our uniforms, especially pants, are giving out." Three days later, Pvt. Stephen H. Draper, Co. B, informed readers of the *Albany Evening Journal* that what he wore was "heavy enough for a Northern winter dress, and made of miserable material."[68] The same day, Capt. Adolph Nolte, commanding the German Volunteers (Co. C), wrote poetically, "The woeful 'packing canvas' of which our uniform consists, falls like autumn leaves from our bodies."[69] Discharged for disability, Pvt. Charles Felt (Co. E) returned to Rochester and on June 28, 1861, displayed his "shoddy" gray uniform at the office of the *Rochester*

(Left) Although listed in the records only as a private in the 3rd New York Artillery in 1861, the military service of George B. Lewis probably began in 1861, with enlistment in the 19th New York Infantry—also known as the Seward Infantry or Cayuga County Regiment—since this regiment converted to the 3rd Artillery in 1862. He wears an example of the "shoddy" iron-gray uniform issued to the 19th Infantry in June 1861. (Right) William H. Denning enlisted in the 13th New York Infantry, or Rochester Regiment, on May 14, 1861, and was killed at Gaines' Mill on June 23, 1862. He poses in the "shoddy" gray jacket and trousers he received with the rest of his regiment on May 22, 1861. *Cartes de visite, Michael J. McAfee collection*

The jacket worn by Sgt. William Brownell, Rochester Light Guard, (Co. A), 13th New York, is based on the pattern established by the Military Board in April 1861. It was fastened by eight M1855/58 New York staff buttons with "Scovill Mfg. Co. Waterbury" back marks. The closed cuffs have for decoration two small buttons of the same type, with "Extra Quality" back mark. Buttons on the shoulder straps and belt loop are of the same pattern. Due to oxidization, the original gray cloth has changed to brown, while the NCO stripes, collar trim, and solid shoulder straps are medium blue. The latter is unusual, since the April specifications seemed to indicate cord trim on the edges only. Note the welt, or slit, pocket low on the right breast. A small oiled-cloth pouch dangles from one of the buttons. Twenty-five-year-old Brownell enlisted for two years at Rochester, New York, on April 25, 1861. He was mustered into Co. A as a sergeant on May 14, 1861. He was reduced to the ranks on May 15, 1862, and captured at Second Bull Run on August 30 the same year. After parole, he received promotion to corporal on February 20, 1863, and was mustered out with his company on May 13, 1863. *Courtesy of the Rochester Museum and Science Center*

Evening Express. This journal commented, "It is very curious spectacle, and has attracted many visitors during the day."[70]

On June 7, 1861, the *Washington Star* described the 19th New York—called the Seward Infantry or Cayuga County Regiment, also recruited at Elmira—as wearing "iron-gray jackets and pants with light green facings, and gray overcoats."[71] The *National Republican* of the same city simply reported that they were "badly uniformed,"[72] while the chaplain of the regiment commented, "The uniforms which our volunteers of Auburn and Rochester received from the hands of the military board, are the meanest, funniest, felonest dress which ever appeared on a

(Left) This detail shows the crudely sewn chevrons and trimmed belt loop on the left-rear waist. (Right) The shoulder straps had solid color facing, rather than trim around the edges. *Courtesy of the Rochester Museum and Science Center*

public street without being hauled along by a squad of police. . . . There is not a man in our regiment who ever before was dressed so poorly."[73] The regimental historian recalled:

> The uniforms had been made of a coarse, fluffy, flimsy material, called shoddy, full of fine flocking, which on shaking sifted out, filling the eyes, irritating the skin, and covering the floor with refuse. A heartless fraud had been perpetrated. . . . Stripes of dark gray ran through them, with streaks of butternut intermingled. Patches of green, spots of brown, and splashes

Drummer George Carmichael wore this example of the "heavy grey overcoats" issued to the 13th New York on May 22, 1861. Loosely based on the sky-blue US Army–regulation overcoat for enlisted infantrymen, it was single breasted but had only four—as opposed to five—buttons at the front. These have been lost from this garment. A fifth button appears to have been attached to the underside of the broad, falling collar, which could be fastened when the collar was turned up. The elbow-length cape has only five small M1855/58 New York staff buttons with "Extra Quality" back mark. This again differs from the regulation overcoat, which had seven small buttons. The cuffs were turned up as per the regulation pattern. It was lined to the waist minus sleeves with red flannel stamped "COMPY / E / 22," and has two welt, or slit, pockets let in the rear waist made from cotton ticking. This garment has also been affected by oxidation and has faded from gray to brown. Twenty-two-year-old Carmichael enlisted at Rochester on April 23, 1861, and was mustered-in as a drummer in Co. E on May 14, to serve two years. He was mustered out with his company on May 13, 1863, and subsequently served in the 22nd New York Cavalry. *Courtesy of the Rochester Museum and Science Center*

> of other colors, dotted the surface, and no less than eighteen different hues were counted in them by an inquiring volunteer. Shabby in color, uncomfortable from gritty dust in them, flabby in texture, they were ungainly in cut. Few were able to get a suit that fitted them. Nearly all were too large. Two men could button around them one overcoat. Many men could button up their folded overcoats in their pants. . . . They had a most depressing effect on all. Men, wanting furloughs to go home to bid farewell to dear ones, before marching to the seat of war, were ashamed to show themselves and went to the front without seeing the friends they so longingly desired to.[74]

The uniforms acquired by the 21st New York, or Buffalo Regiment, were originally purchased for the 74th NYSM from A. & G. Arnoux, of New York, by the Buffalo City Council. Because that militia regiment was not required for three months' service in 1861, the city council sold the uniforms to the state, which in turn issued them to the Buffalo Regiment on May 21. A report in the *Buffalo Daily Courier* of June 5 stated, "The uniforms of the 21st are at least 25 per cent better in quality [than New York State clothing] and one hundred in color." According to Brig. Gen. H. R. White, who visited the military camp near Elmira, at this time the 21st New York wore a "neat and finely fitting gray uniform. . . . It is the same style as the regular State uniform—jacket, cap and pants alike—but fits the men beautifully."[75] In his regimental history, J. Harrison Mills described the uniform as consisting of "a cap, jacket and pants of gray cloth, trimmed with black, and an overcoat of bluish black lined with red."[76] After escorting the Buffalo Regiment to the railroad depot on their departure for Washington, DC, a man in the 27th New York remarked that they "looked well, and very neat in their gray uniforms."[77] When the 21st reached the federal capital on June 19, it was reported to be wearing "dark gray jackets, pants, and cap, trimmed with black."[78]

Other regiments uniformed at Elmira included the 24th New York, or Oswego Regiment, which on May 21, 1861, received "pants and jackets of grey, and coarse grey overcoats. The caps were blue." Most of this was described as "ill fitting."[79] The 26th New York, also called the 2nd Oneida Regiment or Utica Regiment, wore "dark grey jackets and pants" and "serviceable overcoats" when they arrived at the capital from Elmira, New York, on June 22.[80] After visiting this regiment at Camp Douglas the next day, a man in the 14th New York wrote, "Found the boys in good spirits. . . . The uniforms with which they were supplied by the State are a miserable apology for a dress. They are much worse than those supplied the 14th, and they are bad enough [see below]." According to the *Utica Daily Observer* of July 9, when the 26th New York "hove in sight of the White House," President Lincoln asked, "what Rag-mill that body of men represented," and that it was "the opinion of all that the boys ought to have a new uniform."[81]

Those regiments receiving either the dark-blue kersey or dark-blue felt uniforms also—probably as a result of the April 25 contract—included the 3rd New York, or Albany Regiment. Disembarking at New York City from the steamer *Alida* on May 19, this regiment occupied the Park Barracks, with the officers assigned quarters at the Astor House. According to the *Tribune*, the latter wore "dark blue throughout, with a green cord down the pantaloons, the uniform of the Rifles, of which the regiment consists. The cap of the officers is the United States cap. . . . The men are uniformed in the dark blue Chasseur jacket and overcoat, and light blue army cloth pants."[82] Known as the Syracuse Zouaves, Co. E of the 3rd Regiment was formed in July 1860. Modeled on "the famous Chicago Zouaves," this corps wore full dress based on "the renowned Guard Imperial of France," and a fatigue uniform consisting of "blue pants with cord down the seams, red shirt, blue jacket with red trimmings and red fez." On April 22, the *Syracuse Daily Courier and Union* stated that the Syracuse Zouaves would parade in "the regular Zouave uniform, being the only one they will have an opportunity to appear in at home until peace is restored to the country"[83]

While in barracks at Albany, the 14th New York, or Oneida Regiment, received their uniforms on May 23, following which a member of the regiment wrote, "The uniform is not gray as was expected . . . but is blue. Blue pants (with two pockets), jacket (with one pocket) trimmed with red, blue fatigue cap, and blue overcoat with capes. . . . The regulation button is worn. . . . Can't say much in praise of the fit of the garments, but most of the men are having them refitted, which can be done at very little expense." When this regiment made its first dress parade the following day, the *Utica Morning Herald* commented, "The suit is a very dark blue, and consists of overcoat, jacket and trousers." Its clothing was stated as being of "dark-blue cloth, trimmed with red cord" when the 14th New York arrived at Washington, DC, on June 20, 1861.[84]

The 2nd NYSM, also known as the State Grenadiers, commanded by Col. George Tompkins, volunteered for three years and was redesignated the 82nd New York Volunteers. Passing through Baltimore on May 21, 1861, this regiment was reported as wearing "light blue pants, with a broad white seam stripe, blue jacket and cap." Accompanying it was "four brass howitzers and a field piece" worked by a "howitzer corps . . . numbering seventy-five men," plus "an engineer corps, numbering twenty-five men," and a "crack drum corps of twenty-two pieces." According to a *Baltimore Clipper* report, the howitzer corps was commanded by Capt. Thaddeus P. Mott and was "composed entirely of seamen, many of whom had served for years in the United States Navy." In a letter written on May 22 by a Rhode Island volunteer to the *Providence Daily Post*, it was further described as "a company of old salts . . . proverbial for their dexterity in handling such pieces."[85]

Several of the above regiments received federal-issue clothing consisting of 1858-pattern dark-blue flannel sack coats and sky-blue pants, sometimes as an interim measure until the state replaced their shoddy clothing. Correspondence by a lieutenant of the Rochester Light Guard (Co. A), 13th New York, dated June 14, 1861, stated, "It consists of navy flannel coats and hemp-drilled pants. They look very neat and I think will do good service and be very cool for this warm climate. The uniforms from the State to replace the old ones have not yet arrived. When we get them we shall be well supplied with clothes."[86] This regiment was again in receipt of federal uniforms in mid-August, prior to being moved to Fortress Monroe. This probably replaced clothing suffering from the effects of the Bull Run Campaign. At this time, a member of the German Volunteers (Co. C) wrote, "Tomorrow the Lieutenant Colonel will make a requisition upon the Government for our uniforms, which we will get by day-after-to-morrow." Later in this piece he states, "We are satisfied with new and serviceable uniforms."[87] On August 24, a correspondent of the *Syracuse Standard* visited the camp of the 24th New York and wrote, "The regiment are all handsomely uniformed and furnished with the best Enfield rifles, and a large supply of new clothing is in camp which they have no need for."[88]

Rollin B. Truesdell was a twenty-one-year-old farmer when he enlisted in Co. F, 27th New York Volunteers—or Union Regiment—at Binghamton on May 21, 1861. Hailing from Liberty, in Susquehanna County, Pennsylvania—just over the state line from New York—it was a shorter distance from his home town to Binghamton than it was to travel to Harrisburg, or any other places of enlistment in his home state. He was promoted to corporal on November 1, 1861, and sergeant on February 20, 1863. He was mustered out at Elmira on May 31, 1863. His surviving jacket is a fine example of the pattern issued to New York volunteers from June 1861. Fastened by eight buttons, these garments had shoulder straps, a belt loop on the left side, and a breast pocket. The standing collar and shoulder straps were trimmed with sky blue. The nonfunctional cuffs have two small buttons attached. The NCO chevrons are in line with 1858 regulations. *Historical Imagebank, CWu118d & Cwu69ds*

To replace shoddy clothing with better-quality uniforms, the New York State Quartermaster Department advertised new contracts on May 23, 1861—which were let within several days—for 15,000 blue state uniforms "to be made of the regular army standard weight . . . of cloth of pure fleece wool and indigo dye . . . overcoats and pantaloons of [sky blue] and jackets of a deep blue color." This brought the total number of enlisted men outfitted by New York State to 28,000, including all of the first thirty-eight volunteer regiments, plus several of the militia regiments reorganized for federal service. Following a "spirited contest" among 198 tenders, the firms contracted to produce 2,500 suits of clothing each were Devlin, Hudson & Co.; Wilhelm Seligman & Co.; Arnoux & Co.; Baldwin & Co. and Charles Barnum, of

Lifelong friends Hugh Donihue and Reuben Van Leuven both were mustered-in for three years in Co. D, 20th NYSM, on September 5, 1861. Born of Irish parentage in Albany, New York, in 1842, Donihue was a farmer when he enlisted. He was wounded in the left shoulder at Second Bull Run on August 30, 1862, and reenlisted as a veteran in the same regiment in February 1864. Promoted to first sergeant by July 1865, he was mustered out at Portsmouth, Virginia, on January 29, 1866. Van Leuven was born in Marbletown, in Ulster County, New York, in 1844, and was also a farmer. He was wounded in the abdomen and bled to death on the field of battle at Gettysburg on July 3, 1863. Both men wear the state-issue blue jacket. In this reversed image, the belt loop on Donihue's state-issue jacket appears on the right hand side. *Quarter-plate tintype, Seward R. Osborne collection*

Photographed brandishing personal weapons in camp at Bethlehem, New York, on June 24, 1861, these enlisted men of Co. G, 16th New York Volunteers, wear the good-quality May contract blue uniforms issued to their regiment nine days earlier (left to right): Luther Lee Partridge, Andrew Christie Bayne, John Henry Austin, and Edwin O. Betts. All four men were promoted to the rank of sergeant and had been mustered-in a month earlier at Albany. All four resided in De Peyster, a hamlet in the far north of the Empire State. Partridge was wounded on May 3, 1863, in the fighting at Salem Church, Virginia, during the Chancellorsville Campaign. Scottish-born Bayne enlisted in the Veteran Reserve Corps after he left the 16th New York and had risen to the rank of captain by the end of the war. He then joined the regular army and remained in service until 1871. Austin became second lieutenant of Co. G and mustered out on May 22, 1863. Betts was reduced to the ranks on September 29, 1862, and remained in Co. G until its term of enlistment expired. *Carte de visite, Ronald S. Coddington collection*

New York City; and P. P. Kellogg & Co., of Utica, in Oneida County, New York.[89] The uniforms these firms supplied were described in the press as being "made of the best cloth, and in workmanship are far superior to the clothing made for the United States Army."[90] The contract for fatigue caps was awarded to Murphy & Childs, of New York City, and shirts and drawers were produced by Pierce Brothers, of Boston. Shoes were supplied by Benedict, Hall & Co. at $1.25 per pair, and blankets by Cronin, Hurxthal & Sears, also of New York.[91] The issuance of these uniforms began by mid-June 1861.

Having refused to receive the gray uniforms produced via the April 24 contract, Col. Thomas A. Davies, commanding the 16th New York Volunteers, or St. Lawrence Regiment, finally received good-quality blue uniforms for his men on June 15, 1861, while at Camp Morgan near Albany. His regiment was reported as being uniformed in "the regulation [New York] style, except that the men wear a fatigue cap" upon arrival at Washington, DC.[92] The *Atlas and Argus* of June 16 reported that the uniforms worn by this regiment were "made by Mr. [Palmer P.] Kellogg, of Utica," and that every suit was "fully up to sample. Indeed, Messrs. [William W.] Parker and [Henry] Carpenter, tailors of this city, who were appointed to inspect them, rejected only one pair of pants."[93]

Already encamped at Washington, by June 20 the 12th New York had received new uniforms in place of its shoddy gray. In defense of his much-maligned regimental quartermaster, Capt. Henry I. Barnum (Co. I) wrote, "The pants are of dark blue army cloth, and the coats of navy flannel, also dark blue. The pattern of the coat is a short sack, loose enough to be comfortable."[94] A letter believed to have been written by the same officer dated July 4, 1861, mentioned that the men of this regiment "put on the blue flannel jackets and pants furnished by Uncle Sam" and arranged the plumes on their "regulation hats" in preparation for the Fourth of July parade.[95]

The 17th New York, also known as the Westchester Chasseurs, were neatly uniformed in "dark and light-blue cloth" on arrival at the federal capital on June 23.[96] En route for the capital, the 18th New York, or New York State Rifles, under Col. William A. Jackson, passed through Wilmington, Delaware, on June 20, wearing "short jackets made of dark blue cloth, handsomely trimmed; pants of light-blue cloth, and the usual military cap." The 18th New York carried a regimental flag presented by the ladies of Albany bearing "the descriptive charge, 'Rally around it.'"[97] When sworn in on June 22, the 24th New York was reported to be "uniformed as it should be," with overcoats and pants of "all wool army blue, and the jackets of navy blue."[98]

Some of the 27th New York, or Union Regiment, had received "one pair of blue overhauls" by June 19, 1861. On June 29, this regiment was "fully uniformed." According to the *Rochester Evening Express*, this was:

Photographed by a cameraman from Matthew Brady's studio while encamped near Washington, DC, three of these volunteers of the 29th New York, or Astor Guard, wear the state-issue uniform provided via the contract issued in May 1861. The musician at left has an M1840 musician's sword suspended from his shoulder belt. The man at second left is fully equipped with a knapsack, blanket roll, and canteen, while the volunteer to his right wears a four-button sack coat. All but one wears a "SNY" oval belt plate. They are armed with M1842 muskets. *Carte de visite, Michael J. McAfee collection*

> not in the shapeless and worthless material imposed on the Quinby [13th] regiment, but in serviceable and well fitting *clothes*. The uniform consists of overcoat, jacket and pants. The overcoat is of the best army cloth, light blue, well made, durable and impervious to wind and weather of any description. The jacket is of dark blue, close fitting, provided with crescent pockets at the side, tastefully trimmed and provided with officer's buttons. The pants are of light blue, of excellent material and well made.[99]

The more substantial blue uniform was not always welcome. Writing from Camp Anderson, Washington, DC, on August 10, Pvt. Oliver A. Kilmer (Co. D), 27th New York, stated, "The weather for the past ten days has been very warm, so that in the middle of the day, the heat is intolerable. The Government has furnished us with a suit of woolen clothes, suitable for winter wear in a Northern latitude, these we are compelled to wear on duty. This may be according to the army regulations, but I think the regulations of Nature suggest a different dress."[100]

Having apparently been reuniformed, the 28th New York arrived in New York City on June 27, 1861, wearing "light blue overcoats, dark blue jackets, light blue pants and dark blue caps." The product of Kellogg & Co., these uniforms were also inspected by Albany tailors Parker and Carpenter. Each man was also provided with "an India rubber cloth knapsack, haversack, canteen, blanket, and a stout pair of shoes."[101] Organized at Albany, the 30th New York received their uniforms on June 22. When volunteers visited the city several days later, the *Troy Daily Whig* remarked that their clothing "showed the neat colors and excellent texture to good advantage. The uniform is by far the best yet given to any Volunteer Regiment in the State. It consists of a dark blue jacket, light blue pants and overcoat, of excellent quality, and generally a good fit."[102] Composed of "the Hibernian element of the Empire State," the 37th New York, or Irish Rifles, wore "light blue pants, dark blue jacket and fatigue cap." This regiment carried guide flags made of "the most costly green silk, bearing a representation of 'The Harp that once.' &c., &c., in bold relief."[103]

When they finally left camp at East New York, the 38th New York Volunteers, or Second Scott Life Guard,

Although the officers in most New York regiments wore dark-blue uniforms, Col. Louis Blenker and other officers of the 8th New York Volunteers, or "German Rifles," wore gray coats with green cord around the cuffs, gray trousers with double red seam stripes, and red chasseur caps trimmed with gold braid. Also note the black leather stock around his neck, plus the monocle in his eye. Born in Germany in 1812, Blenker fought in an *Uhlan* regiment in the Greek Civil War and, upon return to Germany in 1837, became a colonel in the Worms militia. Driven into the German Revolutionary party due to political corruption, he commanded the *Freischaren*, or Free Corps. Following the failure of the revolution of 1849, he fled to Switzerland, whence he immigrated to the US. Initially in reserve at First Bull Run, his regiment effectively helped cover the Union retreat. He later commanded a division in Virginia and West Virginia but was recalled to Washington in June 1862, following which he saw no further service. Discharged on March 31, 1863, he died seven months later of injuries sustained in a fall from a horse earlier in the war. *Massachusetts Commandery, Military Order of the Loyal Legion of the United States (MASS-MOLLUS), Vol. 59, PL 2906,USAHEC*

wore "light blue overcoats, dark blue jackets and Havelock hats," the latter possibly being a reference to the unusual headgear invented by Chicago hatter James Loomis in April/May 1861, and either ordered from him or copied by suppliers in New York.[104] Regarding headgear, the 33rd New York, or Ontario

Regiment, requisitioned "1700 straw hats" while at Camp Lyon, near the Chain Bridge at Washington, DC, during August, following which an officer stated, "All the 33d, including the Colonel, wear straw hats in hot weather."[105] A predominantly German regiment commanded by Col. Adolph Von Steinwehr, the 29th New York, or Astor Guard, wore a uniform provided by millionaire William B. Astor consisting of "a dark blue jacket, gray pantaloons, corded with blue at the sides, and gray overcoat" when they departed for the federal capital on July 23, 1861. Earlier that month, this unit was reported to be "sadly in want of gray flannel shirts, brown drilling pantaloons, socks, &c."[106] When this regiment passed through Philadelphia, *The Press* commented, "The men wore sprigs of evergreen in their caps, which in Germany is the emblem of riflemen."[107] The embarkation of the 25th New York from Staten Island at the beginning of July was delayed because "about 500 of the uniforms were made large enough to fit the most stalwart of the Green Mountain Boys. As the men could not be enlarged to the requisite proportions the uniforms had to be cut down."[108]

This unidentified young volunteer is possibly a member of the 8th New York Volunteers. His gray coat would have been trimmed with green collar and cuffs, with a wide green seam stripe on the trousers and cap with a green band. A brass, 1858-pattern Infantry "Looped" horn insignia is attached to the front of his cap, and a rigid militia-style knapsack is properly secured to his back via light leather straps. *Michael J. McAfee collection*

The 21st New York did not receive their second state issue until late August 1861. In his regimental history, J. Harrison Mills wrote, "The gray uniforms given us at Elmira had . . . become threadbare, and were replaced with Uncle Sam's livery. On the 29th of August we received caps, jackets and pants of dark blue, with a gray woolen blouse for fatigue duty. The pants were afterward replaced by others of light blue."[109] The 13th New York did not receive their May contract clothing until late August. On the nineteenth, Pvt. J. A. Gault (Co. A) wrote, "Yesterday the boys got the long promised suit of clothes from New York State. They are light blue pants and dark blue jackets. . . . The suit, though superior to that given them at Elmira, might be greatly improved upon, for the money paid for them. But at least the time of torn pants and bare feet is gone."[110] The same day, a lieutenant in the regiment commented, "What had we better do with the old 'shoddy' uniforms now in our possession? Would it not be advisable to send them to the Governor to be placed among the *relics* of the State? Or shall they be sent to Brooks & Bro. to manufacture over for the 25,000 new volunteers now being raised?"[111] The late delivery of these state blue uniforms clearly had a detrimental effect on the soldiers. On August 24, Cpl. W. A. Sands (Co. A) reported:

> This, though better than the other, is not much worth, for they have been so long in the boxes, that they have become mouldy and rotten; some of the pantaloons that I saw on the men on Sunday, neat and whole, are now all torn on account of their rottenness, besides only about half of each company can get fitted with them, so that the men were so unfortunate as to get a jacket or pair of pantaloons too large, can have the privilege of getting them altered, and paying the expense themselves.[112]

By September 13, 1861, much of these problems appear to have been solved, since on that date, a report from the regiment in the *Rochester Evening Express* stated, "The men are well clothed."[113]

The state also paid for the distinctive uniforms worn by some New York regiments. Commanded by

Probably photographed by George Stacy, this detail from a stereoscopic view shows officers and civilians gathered around a table with a cloth painted with the unit designation "8th N. Y. St.[ate] R.[ifles]." The officer with a lady seated at the table may be John Trzeciak, who was mustered in as first lieutenant and adjutant of the 8th New York on April 23, 1861. The officer seated in the chair at left is probably Col. Louis Blenker. These and other officers present wear gray uniforms and red chasseur-pattern caps, while at least nine enlisted men in plainer gray uniforms stand in the rear. *Michael J. McAfee collection*

Col. Louis Blenker, the 8th New York Volunteers, or First Regiment German Rifles, were recruited among the German population of New York City. They received their uniforms on May 12, 1861, which were reported in the *New York Tribune* to consist of "a gray sack with a strap and buckle behind, green cord facings and green shoulder-straps, gray pantaloons with a broad green stripe down the side, and a gray cap with green cord. The officers' uniform is the same, with a red cap."[114] Passing through Wilmington, Delaware, en route for the capital, the German Rifles were described as wearing "gray pants and a loose gray coat, with a short belt, by which it can be loosened or tightened about the waist, at pleasure." Expecting to receive a full complement of arms upon reaching Washington, the Germans carried only "200 muskets, and 112 Sharp's rifles." The regiment was also reported to have "two ambulances, and about eight horses, some of which belong to the officers. Each company has two portable cases containing bandages, lint, plasters, chloroform, and other articles necessary for hospital use."[115]

While encamped at Turtle Bay Park, New York City, during mid-May 1861, the mostly German 20th New York Volunteers, or United Turner Rifles, commanded by Col. Max Weber, were provided with uniforms reported in the *Morning Express* as being "made of cloth of a very inferior quality, but of three different colors, so that the Turners would have looked like clowns or convicts, rather than soldiers and sharpshooters." As a result, Weber determined to acquire better uniforms either by private subscription or via the Union Defense Committee.[116] Departing for Fortress Monroe in what was probably replacement clothing on June 13, the 20th New York were reported to be wearing "blue coats, blue pants, and gray fatigue caps."[117] On December 5, 1861, the *New York Times* reported that this regiment presented a very fine appearance at "Camp Hamilton" near Fortress Monroe, Virginia, with "their bright rifles and green decorated uniforms."[118]

Largely recruited and organized in New York City by Col. Calvin E. Pratt, the 31st New York, also known as the Montezuma Regiment, contained a company consisting entirely of Polish Americans. Designated Co. C and commanded by Capt. Alexander Raszewski, this unit originated as part of the "Polish Legion" raised by Col. Julian Allen. Indeed, on May 9, 1861, the *New York Evening Express* described Raszewski's company as being "clothed in the uniform of the Polish Army, and from part of the Polish Legion raised in this city."[119] When the 31st New York arrived at the federal capital on June 25, 1861, it was reported as being uniformed in the state uniform of "dark blue jacket, light blue pants, and fatigue caps. Their overcoats are of the regular army pattern, and [to] their caps are attached oil cloth capes, as a protection from rain." The same day, a correspondent of the *Baltimore Clipper* observed that the men of this regiment wore "dark blue caps, with a sort of havelock behind as protection against the weather." Each man also had "one good pair of shoes, two pair of drawers, two grey flannel shirts, two pair of socks, and a white blanket." They were armed with "the improved Springfield smooth-bore muskets."[120]

Earlier, on May 2, the *New York Herald* had reported a company of the Polish Legion amounting to "seventy seven men, wearing the crimson Lancer cap" as they marched by on their way to be measured for uniforms.[121] On the basis of an 1861 lithograph, the legion wore red *chapskas*—distinctive square-topped

Polish caps, dark-blue frock coats with red collar and cuffs, and trousers of bluish gray. Formed on October 19, 1861, by a consolidation of the "Polish Legion," under Allen, plus the "United States Rifles" and "Morgan Rifles," the 58th New York contained Germans, Danes, Italians, Russians, and French, as well as Poles.

An outgrowth of the 69th NYSM, the 69th New York Infantry was the first regiment of the Irish brigade organized by Thomas Meagher. Commanded by Col. Robert Nugent, this regiment was described as being dressed "entirely in grey uniforms, with the regulation hat, to which a green feather is attached" when it passed through Baltimore, Maryland, on its way to Washington, DC, on November 18, 1861.[122]

Some New York volunteer regiments were not prepared to wait for the state clothing that Brooks Brothers was contracted to produce in April 1861, and with the help of various volunteer aid societies, including the Union Defense Committee, procured their own uniforms. Established by the merchants and businessmen of New York City on April 20, 1861, the Union Defense Committee appropriated money for "the purpose of procuring the necessary equipment and outfit of the military force." According to a report in the *New York Times*, some of the cloth purchased by

This detail from a stereo view titled "Volunteers at the Park Barracks, New York," where the 31st New York was organized, includes an officer wearing a *chapska* with a white band in the group in the foreground. This may well be Capt. Alexander Raszewski. The unarmed enlisted men formed in the rear wear plain white shirts, gray or sky-blue trousers, and darker-colored caps. *Michael J. McAfee collection*

this means was made up into uniforms by the prisoners at the state penitentiary and the inmates at the city almshouse and lunatic asylum under the supervision of "the ladies of the city."[123] Five of the early-war "Zouave" regiments clothed via volunteer means were the 5th, 6th, 9th, 10th, and 11th New York Volunteers.

The bulk of the contract for the first uniform received by the 5th New York—also known as the Advance Guard or Duryee's Zouaves—was given to Devlin, Hudson & Co., while Seligman & Co. produced 209 of them. Headgear was made by the Seamless Clothing Manufacturing Company, of New York City.[124] When this regiment left New York on May 23, 1861, its uniform was described in the *New York Times* as being "that of the French Zouave, with full flowing pants of red flannel, and the red cap, with a cape of white flannel, which partially concealed the face."[125] A correspondent of the *Burlington Free Press*, of Vermont, reported:

> Their loose, baggy, red trousers with a sort of drab-colored gaiters reaching from just below the knee down, their blue jackets trimmed with other colors, their cap, a sort of close fitting Turkish fez, red with black tassel, (the face being wholly exposed to the sun, but the neck and shoulders protected with a loose white flannel curtain coming out beneath the cap, something like the loose part of a havelock) and the bronzed faces of the men, gave the Regiment a very picturesque and dashing appearance. Each man had his gun and bayonet on his back, and were mostly quite uniform in height and as resolute a looking and moving set of fellows as are often to be met with.[126]

A veteran later recalled that the uniform of Duryee's Zouaves consisted of:

Commanded by Capt. Hiram Duryee, Co. E, 5th New York Volunteers—also known as Duryee's Zouaves—were photographed near Fortress Monroe by George Stacy in June 1861. The Zouaves wear the first version of the Duryee uniform, which included a red fez with short blue tassel, white cotton turban, and havelock; blue jacket with red trim; red-trimmed blue waist band; red pantaloons; and white canvas leggings. Only two men in the front rank appear to be wearing the turban. The NCO at extreme right, plus the officer at the extreme left, wears a red kepi. Later in their service, this regiment would receive pantaloons of a fuller cut, fezzes with long yellow tassel, and leather jambieres to be worn over their leggings. *Library of Congress, PR13 CN 2008:007*

An ex-pugilist and ex-alderman of the First Ward, New York City, William Wilson (seated at center) was involved in paramilitary organizations affiliated with the Democratic Party in New York since at least 1857. In that year he was elected "Major General" of an anti-Republican faction called the "Citizen Volunteers." By 1861, this had evolved into the Union Volunteer Battalion, which on May 22 was accepted into federal service as the 6th New York Volunteers, also known as Wilson's Zouaves. Seated on his left is Lt. Col. John Creighton, while on his right is Maj. William B. Newby. Creighton faced court martial for drunkenness on October 26, 1861, and was expunged from the regimental records. The unidentified enlisted men wear the gray shirts and pants provided by the Union Defense Committee. *National Archives, NWDNS-111-B-4388*

wide flowing Zouave pants of bright red, narrow and pleated at the top, wide at the bottom and baggy in the rear. These were topped with a broad sash of the same color edged with blue tape and falling nearly to the knee on the left side. The jacket was of coarse blue material, trimmed with red tape, short, loose, low-necked and collarless and rounded in front. The shirts were of the same material with a broad stripe of red down the bosom. The leggings were heavy white canvas, buttoned at the side and reaching to the knee and the shoes were clumsy, square-toed scows. The caps were close-fitting red fezzes turned back from the top of the head, to which was attached a cord with a blue tassel that dangled in the middle of the back.[127]

Of this clothing, Sgt. Alfred Davenport, Co. G, recalled that it looked "very pretty" but was not of "the finest texture or the best made in the world."[128] The greatest complaints were made about the cut of the pantaloons, which were adjudged to be too tight at the calf and not baggy enough. On May 8, 1861, Devlin, Hudson & Co. wrote to Col. Abram Duryee, stating they had been informed that many of the Zouaves were wearing "the uniform pants over others, which will of course destroy the fit." Nevertheless, the last 125 pairs of Zouave pantaloons delivered by this firm were lengthened by two inches.[129]

According to Davenport, by the time it had arrived in Baltimore on July 27, 1861, the 5th New York looked "shabby, some of the uniforms being almost worthless."[130] The whole regiment received new uniforms in September 1861, the quality of which was also poor, and Gouverneur K. Warren, who succeeded Duryee in command, remarked later that it "did not have half the cloth it should have had." "The breeches," he added, "were not nearly large and full enough and the linings of the jackets was made of stuff not shrunk and when it became wet, drew the jacket all out of shape."[131] A third and more substantial Zouave uniform was received in February 1862 and was worn

Col. Rush Hawkins and Lt. Col. Edgar A. Kimball (standing second and third from left) pose with other officers and men of the 9th New York Volunteers, also known as Hawkins' Zouaves. The officers wear fine-quality dark-blue uniforms trimmed with gold braid, plus shoulder knots of the same color. Other, more-junior officers have conventional shoulder boards to distinguish their rank. The enlisted men wear red fezzes with large blue tassels and have jackets, vests, and pantaloons trimmed with magenta. Waist sashes were also magenta. The NCO and other enlisted men seen sitting and lying on the floor are fully equipped with knapsacks, blanket rolls, waterproof haversacks, and canteens. Note both the sergeant and officer to his right have "flaming bomb" plates fastening their belts. *National Archives, NWDNS-111-B-5886*

throughout the regiment's most significant period of service until its muster-out in May 1863.

Although Col. William Wilson was probably one of the first to offer New York State a regiment of volunteers, on or around January 20, 1861, his "Union Volunteer Battalion" was not accepted due to circumstances at that time. His regiment was finally mustered-in as the 6th New York Volunteers on May 22, 1861. Poorly led, this unit became more notorious for crimes committed by its officers and men than for its effectiveness in combat. On May 18, 1861, Wilson's Zouaves were described in *Harper's Weekly* as being "roughs and b'hoys of New York City. Their uniform is a gray shirt, gray pants, brown felt hat, belt, and brogans."[132] After a visit to the camp of the 6th New York on Staten Island at the beginning of May 1861, a reporter for the *New York Commercial Advertiser* observed that they had "not yet been fitted with their uniforms, but were clothed in undress, composed of gray shirt and pants, with the addition of a blue blanket, which, true to the instincts of their class, they wore in a most careless but picturesque manner. Thrown over their brawny shoulders, it gave them the appearance of Italian beggars." With funds provided by the Union Defense Committee, the firm of Smith Brothers supplied "700 pairs of pants and shirts" to this regiment.[133] By the time of the presentation of flags in New York City on June 15, 1861, the 6th New York appear to have received some state clothing, since on that occasion they were described as being "attired in their gray jackets furnished by the State which were of the very worst sort of shoddy cloth."[134]

Originating as an independent military club formed in New York City by Rush Hawkins on July 23, 1860, the "New-York Zouaves" was purely a social organization—probably inspired by the visit to the city of Elmer Ellsworth and his United States Zouave Cadets—and without affiliation to the state militia. Despite their intention of adopting a uniform "similar to that of the French Zouaves," this unit originally wore a sparsely trimmed dark-blue jacket and straight-legged trousers, plus red fez.[135] With the outbreak of civil war a year later, Rush Hawkins was the first man to present the state governor at Albany with an offer to raise a volunteer regiment. Designated the 9th New York Volunteers and quartered in Castle

The staff officer uniform worn by Col. Rush C. Hawkins was made by Brooks Brothers, of New York City. Both the jacket and vest were made of the finest wool. Similar in cut to the enlisted men's pattern, the jacket was trimmed with gold braid and had two sets of rank designation. On the shoulders was a Russian knot, over which was sewn a cloth "eagle," and on each sleeve was a Hungarian knot with red wool inserts. *Annmary Brown Memorial Collection, Brown University*

Photographed at the Brady National Photographic Art Gallery in Washington, DC, ca. 1860–61. Rush Hawkins wears the Zouave uniform for officers of the 9th New York Volunteers. His gold-laced red cap with numeral "9" within a hunting-horn insignia at front has a tall, white feather plume attached to its stiffened top. The trousers were similar to the other staff officers, with the exception of an intricate pattern of fine gold braid near the hip, which then ran in a straight line down the length of the leg. *National Archives, 528150*

(Left) The eagle insignia on each shoulder knot was handmade by first making a template, padding and stitching it, and then applying the bullion. (Right) The vest is edged with gold trim and originally had fifteen General Staff "eagle" buttons attached to the red wool strip on its false front. It was fastened at the shoulder and either side with plain wooden buttons. *Annmary Brown Memorial Collection, Brown University*

The cartridge boxes carried by Hawkins Zouaves were made by Peter & Brenner of Newark, New Jersey. Constructed of black enameled leather, they carried .58-caliber ammunition for the Model 1842 smooth-bore musket issued to the regiment in 1861. Solder-filled brass script letters "NG" served to weigh down the front flap, underneath which was an implement pouch. Unlike federal issue, the front flap was stitched around the edge, and the belt loops ensured that the cartridge box was slung low on the waist belt. The tin insert measured 513⁄16 in. wide, 45⁄16 in. high, and 15⁄16 in. deep. The top four partitions are 41⁄2 in. square and 13⁄4 in. deep. The bottom two partitions are 215⁄16 in. wide and 27⁄16 in. high. *Dennis Schurr collection*

This fez was worn by Pvt. Charles W. Lyon, Co. A, 9th New York Volunteers, on May 4, 1861. Aged twenty-one, he enlisted at New York City on April 23, 1861, and was mustered-in for two years on May 4, 1861. *Dennis Schurr collection*

Garden, the unit that evolved adopted a uniform that was based on that worn by the company of original New York Zouaves made by T. Menzesheimer & Sons. Several days prior to its departure for the front, this regiment was vaguely described in the *Commercial Advertiser* as wearing "a blue flannel jacket and pants trimmed with red, a gray shirt, red sash, brown linen leggins [*sic*] or gaiters, and a linen cap and cape to protect the neck."[136] Acquired by private contract, which was paid for by the state, this uniform was described more accurately in the regimental history as being of "the Zouave pattern: close, easy-fitting, permitting full action of body and arms, artistic in form and picturesque, but of modest tone; of army blue, the trousers slightly full, plaited at the waist, with magenta braid down the outer seam; jacket and vest with magenta trimmings, a sash of the same color of woolen material, wide enough to cover the stomach and bowels of the wearer; white leggings, and red fez with a blue tassel."[137]

Formed from various independent Zouave companies with the "National Zouaves" of New York City—commanded by Capt. Waters W. McChesney as its nucleus—the 10th New York Volunteers were originally issued "a dark blue flannel costume, of the zouave pattern, with gray fatigue caps," according to the regimental history.[138] The *New York Herald* published several additional descriptions of this uniform. On May 9, 1861, it reported that this was to consist of a "dark blue flannel jacket and trousers, trimmed with red stripes." Leggings of russet leather had already been furnished by that date.[139] On June 1, the same journal stated that it was the "improved Zouave costume, the jacket and pants being of blue pilot cloth, trimmed with red, with vest of the same cloth, trimmed with stripes of blue, and ornamented in front with a row of gilt buttons; a havelock of linen, Zouave boots, and a blue sash with crimson border, complete the costume." The reporter added, "Several tailors are sent with the uniforms, and each man is to be properly fitted."[140] Clearly made of "shoddy" instead of flannel, these uniforms did not fare well. While encamped at Sandy Hook, New Jersey, the men began to complain that they had been "compelled to pass the inclement weather of the last few days with no warmer apparel than the open flannel jacket and pants commonly styled the 'Zouave uniform.'"[141]

By mid-June, the 10th New York was in receipt of new uniforms paid for by the New York State Board at a cost of $5,920. This was described in the regimental history as being of "the same pattern as the old, but of heavier cloth, the color being dark brown with red trimmings."[142] By August 1861, this uniform had also begun to fall apart, and at least half of each company was described as "incapacited [*sic*] from duty on account of the now stale excuse 'no uniform' and it became a matter of necessity to wait no longer for that which might never come."[143] Hence, the regiment requisitioned regulation fatigue uniforms, which were also slow to be supplied. The long-promised, improved Zouave outfits finally arrived in September 1861, consisting of "light blue trousers, dark brown jacket, red vest[,] white canvas leggings and fez. The trousers and jacket were trimmed with red; the costume fitted easily and yet not too loosely."[144]

The 11th New York Volunteers, also known as the First Fire Zouaves, originally adopted a gray Zouave uniform based on a design proposed before the war by its commander, Elmer E. Ellsworth. The complete outfit of this regiment was reported in the *New York Herald* on April 30, 1861, as consisting of:

> a gray jacket, trimmed with blue and red, gray pants and red shirt, red cap with a blue band, and regulation overcoat. They are all armed with Sharp's breech loading rifles, worth $67 a

Both of these 11th New York Volunteers images were produced at Matthew Brady's Gallery. (Left) Assistant engineer of the New York City Fire Department before the Civil War, Noah Farnham was appointed lieutenant colonel of the 11th New York Infantry (Fire Zouaves) on May 7, 1861, and led the regiment after Elmer Ellsworth was killed during the occupation of Alexandria, Virginia. Nicknamed "Pony" because of his small stature, his horse was shot from under him and he was mortally wounded at Bull Run by a musket ball that deflected off the side of his skull. He wears the officers' first uniform, consisting of a gray frock coat with light-blue cuff facing and gold-lace loops trimmed with red piping; gray pants with gold-lace seam stripes piped with red; and a French-style red cap. (Right) The avenger of Ellsworth, Pvt. Francis Brownell wears the first version of the enlisted men's uniform of the 11th New York. The gray jacket had a medium-blue collar, cuffs, and border, all edged with red lace. His full gray pantaloons have a blue seam stripe, and his red cap has the reversed Roman numerals "XI" on a medium-blue band. He also wears a red fireman's shirt and russet leather leggings. The black arm bands worn by both men are as a result of the death of Elmer Ellsworth at the Marshall House in Alexandria on May 29, 1861. *Library of Congress, LC-B813-1628 C / LC-DIG-cwpbh-00840*

The full dress coat worn by Col. Elmer Ellsworth, 11th New York Fire Zouaves, when shot to death in Alexandria, Virginia, by James W. Jackson on May 24, 1861. Made of "cadet gray" cloth with light-blue cuffs edged with red, it had two rows of seven New York buttons and four smaller buttons of the same pattern set on gold-braid loops edged with red and light blue on each cuff. Shoulder straps were dark blue with red edging. Following receipt of this uniform from the tailor, Ellsworth stated prophetically, "It is in this suit I shall die." Note the gunshot hole on the left breast. It is believed that Ellsworth had pinned to this spot a company badge of the Baltimore City Guard, a memento of the tour of the Chicago Zouave Cadets' 1860 drill tour, which was driven into his breast by the force of the ball. His sword belt was fastened by an 1832-pattern artillery enlisted and infantry NCO sword belt plate. Patterned after a French style dating from the Napoleonic era, this was designed by New York City–based accoutrement maker Robert Dingee and consisted of two S-link-connected brass discs; in Ellsworth's case, both bore the letter "Z" within a wreath. The dress trousers worn by Ellsworth when shot were also "cadet gray," with broad gold seam stripes of embroidered lace edged in red. Note the rear tie with buckle to adjust the waist band. *Courtesy of the New York State Military Museum & Veterans Research Center, Division of Military and Naval Affairs*

piece, and huge bowie knives which can be attached to the muzzles of their rifles, to answer the purpose of bayonets. Their knapsacks are made of rubber cloth, and in case of rain they can be used to protect the entire body from the wet. A blanket, tin plate, knife, fork and various other articles can be carried in each knapsack without inconvenience. A fatigue cap of gray felt, and a tin cup strapped on the outside of the knapsack, and a stout pair of shoes, completes the outfit.[145]

Having seen the 11th New York replace his own regiment as "guardians of the Capitol," a member of the 6th Massachusetts wrote on May 9, 1861, "It is impossible to imagine anything more picturesque than the Zouave sentinels in their red shirts and with their Sharp's rifles, as they pace the precincts of the Capitol, under the vernal foliage of the numerous shade trees."[146] On meeting with several "Fire Zouaves," a member of the 1st Rhode Island Detached Militia commented, "Their uniform consists of a pair of loose breeches tight at the ankle, a loose jacket and forage cap, all of a grey color."[147] Made of poor material, this clothing quickly wore out and, according to the *New York Daily Tribune*, by July 1 had been

Frederick George D'Utassy was born in Hungary as David Strasser but created a new persona when he arrived in the US before the Civil War, claiming he was a member of a prominent military family with noble roots who had served in the Austrian army until the Hungarian revolt of 1848–49. He was employed as a teacher of languages and as a life insurance agent in New York City when he was appointed colonel of the 39th New York Volunteers, or "Garibaldi Guard," on May 28, 1861. Photographed at the studio of Matthew Brady, he wears the full dress of his regiment, consisting of a dark-blue coat and pants trimmed with red cord, with distinctive Hungarian-style gold lace across the breast and elaborate cuff braid. Collar rank was similar to the Austrian system of six-pointed stars. He holds the green, red, and white "Hungarian standard" presented to the 39th New York five days earlier. D'Utassy was cashiered on May 29, 1863, after being found guilty of numerous offenses, including selling appointments and receiving payment of a false and fraudulent account amounting to $3,265.40. He was subsequently sent to Sing Sing Prison. *Carte de visite by Brady's National Photographic Gallery, Broadway & Tenth, New York; courtesy of USAHEC*

Capt. Charles Schwarz commanded the Third Company (Co. C), 39th New York, which was composed of volunteers from the German immigrant population of New York. He wears the original fatigue uniform of the regiment, including the famous red shirt and knotted scarf, or neckerchief, worn by so many *Garibaldini* in Europe during the Civil War period. He takes aim with a .36-caliber Savage Navy revolver and holds a Model 1840 cavalry officer's saber. Note the small ivory-handled knife in the sheath attached to his waist belt. *Library of Congress, LC-B 8161:2423*

Of particular interest in this Brady image of Col. D'Utassy and the staff of the 39th New York is the enlisted men standing at either side wearing full dress, consisting of a *bersaglieri*-style uniform of a black, round-topped hat with feather plume and eagle insignia. The coat was blue black with red facings on cuffs and collar, the pants having a narrow red stripe. Their hats are black and round topped, with wide, stiff brims along with a black feather and eagle. They have shoes with gaiters protecting the ankle and calf. *Massachusetts Commandery, Military Order of the Loyal Legion of the United States (MASS-MOLLUS), Vol. 73, p. 3638, USAHEC*

replaced by a new uniform that the Fire Zouaves wore during the battle at Bull Run, composed of "a red fez cap, red fire shirt, dark blue pants, and Zouave jacket."[148] Three days later, the *National Republican*, at Washington, DC, concurred that the replacement clothing consisted of "a red cap with blue fez [*sic*], red shirt, and blue pantaloons." The latter journal also stated that their first uniform was "of such material and make that it did not serve them long."[149] As the Army of Northeastern Virginia advanced toward Bull Run on July 21, 1861, a man in the 2nd Maine observed "the red-shirted and red-capped Zouaves" of the 11th New York disappear by "at the double quick" toward the Confederate forces.[150]

Four volunteer regiments were directly organized by the Union Defense Committee of New York City. The first of these was the cosmopolitan 39th New York Volunteers, or Garibaldi Guard, composed of three Hungarian companies, three German, one Swiss, one Italian, one French, one Spanish, and one Portuguese, most of whose members had already seen active service in Europe. Raised in New York City, this regiment was accepted by the state on May 27, 1861, and mustered-in for three years at Washington, DC, on June 6, 1861, to date from May 28, 1861. Elements of the Garibaldi Guard paraded for the first time in full dress uniform and carrying arms on May 23, 1861. On this occasion, the *New York Evening Express*

This detail from a Brady glass stereoscopic view shows a band member of the 39th New York holding an over-the-shoulder horn and a Model 1840 musician's sword in a leather frog attached to his waist belt. Standing behind him at right are two enlisted men wearing examples of the full-dress *bersaglieri* hat of the regiment, embellished with broad leather band and brass eagle plates, and fatigue clothing consisting of four-button sack coats and dark-blue trousers. They both have saber bayonets attached to their 1855-pattern rifle belts to accommodate the Model 1855 rifles with which the regiment was initially armed. *National Archives, 111-NA-B-5560*

described Co. B (the Swiss company)—the only members of the regiment to be armed at this stage—as wearing "a black cloth coat and pants, bound with narrow red cord." Although the enlisted men of this company still wore their fatigue caps, the officers sported "the Bersiglieri [*sic*] circular hat, of felt, distinguished by its broad brim and tall green feathers." Two days later, the *New York Times* reported the whole regiment uniformed in "a suit of blue-black, the pants having a narrow red stripe, and the facing of the frock being red. Their hats are black, round-topped, wide, stiff brims, with a black feather and eagle. They have shoes with gaiters protecting the ankle and calf."[151] As the regiment departed for Washington, DC, on May 28, a reporter for the *New York Herald* observed, "They were dressed in blue frock coats, blue pants trimmed with red cord, red undershirts, and felt hat ornamented with feathers and green leaves. Their knapsacks contained blankets and comfortable under clothing, while the haversacks were crammed with bread, cheese, Bologna sausages, and all manner of eatables and drinkables."[152] Following the passage of the 39th New York through Wilmington on May 29, the *Delaware State Journal and Statesman* observed that their full-dress headgear consisted of "a Garibaldi hat, which is of black felt, with a round top, banded with a wide leather belt bearing a medallion of the American eagle, a tricolor badge and a small plume of black feathers."[153]

Three *vivandières* (female attendants) accompanied the regiment when it left New York. According to a report in the *Daily State Gazette & Republican* of Trenton, New Jersey, two young girls ran away from their parents in Jersey City and accompanied the Garibaldi Guard to Washington, although the father of Rebecca Ellestein, alias Edelstein, returned home with the "two truants" on June 1, 1861, and expected to keep his daughter in "durance until her romantic ideas have vanished."[154] The *Evening News* reported that the *vivandières* "dressed in blue gowns with gold lace and facings, red jacket, and Garibaldi hats, decorated tastefully with feathers and colored plumes." The *Daily News* mentioned their "blue frocks with red flannel waists, and their jaunty regimental caps, crowned with black and red feathers." The *Tribune* described them in "the Garibaldi hat of the regiment, a red flannel basque and blue skirt, and the black gaiters."[155] A further report in the *Pittsburgh Gazette and Commercial Journal* of June 6, 1861, stated, "They wear a red basque, blue skirts, reaching a little below the knee, and high leathern leggings, laced close. These and the Kossuth hat, looped up at the side, constitute the dress."[156] In a letter home on June 2, a member of the 1st Rhode Island Detached Militia mentioned the *vivandières* with the Garibaldi Guard, stating, "They carry a small tin keg slung on their left side, filled with a wishy-washy wine, but such as der Deutchman love, and which they retail at five cents for a very small glass."[157]

Born in Germany about 1830, Adolphus Weiss, alias Adolph Wiss, was a saloon owner when he enrolled at New York City on June 6, 1861, to serve for three years. He was mustered-in as a lieutenant of the Zouave Company (Co. A), 41st New York Volunteers—also known as the "De Kalb Regiment" or "2nd Yaeger Regiment"—and was commissioned a captain on August 14, 1861. Discharged on May 16, 1862, he subsequently served in the 8th Infantry. He wears the regimental uniform based on that of the Prussian yaeger, or rifleman, which consisted of a dark-green coat and kepi trimmed with red facings, and gray trousers with red cord seam stripes. *Massachusetts Commandery, Military Order of the Loyal Legion of the United States (MASS-MOLLUS), Vol. 73, p. 3638, USAHEC*

The 40th New York, also known as the "Mozart Regiment" or "Continental Guard," was organized at Yonkers, New York, in May 1861. The uniform received by this regiment was similar to that worn by the 9th NYSM, being of "dark blue cloth, with red facings and trimmings, and large gilt buttons; the coat, pants and caps of the same color." According to a report in the *New York Herald*, this uniform was made by New York clothiers Devlin, Hudson & Co. and Arnoux & Co.[158]

Four companies of Massachusetts volunteers were attached to the 40th New York, plus two companies from Pennsylvania. The Union Guard (Co. H), of Arlington, Massachusetts, wore "the regular gray militia suit, then worn by the Massachusetts troops. Each garment, including the cap, was made of the same material, and the coat was cut with long skirts, frock style, and the breast thickly padded in the manner of the ancient Continental coat." The National Guard (Co. B), of Newburyport, Massachusetts, were uniformed in "dark blue coats and drab pants with white trimming." They also had a gray fatigue dress. Regimental historian Sgt. Fred Floyd, of the Union Guard, wrote, "At first, the Mozart jacket felt strange to us, for the Arlington coat was a double-breasted frock, the skirts of which reached nearly to the knees, while the Mozart jacket ended at the waist, just below the belt."[159]

The nucleus of the 41st New York, also known as the De Kalb Regiment or 2nd Yaeger Regiment, was the De Kalb Zouaves commanded by Capt. Emil Duysing. Formed by "a few patriotic Germans" who were "equipped according to the French bill of Zouave dress," this company wore "a dark blue jacket (braided with red) and pantaloons with yellow and black leggings of the Turcos, the blue sash, red fez and blue tassel." In its report on the De Kalb Regiment, the *New York Times* of May 26, 1861, stated that their uniform consisted of "a fez, black jacket and pantaloons trimmed with red, light blue sash, white gaiters, and yellow leggings faced with black patent leather."[160] The uniform provided for the remainder of the regiment was based on that worn by the Prussian Yaeger, or rifleman, and consisted of "a dark green frock coat, trimmed with red on the collar and cuffs, gray pantaloons, trimmed with a red cord, and cloth caps of the same color as the coats, faced with red." They were also provided with "an overcoat of gray pilot cloth, made after the Prussian army regulations" and "made in such a manner as to serve as a blanket, the skirts thereof are looped up with hooks in order to cause the wearer no inconvenience in marching."

Both of these volunteers wear sewn on the breast of their jackets the shield insignia of the Tenth Legion, 56th New York Volunteers. The man at left strangely wears his upside down. The man at right is probably wearing the New York State pattern issued to the regiment in October 1861. Issued in branch service colors of light blue for infantry, green for sharpshooters, red for artillery, and orange for cavalry, each shield was incised with a large "X" for the Roman numeral 10. The cutout X thus allowed the dark-blue cloth of the jacket to show through the colored device. *Ninth-plate ambrotype / ninth-plate ambrotype, Daniel J. Binder collection*

Officers, including those in the Zouave company, wore the same uniform with the addition of shoulder straps and gold braid on their kepis.[161]

The 42nd New York, also known as the "Tammany Regiment," was provided with a service uniform similar to that worn by the 7th NYSM, which was reported in the *Herald* to consist of "gray pantaloons and jacket," plus gray cap, all trimmed with black.[162] During involvement in the action at Ball's Bluff—or Harrison's Landing—on October 21, 1861, the "gray jacket and pants" worn by Capt. O'Mara caused him to be mistaken for a rebel by a Confederate officer. Approaching in the confusion of battle, he was asked where the "infernal Northerners" were. O'Mara pointed toward the rebels outflanking his position, and when the officer began to fire on his own troops, he "blew his brains out with a pistol."[163]

Organized as infantry during August/September 1861, the 50th New York was designated as the 50th Regiment of Engineers on October 22, 1861. On August 5, the *Rochester Evening Express* reported that the uniform would consist of "first quality army cloth gray, in color, trimmed with green." Two companies were to be armed with "rifles and sword bayonets," and the remainder with "rifled muskets of the best quality."[164]

Recruited at Newburgh during August 1861, the Tenth Legion was raised under the auspices and command of Col. Charles H. Van Wyck, representative of the Tenth Congressional District of New York State, and was named in honor of his district.[165] As with other legion-based units, it was initially a mixed command consisting of infantry, artillery, cavalry, and sharpshooters. This unit was organized as the 56th New York Volunteers on October 15, 1861. Two weeks later, the *New York Tribune* reported that their uniforms—of blue state-contract pattern, on the basis of photographic evidence—had been "prepared with much care. Each soldier has a shield on his left breast, in which is cut an X. The infantry shield is blue, riflemen green, cavalry orange and artillery red."[166]

Upon arrival in New York City on November 7, 1861, the infantry of the Tenth Legion / 56th New York Volunteers was described as consisting of 1,452 men, including two companies of cavalry, two of artillery, and one of sharpshooters, all of which wore "dark blue caps and jackets, and light blue pantaloons." Presumably carried by the infantry, sharpshooter companies, or both, arms consisted of .577-caliber Short Enfield rifles "to the end of which are attached large sword bayonets."[167] By the end of 1861, the artillery had been reorganized as the 7th and 8th New York Independent Batteries, and the two troops of cavalry were assigned to the 1st New York Mounted Rifles. The sharpshooter company remained with the Tenth Legion as Co. L, making it an eleven-company regiment rather than the standard ten company.

This enlisted man of Company B, 2nd NYSM—or 82nd New York Volunteers—wears an 1858-pattern dark-blue fatigue jacket and mazarine blue pants with white seam stripes. The latter faded badly and were replaced with pants of sky-blue twilled kersey army cloth soon after. Note the company letter "B" attached to the front of his dark-blue cap. *Todd New York album; Anne S. K. Brown Military Collection, Brown University*

The service uniform worn by this corporal of the 9th NYSM, or 83rd New York Volunteers, was received by the beginning of July 3, 1861, and consisted of a nine-button, dark-blue jacket faced with red on the cuffs and trimmed with the same color around the shoulder straps. Caps were also dark blue with red bands. A militia box knapsack with blanket roll strapped to the top and the regimental numeral "9" painted beneath the attached mess tin rests on the chair, as does his dark-blue-trimmed red overcoat. *Michael J. McAfee collection*

This unidentified member of the 9th NYSM has deliberately turned back the cape and collar of his dark-blue overcoat to show off its red lining. His cuffs and chevrons were faced with the same color. His small 1839-pattern oval plate displays the company letter "F," as does his cap. *Carte de visite, Michael J. McAfee collection*

Four militia regiments, consisting of the 2nd, 9th, 14th, and 79th NYSM, volunteered for three years' federal service and were redesignated as the 82nd, 83rd, 84th, and 79th New York Volunteers, respectively. Commanded by Col. George Tompkins, the 2nd NYSM, or State Guard, was supplied with "dark blue jackets, light blue pants with wide white stripe, and dark blue fatigue caps with Havelocks" when called into service as the 82nd New York Volunteers in May 1861.[168] Probably part of the original Brooks Brothers contract, this clothing proved unsatisfactory soon after receipt. The *New York Times* of May 13, 1861, reported, "The pantaloons, of mazarine blue, are found to be a mistake, as the rain causes the color to fade. Col. Tompkins has entered into a contract for 900 pairs of pantaloons, made from twilled kersey army cloth."[169]

Having disbanded in 1858, when much of its original Irish membership joined the 69th NYSM, the 9th NYSM, or City Guard, was revived the following year by three non-French companies who had left the 55th NYSM because they felt out of place in a French-speaking regiment. Commanded by Col. John W. Stiles by April 1861, the 9th NYSM was technically considered heavy artillery within the state organization but was redesignated the 83rd New York Volunteers for federal service. According to regimental historian John W. Jacques, who served in Co. D, the fatigue uniform funded by the Union Defense Committee, who also supplied its "knapsacks, blankets [&] equipments," consisted of "dark blue pants with red stripes; jackets with red trimmings on the cuffs; low caps with gilt braid around them, with the letter of the company on the peak; overcoats dark blue, cuffs trimmed with red, and broad capes lined with red." A report published in the *New York Herald* on July 3, 1861, confirmed that it consisted of "a heavy twilled blue flannel jacket, loose pants of the same material, and russet leggings."[170] In line with its role as heavy artillery, the nine-button fatigue jackets worn by the 9th NYSM were faced with red at the cuffs and had red trim around the shoulder straps. Caps were also dark blue with red bands and trimmed with gold, with the regimental number at the front.

Brigaded with the 1st New Hampshire, some of the 9th NYSM exchanged uniforms with the New Hampshire men on the expiration of their term of service. Regimental historian John W. Jacques recorded that the New Hampshire men "started for Sandy Hook, to take the cars for home, and our men went down to see them go[;] we gave them a cheer upon cheer, which they returned; they were eager for us to change uniforms with them, we did so, this one, with our jackets, another one, with our overcoats, still others, with our pants and caps, as they passed through the city of New York, the people must have thought that the 'Ninth' were coming."[171] These borrowed items of uniform must have been turned in to the New York state authorities before they departed on the final leg of their homeward journey, since the 1st New Hampshire men were reported to be in a "miserable" condition regarding clothing upon their arrival at Concord on August 2, 1861. According to Jacques, the 9th NYSM did not receive federal clothing until April 12, 1862, on which date he recorded, "For the first time since entering the United States service, the light blue pants were drawn from the Government, and worn in place of the dark blue pants, with red stripes, we also donned the overcoats, at Camp Claasen, Md., leaving us only our fatigue jackets, as the only apparel, denoting our original uniform."[172]

The 14th NYSM, also known as the 14th Brooklyn, or 84th New York Volunteers, first paraded in its new uniform on April 18, 1861. Supplied by the City of Brooklyn, this had been adopted by the board of officers in 1860 and was described in the regimental history as consisting of "red pants, white leggings, blue jacket and broad red chevrons and shoulder knots, and cap with blue band, red above and blue top."[173] Later, on May 12, 1861, this uniform was reported to consist of "red pantaloons, blue jacket embroidered with red, and red and blue cap, similar to that of the Chasseur a Pied of France." This regiment paraded the next day "enveloped in their large [dark-]blue overcoats."[174] The first uniform worn by the 14th NYSM did not fare well. On the occasion of its departure for Washington, DC, on May 18, 1861, a reporter of the *New York World* observed that it had "a very objectionable uniform, both on the score of color and durability. It was of a kind of red flannel, and though very striking on parade, will make its wearer a peculiarly conspicuous mark for sharp-shooters, while as an outside garment, it will shortly fray into rags."[175] On July 1, 1861, the *New York Daily Tribune* reported, "the whole regiment is to be newly uniformed, their old uniforms having become unserviceable."[176]

This unidentified private of Co. A, 14th NYSM—or 84th New York Volunteers—wears a rare example of the blue trousers issued to his regiment after its involvement at First Bull Run. His chasseur jacket is worn over a separate red vest. Note the company letter on the red cap held on his lap. He has a small Union cockade attached to his breast and sports a checked civilian necktie. *Ninth-plate ambrotype, author's collection*

(Right) Initials "A.T" carved in the butt stock of the musket tentatively identify this private of the 14th NYSM as Alonzo F. Thompson. His jacket has fifteen small, decorative ball buttons on each side and is fastened at top and bottom with pairs of hooks and eyes. The photographer's colorist has neglected to tint red the cuff patch to which three small buttons are sewn. His separate vest would have been fastened at the side. He also wears white canvas leggings and the red pantaloons that later earned the regiment the sobriquet "Red Legged Devils." He has reversed his cap box and bayonet scabbard to counteract the reverse effect of the image. He holds a US Model 1855 rifle musket with socket bayonet attached. *Sixth-plate tintype, Liljenquist Collection, LC-DIG-ppmsca-32081*

After heavy involvement at Bull Run, the uniforms of the 14th NYSM were in such a poor state that regulation blue was worn for a short time. According to Col. Alfred M. Wood, "the red pants were worn out, some with only the strong twilled lining left, the army blue had to be substituted until others could be supplied by contract and, although the blue looked neat and comfortable, the men were not pleased with them as 'they would not be found dead without red pants on.' The central government soon supplied the distinctive uniform of the regiment and continued to furnish it during its term of service."[177]

First organized in November 1858, the Highland Guard was subsequently designated the 79th NYSM, after the 79th Regiment, the Queen's Own Cameron Highlanders, of the British army.[178] Adopting the Cameron of Erracht tartan, which was specially shipped from Scotland, this regiment first paraded in undress uniform composed of "plaid pants, polka jackets and small caps" on September 17, 1860. This was further described by regimental historian William Todd, Co. B, as consisting of "handsome State jackets with red facings, blue fatigue caps and Cameron tartan pants." In wearing this uniform for the first time in June 1861, Todd recalled that recruits found "the pants were too long—or too short, the coat or

Born about 1834 in Scotland, James A. Farrish (Farrish House, 16 East Houston Street) was mustered in as captain of Co. B, 79th NYSM, in April 1861. Wounded and captured at First Bull Run, he was held as a prisoner of war in Richmond, Virginia, and Columbia and Charleston, South Carolina, until May 1862, when he was exchanged near Washington, DC; he did not rejoin the regiment. He appears to have enlisted in the Regular Army after the war and is listed as a "Soldier" serving at Fort Omaha, in Douglas County, Nebraska, in the 1870 census. Probably photographed in April 1861, Farrish wears the plaid pants, or trews, assigned for undress with a four-button sack coat. Note the crossed-cannon Militia Artillery insignia pinned to his cap front, over which is the miniature numeral "79." *Todd New York album, Anne S. K. Brown Military Collection, Brown University. Original carte de visite in the Military Order of the Loyal Legion Museum, Philadelphia.*

jacket collars so high and stiff that we could hardly turn our heads without scratching our necks or chins, while the tips of our fingers could scarcely been seen, so generous was the length of the sleeve."[179] By February 1860, a few members of "the new Scotch regiment were present in their kilts" for a grand military fete held at the Academy of Music in New York City on the twenty-second. Company B of the regiment escorted Elmer Ellsworth and the Chicago Zouaves on their departure from the city on July 20, 1860, dressed in "kilts, polka jackets, plaid stockings and bright buckled shoes."[180]

Increased in regimental size to 895 officers and men when mustered into federal service on May 29, 1861, the 79th NYSM found great difficulty providing its whole complement with kilted full dress. According to William Todd, "All of the officers and many of the men wore the kilts while the rest of the men were dressed in handsome State jackets with red facings, blue fatigue caps and Cameron tartan pants."[181] Upon the regiment's departure for Washington, DC, the *New York Times* reported that "the kilted pipers were seen treading their way through the multitude, preceded by an admirably drilled squad of our Metropolitan Police. Then came the officers, variously clad in the tartans of their clans . . . then the men, dressed in dark jackets tipped with red, and plaid pantaloons."[182] Arriving via steamer at Philadelphia, the *Inquirer* reported, "The

Photographed prior to the Civil War, two 79th NYSM soldiers pose in Highland full dress consisting of a glengarry cap with red, blue, and white dicing, blue jacket or doublet edged with red cording, and red facing on collar and cuffs trimmed with white piping, kilt of Cameron of Erracht tartan, white horsehair sporran with three black tassels and five-lobe cantle, diced stockings, and buckled shoes. Seated at center, Cpl. William Beattie wears undress consisting of plaid pants, or trews, polka jacket, and cap. Besides his chevrons, Sgt. Robert S. Gair (left) is distinguished by an NCO's sword and waist sash. The unidentified enlisted man at right has a Colt Pocket revolver tucked in his waist belt. Born in Scotland, Gair became a multimillionaire after the war on the basis of a paper box and bag business he established in Manhattan in 1864. *Todd New York album, Anne S. K. Brown Military Collection, Brown University. Original image owned by General Lawrence Beattie.*

This 79th New York corporal wears trews of Cameron of Erracht tartan and an 1858-pattern frock coat. Increased in size to 895 officers and men when mustered into federal service on May 29, 1861, the regiment found great difficulty providing its whole complement with full Highland uniform, and some new recruits received federal-issue clothing. As the war progressed, the 79th wore government-issue uniforms combined with vestiges of their Highland garb. This image was taken at the studio of Jesse Harrison Whitehurst, at Washington, DC. *Carte de visite, Michael J. McAfee collection*

One of a series of stereoscopic views taken of the Fourth of July parade in New York City in 1860 by photographer Edward Anthony. The 79th NYSM, or "Cameron Highlanders," are shown halted on Tryon Row, Manhattan, with pipers in advance and Robertson's band of "30 pieces" to their fore. The Hall of Records stands behind the trees at left. *Detail from "Anthony's Instantaneous Views." No. 433 by "E. & H. T. Anthony & Co., 501 Broadway, New-York," author's collection*

different companies were somewhat diversified as to style of uniform, but the national plaid marked all. Some were accoutred in the full Highland costume, kilt and bare knees; others were in plaid pants."[183] Of this occasion, *The Press* added:

The drummer boys in the van wore havelocks, and were led by a drum major. Many of the boys along the route, not willing to be outdone in nudity, had their pants rolled up to the highest possible degree. . . . About half the officers and a couple hundred men, without the fear of

Quartermaster Sgt. Edward H. Welch wears the uniform of the 65th New York Volunteers, consisting of an 1858-pattern "Hardee" hat with numeral "1" for "First U.S. Chasseurs" set within a die-struck brass horn. He wears the "army blue" chasseur jacket, trimmed with light blue, and "cadet gray" pants. Gray caps were used for undress. Rank is distinguished via the M1840 NCO's sword he holds, plus light-blue "bars and a tie" and red worsted waist sash. Enlisting as a corporal in Co. H, 65th New York, on November 6, 1861, Welch was promoted to quartermaster sergeant on August 22, 1861. He received a commission as second lieutenant on July 22, 1862, and became first lieutenant on March 1, 1863. He was mustered out on September 12, 1864. *Carte de visite, Michael J. McAfee collection*

> rheumatism and briars before their eyes, had hazarded the entire Scotch. The privates who adopted the Highland style of equipments were mostly men largely abounding in the calf element, and were not, as one would expect, mustered into platoons, but mixed up indiscriminately with the rest. . . . They marched on, covered with knapsacks and perspiration.[184]

Of the passage of the 79th NYSM through Baltimore, Maryland, the local press expressed disappointment that the whole regiment did not wear kilts, stating that "only a third of the force was apparelled [*sic*] in Highland style."[185] When the 79th regiment arrived at the federal capital, the *Evening Star* stated, "About one third of the members wear the full Highland uniform, the remainder being dressed in blue jackets trimmed with red, dark green plaid pants, and blue fatigue cap."[186] According to the *Herald* of July 5, 1861, when the regiment took part in the review of New York troops in Washington, DC, "But three or four of the officers wore the full Highland rig (bare legs)."[187]

In a last effort to provide the whole of the 79th New York with full Highland dress, Lt. Col. Samuel Elliott wrote to the *Tribune*, "I purpose going to New-York on furlough to attend to the unfinished business of the regiment, which may occupy me some time, as I am anxious to obtain pipers, for whom I may have to go to Canada, and also to procure kilts for the entire regiment, without which the Highlander is shorn of half his martial spirit and all his martial splendors."[188] As McDowell's Army of Northeastern Virginia began its march to Manassas Junction four days after the publication of this letter, Elliott clearly had no time to fulfill his mission. Of that occasion, Todd wrote, "At two o'clock in the afternoon in 'light marching order' the march began; our knapsacks containing our uniform jackets and tartan pants . . . having been packed and left at camp in charge of the 'Invalid Corps.' If any of our men wore anything other than the regulation dark blue blouses and light blue pants during the campaign . . . they were few."[189]

Composed entirely of men of Gallic descent, the 55th NYSM (redesignated 55th New York Volunteers on October 15, 1861), or Garde Lafayette, was slow to organize for war, not having sufficient numbers to volunteer for three years until the end of August 1861. Commanded by Col. Philipe Regis de Trobriand, this regiment changed its prewar French infantry-style uniform of "dark blue frock coats, scarlet pants, uniform caps, neatly trimmed with scarlet cord and braid, and pompons of scarlet worsted" (shako, dark-blue frock coat with red trim and epaulets, and "dark Crimson pants") for a red kepi, sky-blue frockcoat with red trim, which could be fitted with red epaulets, and red pants. Due to a shortage of imported materials for the latter, many men temporarily received heavy duck trousers. First formed in August 1860, the "New-York French Zouave Corps" became Co. I of the 55th

Regiment and adopted "navy blue poncho jackets, trimmed with scarlet, blue shirts and sashes, blue turban for full dress, and for fatigue the red Fez cap, with blue tassel. The pantaloons will be made of scarlet cloth, to reach to the knee, yellow leggings, and heavy shoes, to lace up in front."[190]

Several other volunteer regiments adopted a chasseur-style uniform, among them the 51st, 57th, 65th, 73rd, and 74th New York Volunteers. The 51st New York, or Scott Rifles, chose to adopt a version consisting of "a dark blue tunic, slashed at the skirts, embroidered with green, dark blue pants, with green stripes, and the regulation cap."[191] Composed largely of those who had served in the three-month regiments, the 57th New York, also known as the Clinton Rifles or US Voltigeurs, wore a chasseur blue jacket with "yellow facings and silver lace."[192] In September 1861, Col. Page, commanding this regiment, also received orders from Quartermaster General Meigs to purchase "all shoes, leggins, and gaiters of the French pattern, requisite for his command."[193] Stationed at Willett's Point but recruited in New York City, the 65th New York, also known as the First United States Chasseurs, adopted a uniform consisting of "an army blue chasseur jacket, trimmed with light blue braid, cadet gray pantaloons and gray cap."[194] According to photographic evidence, 1858-pattern Hardee uniform hats were also worn. On July 29, a report in the *New York Tribune* added, "So well adapted is the uniform of this regiment to military purpose, that already it

Recruited throughout New York State following the death of Elmer Ellsworth, the People's Ellsworth Regiment, or Ellsworth's Avengers, became the 44th New York Volunteers. Sgt. William M. Rexford, Co. D, was photographed wearing both the zouave and blue state uniforms issued to his regiment. The zouave uniform at left consisted of a dark blue jacket and pants trimmed with red, a red shirt, and russet leather leggings. The cap worn with his state uniform (right) has the letters "PER" for "People's Ellsworth Regiment" attached to its front. In both images he holds an NCO sword. *Carte de visite, Michael J. McAfee collection*

Enrolled as lieutenant colonel of the 53rd New York Infantry, or D'Epineuil's Zouaves, Joseph Antoine Vignier De Monteil wears the showy officers' uniform of his regiment. Based on that worn by the officers of the Imperial Guard Zouaves of France, this consisted of a red kepi quartered with gold-lace, dark-blue frock coat with elaborate gold sleeve braid, red cuffs, and a single row of eighteen plain bell buttons, and light-blue pantaloons with knee-high black rubberized coating. Often at loggerheads with his younger commanding officer, Col. Lionel Jobert D'Epineuil, and unpopular with his other fellow officers, De Monteil eventually detached himself from the 53rd New York during the battle for Roanoke, North Carolina, and volunteered as a private with Hawkins' Zouaves. He was killed in action on February 8, 1862. *Carte de visite, Michael J. McAfee collection*

Published in *New York Illustrated News* on October 14, 1861, this engraving shows the uniform of an enlisted man and an officer of D'Epineuil's Zouaves. Also on the basis of that worn by the French Imperial Guard Zouaves, the enlisted man wears a red fez with yellow tassel, dark-blue jacket and vest trimmed with yellow braid, blue sash, light-blue full pantaloons trimmed with yellow, and yellow leather greaves over white linen leggings. Another Zouave wearing a hooded cape, or *collet á capuchin*, can be seen in the background. *Author's collection*

has been imitated by several other regiments in process of formation."[195]

In anticipation of further calls for troops following the Union defeat at Bull Run on July 21, 1861, Gov. Morgan contracted with Devlin, Hudson & Co. and Arnoux & Co. for 10,000 additional sets of 1861-pattern state uniforms toward the end of that month. This clothing was supplied to many of the remaining volunteer regiments raised by New York throughout the remainder of 1861.[196] Meanwhile, other New York units organized in 1861, with either companies or the entire regiment wearing Zouave or semi-Zouave uniforms, included the 44th, 53rd, 62nd, and 73rd New York. The 44th New York, also known as the People's Ellsworth Regiment, or Ellsworth's Avengers, was recruited throughout the state following the death of Col. Elmer Ellsworth on May 24, 1861. Recruited under the auspices of the Ellsworth Association of Albany, New York, this regiment wore semi-Zouave dress plus the state uniform. Following its arrival in New York City on October 21 wearing the latter uniform, the *Commercial Advertiser* reported, "The uniform is the blue jacket and light blue pants of the state regiments, with red leather leggings. The initials 'P.E.R.' are attached to the caps of the soldiers, while the officers have the figures 44, which is the numerical designation of the regiment in the New York volunteer forces."[197] The next day the *Daily Tribune* stated that their other uniform was "the zouave dress of dark blue with red facings."[198]

Organized in August 1861 by Lionel Jobert D'Epineuil—an inefficient officer who managed to convince the War Department that he was a veteran of the French army—the D'Epineuil Zouaves were consolidated into the 53rd New York Volunteers on October 12 and wore a uniform that was an exact copy of the 6th Regiment Imperial Zouaves of France. Made by Brooks Brothers, this consisted of a "red fez cap with a long yellow tassel, dark blue jacket trimmed with bright yellow braid, blue sash, and yellow and black leggings and duck gaiters." The officers' uniform was composed of "dark blue coat with plain bell buttons, and heavily braided on the arm, dark blue

Twenty-one-year-old Isaac Cooper was mustered-in for three years as a private in Co. A, 62nd New York Volunteers—also known as the Anderson Zouaves—on June 29, 1861. He was soon after on detached service alongside Elisha Hunt Rhodes of the 2nd Rhode Island Infantry as a clerk at the headquarters of divisional commander Brig. Gen. Erasmus D. Keyes. He wears the Zouave-style uniform issued to most of the companies of 62nd New York, consisting of a dark-blue jacket with red trim; a trimmed shirt with collar turned down over the jacket, which was probably the same colors but may not have been an issue item; sky-blue trousers with one-inch-wide seam stripes, which were not as voluminous as full Zouave pantaloons; and white gaiters. He holds an example of the 1,000 red fez caps supplied to his regiment by the Seamless Clothing Manufacturing Company of New York in August 1861. The jackets, trousers, and sashes were made by William Seligman & Co., of New York City. *Signed carte de visite, Michael J. McAfee collection*

Charles E. Moore enlisted in the Advance Guard, Co. I, 62nd New York, on June 24, 1861, and was promoted to sergeant before the end of the year. He was awarded the Medal of Honor for bravery for rescuing the regimental color at the Wilderness on May 5, 1864. Originally the Zouave company of the 55th New York, or Garde Lafayette, the Advance Guard was commanded by Italian-born Capt. Charles G. La Fata and wore the full Zouave uniform, including red-trimmed dark-blue jacket and vest, voluminous red pantaloons, wide blue sash, red fez with long blue silk tassel, and yellow leather greaves over white gaiters. *Carte de visite with back mark "Hallett & Brothers / 134th & 136th Bowery, / Near Grand Street, N.Y."; Michael J. McAfee collection*

vest, light blue pantaloons covered with rubber from knee down."[199]

Named in honor of Col. Robert Anderson of Fort Sumter fame, the 62nd New York, or Anderson Zouaves, was first organized in May 1861. Parading on the twenty-seventh, a few of the 400 men recruited into this unit by that time wore a uniform consisting of "a blue jacket, with red trimmings, with the initials A.Z. worked on the corner, blue trowsers, [and] a fez cap, with tassel."[200] Further impressions of this unit were included in a report published four days later, stating that this uniform was composed of "a blue Zouave jacket, with a red edge, on which is a row of brass-bell buttons. In the lower corners are the initials A.Z. The pants are blue and the leggins and gaiters similar to those of the French Zouaves."[201] Called the Advance Guard of the regiment and commanded by Capt. Charles G. La Fata, Co. I was composed largely of "French adopted citizens" who originally formed the Zouave company of the 55th New York, or Garde Lafayette, but defected to the Anderson Zouaves in hopes of seeing action sooner.

Based on that of the French Imperial Guard Zouaves, their uniform consisted of a "red fez or skull cap with its long blue silk tassel, the immensely loose, red, baggy breeches, the leggins, gaiters, long blue scarf worn round the middle, the queer, tight cloth waistcoat with only one armhole—the left—in it, fastening on the right, and the short jacket." This unit wore their hair "closely cropped and their necks bare." The officers had "dark blue uniforms, similar to those worn in the United States army."[202] The remainder of the regiment wore the same Zouave-style jacket with light-blue pants and either red fez or dark-blue caps. The whole regiment also received "dark grey seamless overcoats" produced

A Pennsylvania company originally known as the Pittsburgh Zouaves commanded by Capt. John P. Glass, Co. A, 74th New York (5th Excelsior), wore a full Zouave uniform based on that of the French Imperial Guard Zouaves. Unusually this included a yellow *tombeau* both on vest and jacket. The seated soldier wears the modified chasseur-style uniform worn by the rest of the regiment. *Daniel J. Miller collection, USAHEC*

Taken from the original stereoscopic negative, this print shows at least ten enlisted men, plus one officer, of *Les Enfants Perdus* in an abandoned Confederate gun emplacement at Yorktown, Virginia, in 1862. Standing at right, the officer wears a chasseur-pattern cap and white summer pants. His rank is distinguished by three broad, inverted chevrons on the lower sleeves of his coat, plus narrow straps on his shoulders. Three of the enlisted men wear full dress composed of a dark-blue jacket with a triple row of buttons—originally accommodating a yellow plastron—and shako with pompon. Three more have white linen Havelock covers over their headgear. The others have a mixture of fatigue caps and fezzes. *Library of Congress, LC-B811-455*

by the Seamless Clothing Manufacturing Company of New York.[203]

With organization begun in May 1861, and eventual formation as part of the Excelsior Brigade, organized by Brig. Gen. Daniel E. Sickles, the Second Regiment of Fire Zouaves initially wore "red shirts and glazed caps."[204] Toward the end of July, this regiment began to receive its semi-Zouave uniform, consisting of a "light blue cap, dark blue chasseur jacket, trimmed with light blue braid, red flannel shirt, the collar of which is large and turns over the jacket, light blue trowsers, which are enclosed just below the knee in strong white duck linen leggings, and fall loosely over." In addition to this, they were supplied with "army cloth overcoats."[205] This regiment received its numerical designation 73rd New York Volunteers on December 11, 1861. Originally known as the Pittsburgh Zouaves of Pennsylvania, Co. A of the 74th New York—or the Fifth Excelsior Regiment—wore full Zouave dress that was a variation of the French Imperial Guard Zouave uniform, composed of a red fez with blue tassel and a dark-blue jacket and vest—both of which had a yellow lace *tombeau*—full red trousers, light-blue sash, yellow leather greaves, and white canvas gaiters.

In contrast, the 71st New York Volunteers, also known as the Second Excelsior Regiment or Jackson Light Infantry, was described as "the worst supplied regiment" when it passed through Baltimore on July 25, 1861. Composed "entirely of Germans," the "majority of them were in citizens' dress," and "some had their knapsacks secured to their backs with rope, while others had no accoutrements whatever, while upwards of one hundred were without arms."[206]

Commanded by Col. Felix Confort—a veteran of the French army—*Les Enfants Perdus*, or "Lost Children," was possibly named after a French unit known as the *Enfants Perdus de Crimee*, which served during the Crimean War. Officially known as the Independent Battalion, New York Volunteer Infantry, Confort's command was also referred to as the Independent Corps of Light Infantry, or German Legion. Recruiting began in New York during August/September 1861, and by November, enlistees for *Les Enfants Perdus* were fully clothed in a uniform resembling that of the French *chasseurs a pied*, which the *New York Herald* reported as resembling "in some respects the Zouave dress, [but] differs from it in a more comfortable arrangement of the loose pants and in the cap, which is a kepi, and not a fez. The jacket has short tunic lappels [*sic*], while the color of the uniform is a dark blue throughout, trimmed with yellow."[207] This was further described as consisting of a "blue tunic and pantaloons of the Chasseur-a-pied in the French service. . . . By attaching a yellow plastron to the front of the coat, a brilliant uniform is present for dress parade. The shako is blue, with yellow trimming, and light, yet very strong."[208] According to photographic evidence, the coat was triple breasted, and the low-crowned shako was fitted with a small round pompon over which white cotton Havelock covers were later worn. Blue fatigue caps were also acquired for undress. Pantaloons were tucked into white canvas gaiters, over which were dark leather greaves.

The mounted contribution from New York began with the Jackson Horse Guards (Co. A), 1st Cavalry, NYSM, and the Hussars (Co. C), 3rd Cavalry, NYSM, both of which arrived in the federal capital during July 1861 and served for three months until October 23 and November 2, respectively.[209] Authorized by the president on May 1, the 1st New York Cavalry, or Lincoln Cavalry or Carbine Rangers, was supplied with 800 US-regulation cavalry uniforms—including twenty for musicians—made by Arnoux & Co., which the *New York Herald* reported consisted of "a dark blue tight fitting jacket, trimmed with orange; light blue pants, and a high crowned felt hat, ornamented with a black plume and fastened up at the side with a brass eagle."[210] However, the *Tribune* of August 27 stated that the uniform had "lemon colored facings," which would have been more in line with a cavalry unit.[211] On August 25, 1861, complaints concerning the uniform of the 1st New York Cavalry appeared in the city press, stating, "Some of the men who desired good fitting clothes, paid the firm to have their suits cut to fit, and in the end did not get their clothes, nor could they obtain a return of their money. The garments are so badly put together, and in numerous instances have been sent to the company tailors to be sewed over again."[212] Two days later, one of the companies in this regiment made up predominantly of Germans was reported to be wearing "green sprigs on the front of their caps, and another . . . had gray blankets rolled up and slung over the right shoulder, and under the left arm."[213] On February 3, 1862, Pvt. James Hudson, Co. H, 1st New York Cavalry, wrote to his cousin from Camp Kearney, near Alexandria, Virginia: "We received new uniforms a few days ago

Photographed at Brady's National Photographic Gallery, William A. Howard was described as "a handsome, plausible man with a breezy salt-water manner and in neat semi-nautical attire." Wearing the uniform of a colonel of the 1st Regiment, New York Marine Artillery, the cuffs of his frock coat have an unusual row of four small buttons set within a narrow band of trim that was probably red. His red shoulder straps have an oak leaf, either end of which was probably a cross cannon and anchor wrought in silver. His 1850-pattern foot officers' sword has an unorthodox cutlass-style brass "basket" attached to the hilt. *Albumen silver print from original negative by Brady, National Archives, 111-B-2785*

Although both these men enlisted in 1862, their uniforms are representative of what the Marine Artillery, New York Volunteers (nicknamed "the Horse Marines"), adopted in 1861. (Left) Andrew Wenz, alias Wenc, was born in Bavaria ca. 1834. He enlisted for three years service in Co. G, Marine Artillery, at Chicago on July 30, 1862, and was discharged at New Berne or Hilton Head, North Carolina on January 25, 1863. Although Companies A to C, Marine Artillery, appear to have formed the garrison at New Berne throughout their service in North Carolina, the high boots worn by Wenz indicate he may have been involved in mounted land operations. The rest of his uniform consists of a plain navy cap, plain "round jacket" with two rows of five buttons plus three buttons on each cuff, and plain trousers. (Right) Twenty-two-year-old A. L. Castle enlisted as a private in Co. D, Marine Artillery, on August 18, 1862, and was honorably discharged on January 15, 1863. He wears a plain blue overshirt with three-button placket front as part of his uniform. *Carte de visite with back mark "Photographic Artist / P. H. Rupp / 13 Avenue A, N.Y."; author's collection. Carte de visite by Charles D. Fredricks & Co. / "Specialite" / 587 Broadway, New York; Michael J. McAfee collection.*

and as our old ones are not worn out yet, we are pretty well supplied in that line."[214]

Both the 1st New York Mounted Rifles and 4th New York Cavalry, also known as the Lincoln Greens or Dickel's Mounted Rifles, were initially issued with cavalry uniforms trimmed with green lace. Known as the Northern Black Horse Cavalry, the 7th New York arrived in New York City on November 23, 1861, with the officers, including Col. Andrew J. Morrison, riding "jet black horses, principally of 'the Blackhawk and Morgan stock.'" The *Herald* commented that Gov. Gen. Morgan had "received an order from Washington to procure all of the horses of these breeds needed by the regiment," but this unit was never mounted.[215] Organized during September/October, and mustered-in on November 14, 1861, the 8th New York Cavalry, also known as the Rochester Regiment, received their uniforms on October 15, following which the *Rochester Evening Express* reported, "Each man is apportioned a heavy blue overcoat, dark blue jacket with yellow trimmings, light blue pants, two shirts, two pair of stockings, and one pair of shoes." The next day the same journal added that this uniform was "the best yet given to volunteers."[216] By October 30, 1861, the 9th New York Cavalry, also known as the Westfield Cavalry, had received their uniforms from the state, consisting of "light blue army cloth pants, dark blue jackets, woolen shirts, woolen socks, fatigue caps, brogans—all apparently of good material. . . . The caps are provided with an oil cloth covering, and capes to protect the neck against rains."[217] This regiment was not mounted until June 1862. The 10th New York Cavalry, also known as the Porter Guard, received US-regulation cavalry clothing on November 30, 1861, about which the regimental historian commented, "The suits were mostly of generous size. Had the cloth been judiciously used there would have been sufficient in the suits to have clothed the entire regiment, but, as it was, some of the smaller fellows got suits so large that they rattled around in them, to the great amusement of their comrades. However, the uniforms, like everything else, finally became adjusted."[218]

Composed largely of ex-seamen, the Naval Brigade, later known as the Virginia Coast Guard or Union Coast Guard, was recruited in New York City by former US Navy lieutenant Washington A. Bartlett. Although he received presidential permission to raise this unit after a meeting with Abraham Lincoln on May 21, 1861, Bartlett did not receive the necessary authority from Secretary of War Simon Cameron, or the state of New York. Consequently, the Naval Brigade initially experienced great difficulty gaining official recognition or obtaining uniforms, arms, and equipage, since neither the state authorities nor the Union Defense Committee wished to assume responsibility for outfitting it.[219] Thus, the cases of uniforms plus weapons—including 500 Sharp's rifles and 200 Savage revolvers—loaded with it aboard the steamer *Coatzacoalcos*, bound for Fortress Monroe on May 27, 1861, remained unissued, and the Naval Brigade was reported to be devoid of "decent clothing" or footwear. According to the *Commercial Advertiser*, many men had thrown away "worn out garments, as they were promised new uniforms on their arrival at Fortress Monroe."[220] Within days of arrival on the peninsula, Bartlett was seriously injured by a fall while superintending the locating of guns at the Rip Raps.[221] At the same time the unit began to break up, as about 180 men returned to New York, while 768 remained at Fortress Monroe to be organized by Butler into "a coast guard," or "1st Regiment, B. F. Butler Coast Guard."[222] By mid-June, remnants of the unit led by Maj. Whittemore were consolidated with those elements of the 3rd Massachusetts enlisted for the war under the command of Col. D. W. Wardrop, and detachments had been detailed to man guns and operate barges to transport troops across Hampton Creek above Fortress Monroe. Meanwhile, recruiting began at Park Barracks in New York City for the reorganized Coast Guard, which was officially formed into a regiment by an order from the adjutant general's office on August 21, 1861.[223] Elements of this regiment served on the Atlantic coast aboard various naval vessels and manned gunboats, including the frigate USS *Congress* and steamers *Hunchback* and *Southfield*.

It is assumed that this unit was eventually issued navy-style uniforms. On June 14, 1861, about fifty of the Naval Brigade received "naval accoutrements," and by August 23, it was revived and renamed the Union Coast Guard and was reported to be "well uniformed, and much improved in drill." However, a report dated November 1 stated that it was still "deficient in clothing, hats and shoes."[224] This unit received the numerical designation 99th New York Infantry in January 1862.

Consisting of "sailors, fishermen, and experienced boatmen," the 1st Regiment, New York Marine Artillery, was organized in New York City beginning during November 1861. On the basis of "the principle of the Royal Marine Artillery" of the British Royal Navy, this unit was recruited under Col. William A. Howard, who was a midshipman in the navy but was a captain in the US Revenue Marine when the Civil War began. Pvt. Oliver White (Co. C) recalled that this unit was "at all times ready for service on land or water." As artillerists, it manned naval howitzers "used either in launches on the slide, or on shore mounted on a carriage with trail-wheel and drag-rope. We were especially well drilled in the use of naval light artillery, either afloat or ashore." The regiment also manned small vessels carrying various sizes of ordnance, which in reality were "army gunboats."

According to White, the uniform of the Marine Artillery was:

> nearly like that of the navy. The officers wore a gold band on the cap, but no sash under the belt. The shoulderstrap was red, with a cross cannon and anchor wrought in silver, afterwards adopted by the general as the emblem of the Ninth Corps. The line officers wore double-

> breasted coats, and the clothes of the men were all dark navy blue. The arms were short Belgian rifles with the sword bayonet for those who acted as infantry, and pistols and cutlasses for those who worked the howitzers.[225]

During mid-1862, men recruited for the unit in Chicago were advised that their "List of clothing" would consist of "1 Long Pea Jacket, 1 Blue Cloth Pea Jacket; 2 pairs Duck Trowsers; 1 Black Silk Handkerchief; 1 pair Long Stockings; 1 pair Blue Cloth Trowsers; 1 pair blue Satinet Trowsers; 1 pair Boots; 1 pair shoes; 1 blue Cap; 2 pair Drawers; 2 flannel Shirts; 2 Linen Frocks; 2 Blankets; 1 Mattress; 1 Glazed Hat."[226]

On the basis of documentary and photographic evidence, enlisted men of the Marine Artillery wore blue navy-style clothing, including cloth caps, "round jackets," jumpers or overshirts, and plain matching trousers, which appear not to have had a "drop front." Because elements of this unit served in land operations as a mounted force, some men wore knee-high riding boots with their navy uniforms, as a result gaining the nickname "the Horse Marines."[227]

New York Order of Battle, 1861

New York State Militia (NYSM) ("Three-months' Service")

1st Regiment, Co. A (New York Horse Guards)

2nd Regiment (State Grenadiers or State Guard)

3rd Regiment Cavalry, Co. C (New York Hussars)

5th Regiment (Jefferson Guard)

6th Regiment (Governor's Guard)

7th Regiment (National Guard) (two months' service)

8th Regiment (Washington Grays)

9th Regiment (City Guard)

12th Regiment (Independence Guard)

13th Regiment (National Grays)

14th Regiment (Brooklyn Chasseurs)

20th Regiment (Ulster Guard)

22nd Regiment (Union Grays or Home Guard)

25th Regiment (Albany)

28th Regiment (National Guard of Brooklyn)

55th Regiment (Garde Lafayette)

64th Regiment (Cattaraugus Regiment)

69th Regiment (National Cadets)

64th Regiment (Cattaraugus Regiment)

71st Regiment (American Guard)

79th Regiment (Highlanders)

Volunteer Infantry

1st Infantry (National Guard)

2nd Infantry (Troy Regiment)

3rd Infantry Regiment (Albany Regiment)

4th Infantry (1st Scott Life Guard)

5th Infantry (Duryee's Zouaves)

6th Infantry (Wilson's Zouaves)

7th Infantry (Steuben Regiment)

8th Infantry (First Regiment German Rifles or Blenker's Rifles)

9th Infantry (Hawkins' Zouaves)

10th Infantry (National Zouaves or McChesney's Zouaves)

11th Infantry (Ellsworth's Fire Zouaves or First Fire Zouaves)

12th Infantry (Onondaga Regiment or Independence Guard)

13th Infantry (Rochester Regiment)

14th Infantry (1st Oneida County Regiment)

15th Infantry (converted into 15th Engineers)

16th Infantry (1st St. Lawrence County Regiment)

17th Infantry (Westchester Chasseurs)

18th Infantry (New York State Rifles)

19th Infantry (Seward Infantry or Cayuga County Regiment) (converted into 3rd Regiment Light Artillery)

20th Infantry (United Turner Rifles)

21st Infantry (1st Buffalo Regiment)

22nd Infantry (2nd Troy Regiment or 2nd Northern New York Regiment)

23rd Infantry (Southern Tier Regiment)

24th Infantry (1st Oswego Regiment)

25th Infantry (Union Rangers or Kerrigan Rangers)

26th Infantry (2nd Oneida Regiment or Utica Regiment)

27th Infantry (Union Regiment)

28th Infantry (Niagara Rifles or Scott Life Guard)

29th Infantry (Astor Rifles or 1st German Infantry)

30th Infantry

31st Infantry (Montezuma Regiment or Baxter's Light Guard)

32nd Infantry (1st California Regiment, Empire City Regiment, or Cerro Gordo Legion)

33rd Infantry (Ontario Regiment)

34th Infantry (Herkimer Regiment)

35th Infantry (Jefferson County Regiment)

36th Infantry (Washington Volunteers)

37th Infantry (Irish Rifles)

38th Infantry (2nd Scott's Life Guard)

39th Infantry (Garibaldi Guard)

40th Infantry (Mozart Regiment or Constitution Guard)

41st Infantry (De Kalb Regiment or 2nd Yaeger Regiment)

42nd Infantry (Tammany Regiment or Jackson Guard)

43rd Infantry (Albany and Yates' Rifles)

44th Infantry (People's Ellsworth Regiment or Ellsworth Avengers)

45th Infantry (5th German Rifles)

46th Infantry (Fremont Rifle Regiment)

47th Infantry (Washington Grays)

48th Infantry (Continental Guard)

49th Infantry (2nd Buffalo Regiment)

50th Infantry (converted into 50th Engineers)

51st Infantry (Shephard Rifles, New York Rifles, or Scott Rifles)

52nd Infantry (German Rangers or Sigel Rifles)

53rd Infantry (D'Epineuil Zouaves)

54th Infantry (Barney's Rifles, Black Rifles, or Schwarze Yager)

55th Infantry (see 55th NYSM)

56th Infantry (Tenth Legion or Orange and Sullivan Regiment)

57th Infantry (National Guard Rifles, Clinton Rifles, US Voltiguers, or Zook's Voltiguers)

58th Infantry (Polish Legion)

59th Infantry (Union Guards)

60th Infantry (1st St. Lawrence Regiment)

61st Infantry (Clinton Guard, Astor Rifles)

62nd Infantry (Anderson's Zouaves)

63rd Infantry (3rd Regiment Irish Brigade)

64th Infantry (see 64th NYSM)

65th Infantry (1st US Chasseurs)

66th Infantry (see 6th NYSM)

67th Infantry (1st Long Island Regiment or Brooklyn Phalanx)

68th Infantry (Cameron Rifles or 2nd German Rifles)

69th Infantry (see 69th NYSM)

70th Infantry (1st Regiment Excelsior Brigade)

71st Infantry (2nd Regiment Excelsior Brigade)

72nd Infantry (3rd Regiment Excelsior Brigade)

73rd Infantry (4th Regiment Excelsior Brigade or 2nd Fire Zouaves)

74th Infantry (5th Regiment Excelsior Brigade)

75th Infantry (Auburn Regiment or Cayuga County Regiment)

76th Infantry (Cortland Regiment)

77th Infantry (Bemis Heights Regiment or Saratoga Regiment)

78th Infantry (Cameron Highlanders)

79th Infantry (see 79th NYSM)

80th Infantry (see 20th NYSM)

81st Infantry (2nd Oswego Regiment or Mohawk Rangers)

82nd Infantry (see 2nd NYSM)

83rd Infantry (see 9th NYSM)

84th Infantry (see 14th NYSM)

85th Infantry

86th Infantry (Steuben Rangers)

87th Infantry (see 13th NYSM)

88th Infantry (5th Irish Regiment or Meagher's Own)

89th Infantry (Dickinson Guard)

90th Infantry (Hancock Guard or McClellan Chasseurs)

91st Infantry (Albany Regiment or Columbia County Regiment)

92nd Infantry (2nd St. Lawrence Regiment)

99th Infantry (Union Coast Guard or Bartlett's Naval Brigade)

100th Infantry (3rd Buffalo Regiment)

101st Infantry (Union Brigade or Onondaga County Regiment)

Volunteer Artillery

1st Regiment Light Artillery (Morgan's Light Artillery)

1st Regiment Marine Artillery (Howard's Artillery Naval Brigade)

1st Battalion Light Artillery (Baden Artillery or German Artillery Corps)

2nd Regiment Heavy Artillery

2nd Battalion Light Artillery (Irish Brigade Batteries)

3rd Regiment Light Artillery (Seward Artillery)

3rd Regiment Heavy Artillery (German Heavy Artillery)

Volunteer Cavalry

1st Regiment (Lincoln Cavalry or Carbine Rangers)

1st Regiment Mounted Rifles

2nd Regiment (Harris Light Cavalry)

3rd Regiment (Van Allen Cavalry)

4th Regiment (1st German Cavalry, Dickel's Mounted Rifles, or Lincoln Greens)

5th Regiment (1st Ira Harris Guard)

6th Regiment (2nd Ira Harris Guard)

7th Regiment (Northern Black Horse Cavalry)

8th Regiment (Rochester Regiment)

9th Regiment (Stoneman's Cavalry)

10th Regiment (Porter Guard)

Volunteer Engineers

1st Engineers (Serrell's Engineer Corps)

CHAPTER 3:

NEW JERSEY

The state of New Jersey was requested to provide four regiments of militia infantry for three months' service on April 15, 1861. As a result, Governor Charles S. Olden issued orders for each of the four militia divisions to furnish one regiment. Within fifteen days a sufficient number of existing militia companies had volunteered to complete the quota. Designated "Foot Militia," the four regiments of the 1st New Jersey Brigade left the state for Washington, DC, on May 4. Although there is no evidence that New Jersey issued state dress regulations for enlisted men of its volunteer militia during the 1850s, the Hudson Brigade, Second Division, adopted a uniform dress in 1858. Introduced by brigade commander James Hatfield, this consisted of "mazarine blue pants, dark blue frock coat, cap of pattern of 71st [New York State Militia] regiment, with wreath ornaments and enamelled leather body belts."[1] In 1859, the Newark Brigade, Second Division, also adopted "dark blue frock coats and light blue trousers with white stripe," while infantry were distinguished by white belts and riflemen by black belts.[2] As a result of a militia law passed in March 1860, all general, field, and staff officers were required to be uniformed and equipped according to the regulations of the United States. Despite this growing conformity, the uniforms, arms, or equipment in use were considered inadequate for field service in 1861.

In response, Governor Olden appointed a board of commissioners to provide a uniform for the four three-month regiments. Meanwhile, public concern for the "welfare and comfort" of the troops resulted in the publication of a list of articles each man was to receive, consisting of "1 great coat, 1 cap, 1 coat, 1 pair of trousers, 1 pair of boots, 2 flannel shirts, 2 pair of drawers, 2 pair flannel stockings."[3] The *Atlantic Democrat* of May 4, 1861, summed up the situation in New Jersey during the first few weeks of war, stating, "In this matter of uniform . . . there is no uniformity, as some regiments are equipped at home better than those that depend on the State. This is not right, but the exigency of the case, perhaps justifies the difference."[4]

This unidentified enlisted man is possibly a member of the Johnson Guard, a militia company from Salem County that volunteered for three months' service as Co. I, 4th New Jersey Foot Militia, in April 1861. He wears what appears to have been a dark-blue frock coat with white trim around collar, cuffs, and coat front. The photographic artist has not touched his buttons with gold paint, as with the breast plate, which may indicate that they were silver metal as per 1847 regulations for infantry in the US Army. He has 1839-pattern accoutrements consisting of a white buff leather cartridge box sling and bayonet sling and white buff leather waist belt. Although his trousers appear to be of civilian checked pattern, another enlisted man from this unit was photographed wearing exactly the same type of trousers, indicating that they may have been part of the company uniform. *Sixth-plate ambrotype, author's collection*

While the board deliberated, the citizens of New Jersey set about clothing their three-month volunteers. As a result of measures taken in 1859, the 1st Regiment was already uniformed by authority of the US Quartermaster General and left "having also overcoats and blankets."[5] Organized in Trenton—the state capital—the 2nd New Jersey, also known as the "Hudson Regiment," was in receipt of clothing and equipment before the end of April, costing $23,000 and paid for entirely by private subscription by the

A drill company consisting of "about thirty lads . . . between the ages of ten and eighteen," the Stevens' Zouaves were formed in Camden, New Jersey, during June–July 1861 and were named for a cashier of the Farmer's & Mechanic's Bank of that city. Ellis Hamilton was originally listed as a private but was clearly promoted to a first sergeant, since he wears that designation in this *carte de visite*. His uniform is based on that of the Chicago Zouave Cadets. Hamilton became a lieutenant in the 15th New Jersey at age sixteen and rose to the rank of captain. He was killed in action at age eighteen in the Wilderness in 1864. *Special Collections and University Archives, Rutgers University Libraries*

citizens of Jersey City. After visiting Camp Olden, situated "a little below the Arsenal in South Trenton," a correspondent for the *Philadelphia Inquirer* reported seeing "the colored uniforms of the volunteers."[6] Following his visit to the same encampment, a correspondent of the *Daily State Gazette*, of Trenton, wrote, "At the Quarter Master's tent . . . great activity prevailed. Here the soldiers were being uniformed, under direction of Cols. [D. S.] Gregory and Clark, and the constant demand for coats, over-coats, pants, shoes, knapsacks, &c., showed that 'service' was at least expected."[7]

When they arrived at the federal capital on May 5, the 1st and part of the 2nd New Jersey Foot Militia (NJFM), also called the "Jersey Blues," were wearing a "dark blue frock coat, light blue pants trimmed with white cord, blue fatigue cap and army regulation overcoat." Each man carried "a heavy blanket, knapsack and canteen" and was armed with "the Minie musket." A stand of colors carried by the 1st NJFM was presented to the regiment by "the High School in Washington street, Newark."[8] Arriving as Co. H of the 2nd regiment, the New Jersey Zouaves, also known as the Communipaw Zouaves, of Jersey City, wore Zouave clothing consisting of a "dark blue Zouave jacket, slashed at the sides, sleeves tipped with red, and the whole ornamented in true Zouave style with red and yellow trimmings neatly displayed, red fatigue cap with blue and yellow trimmings, goose grey trowsers folding down at the bottom over cow-hide leggings, which reach the calf." They also wore "dark blue shirts with yellow facings down the front" and were "provided for cold and wet weather with heavy dark blue overcoats, having large comfortable capes." This company was armed with "Minie rifles and sword bayonets."[9]

The 3rd and 4th Regiments received clothing paid for by state Quartermaster General Lewis Perrine in Trenton. That received by the Olden Guards (Co. A), Wilkinson Guards (Co. C), and Jersey Blues (Co. D), 3rd Regiment, plus the Anderson Guards, Co. H, 4th Regiment, was made by the "Ladies of Trenton" in

Published in the *New York Illustrated News* on May 25, 1861, this engraving depicts the Communipaw Zouaves (Co. H), 2nd New Jersey Foot Militia, parading past President Lincoln, who stands with hat off on the edge of the carriageway in front of the White House. The accompanying text stated, "The Zouaves especially, with their neat grey and blue uniform, trimmed with red and yellow, and their long sword bayonets, attracted great admiration." *Author's collection*

the "school rooms" of the First Presbyterian Church.[10] The National Guards (Co. B) were recipients of "shirts [and] havelocks" courtesy of the "Ladyes of Mount Holly, N.J." on June 19, 1861.[11] Each member of the Wilkinson Guards and Olden Guards was also provided with an "India-rubber blanket" via private subscription.[12] The Marion Rifles each received "two flannel shirts and two pair of drawers" before they left Burlington to join the 4th New Jersey as Co. K.[13] First formed in the South Ward of Camden, New Jersey, during January 1861, the Camden Zouave Rifle Corps, commanded by Capt. John R. Cunningham, were still wearing their Zouave uniforms when they enlisted as Co. G of the same regiment. Possibly based on that of the Chicago Zouave Cadets, this consisted of blue jacket, full red pantaloons, and red fez or red cap.[14]

Not all of its companies were fully clothed and equipped when the 3rd Regiment left Trenton on May 3, 1861. According to letters written by an anonymous member of the regiment, "two or three companies have been shamefully neglected," while others had been furnished with "every thing necessary—overcoats, plates, knives and forks, spoons &c." Those without overcoats received them five days later.[15]

When the 4th NJFM arrived in Washington, DC, on May 6, they wore "dark blue coats and pants, trimmed with light blue cord; dark blue fatigue caps, similarly trimmed, and grey regulation overcoats." Armed with "the old flint lock muskets, altered to percussion locks," each man also carried in his knapsack "two shirts, two pairs of drawers, two pairs of socks, a tin plate, knife and fork, soap, comb and brush."[16]

By May 18, 1861, the board of commission appointed to choose a "Regulation Uniform" for the New Jersey Militia reported in favor of a "Blue Coat, Light Blue Pants and Army Cockade Hat."[17] This was probably a retrospective description of the uniform provided before the four regiments left for Washington, DC, although it may have replaced the clothing supplied before their departure. What is certain is that according to the *Annual Report of the Quartermaster General of the State of New Jersey for the Year 1861*, the Newark-based firm of N. Perry & Co. had supplied uniforms at a total cost of $30,216. Among the other twenty-nine firms that provided uniform clothing for these regiments were Halsey, Hunter & Co. and Jabez Ticknor & Co.[18]

While at Camp Scott, near Washington, DC, the New Jersey three-month volunteers were issued new uniforms. On June 12, 1861, they received straw hats and linen pants, which seemed more appropriate for the hotter climate in Virginia. According to a report in the *Newark Daily Advertiser*, "The variety of shapes into which a straw hat can be converted, was never before demonstrated. Three cornered hats, and cocked hats, and hats all brim, and hats with the brim all gone to the crown, hats made to imitate all other kinds of hats, and hats which resemble nothing ever before invented, are to be seen through the camp."[19] Three days later they received "summer coats and pantaloons." A report in the *Irish American Weekly* stated that the "former were intended for giants, the latter for dwarfs; the coats were wide enough in the body to wind about you once or twice, and a half yard too long in the arms; stuff, woolen—color, blue—style *a la* sailor boy's roundabout . . . the pantaloons were a novelty in their way. Those which were long enough in the legs, were too narrow at the waistband; those wide enough about the waist, were too short in the leg."[20]

Regarding small arms, all four three-month militia regiments were furnished by the New York Arsenal with 2,880 "National Armory Brown" converted muskets, with 1839-pattern infantry accouterments. A few companies seem to have brought their own arms or received them from the state. A limited amount of ammunition was secured from the New York Arsenal through the cooperation of the Union Defense Committee of New York City. The day before these regiments left for the federal capital, the *Daily State Gazette & Republican* of Trenton reported, "The arms that have been offered to the volunteers of this State (or, at least, a portion of them) are so defective, that great dissatisfaction has been created among the troops."[21] Five companies of the 2nd Regiment exchanged their "old altered flint-lock muskets" for "new Government Minnie muskets" several weeks after arrival in Washington, DC.[22]

A further requisition was made on May 3, 1861, for three regiments of three-year volunteers, which resulted in the 1st, 2nd, and 3rd New Jersey Infantry. As a result of General Order No. 4, dated August 4, 1861, these regiments were formed into the 1st Brigade of New Jersey Volunteers at Camp Trenton, in Virginia, under the command of Brig. Gen. Philip Kearny. The first regiment was formed largely from volunteer

The 1851-pattern dress cap worn and held by this unidentified New Jersey militia corporal displays the numeral "1" inset in the cap plate, indicating he belonged to one of the four 1st New Jersey Volunteer Militia regiments that existed in the antebellum period. Because the Newark Brigade, Second Division, adopted "dark blue frock coats and light blue trousers with white stripe" in 1859, with infantry distinguished by white belts, this man is possibly a member of the 1st Regiment, Newark Brigade. A distinctive feature of many New Jersey uniforms, his coat collar is trimmed only around the base. Trim is also applied to the bridle straps on his shoulder and around his cuffs. The plate on his 1854-pattern cap plate bears a panoply of arms with a scroll plus motto underneath, with a wreath surrounding the inset numeral. His belt plate is the "eagle wreath" pattern of 1851, or the militia variant. Elements of the Newark Brigade formed the 1st New Jersey Foot Militia, which was one of the four three-month regiments provided by New Jersey in April 1861. *Copy print, Michael J. McAfee collection / sixth-plate ambrotype, author's collection*

companies not required as three-month volunteers, several of which appear to have been uniformed before they left their local communities. Enlisting as Co. D, 1st New Jersey—the Garibaldi Guards, of Phillipsburg, were attired in "red shirts with a tri-colored sash around the waist" when they arrived in Trenton on April 27, 1861.[23] The Union County Volunteers of Elizabeth, Union County, were "thoroughly uniformed" and in need only of "arms and knapsacks to complete their outfits" before they were mustered-in as Co. A, 1st New Jersey.[24]

The state also undertook to uniform these three regiments. Contracts were advertised in the press on May 20, 1861, to include 2,000 each of "Uniform Hats, Trim'd U.S. Regulation," "Uniform Coats," "Uniform Trousers," "Flannel Sacks," "Forage Caps," and "Great Coats," plus "Sets of Straps" for the same. For footwear, 2,500 "Pairs [of] Bootees" were required. The amount of each required item suggests that there was sufficient surplus clothing and headgear from that made for the three-month regiments to provide for at least one regiment of three-year volunteers.[25] At the same time, the state contracted with David Oakes, who owned mills at Bloomfield and Baskenridge, to produce "10,000 yards of cloth for uniforms."[26] All the contracts were let by June 1, with the Newark-based firms of N. Perry & Co. and Halsey, Hunter & Co. once again providing "uniforms, great coats and trowsers." Duryea, Jacques & Co., of 326 Broadway, New York City, produced the dress hats, and George Booth & Sons, of Newark, New Jersey, made the fatigue caps. Sack coats were supplied by Merchant & Waldron of Newark. All articles were to be delivered to the arsenal at Trenton by June 16, 1861, with "the clothing much earlier."[27] According to the *History of the First New Jersey Brigade*, Gen. Kearny himself saw that these uniforms fitted the wearers, and if he found any man with ill-fitting coat or trousers, he had the regimental tailors at work at once to correct the fault, contributing from his own purse to defray the expense.[28]

The white buff waist belt worn by this unidentified New Jersey volunteer may indicate that he belonged to a unit of the Newark Brigade, Second Division, NJVM, which was prescribed white belts for infantry and black belts for riflemen since 1859. He holds a Model 1822 musket altered for percussion. *Ninth-plate ambrotype, author's collection*

The uniform worn by the enlisted man in this unidentified albumen labeled "New Jersey Civil War First Defender" represents an example of the type of clothing supplied by the state of New Jersey to men who enlisted in the three-month militia and the first few regiments of three-year volunteers. Probably patterned on the uniform adopted by elements of the Second Division, NJVM, in 1858–1859, his coat has light-colored trim around the bottom edge only of the collar, while the cuffs are trimmed in the normal manner. His light-blue trimmed shoulder straps are also not included in federal regulations. His light-blue trousers have a narrow, light-colored—possibly white—seam stripe. *Unmounted albumen from ambrotype, author's collection*

Having departed Camp Olden on June 28, 1861, the 1st through 3rd New Jersey Volunteers (three years' service) were reported in the New York press as wearing "the regular United States uniform—dark blue frock coat, with light blue trimmings, light blue pants and light blue overcoat, with dark blue trimmings; regulation hat (Kossuth style, turned up at the side)."[29] Following their passage through Wilmington, Delaware, later the same day, the 1st New Jersey men were again described as being "uniformed in the United States regulation pattern, dark blue coats and pants and black hats, the brim fastened up to one side by a button. They carry the percussion musket of 1849; the regiment numbers 1010 in the ranks." The 2nd New Jersey was "uniformed in a similar manner to the first, and is well armed and equipped."[30]

On the basis of photographic evidence, the nine button dress coats produced in Newark were indeed based on federal regulations but differed in detail. The standing collar was trimmed light blue only around its base, and shoulder straps were added and trimmed all around in the same color. Also differing slightly from that found on US-regulation coats, the cuff trim in some cases formed less of a pointed arc.

A requisition for five more regiments—plus one company of artillery—for three years' service was received on August 3, 1861. Designated the 4th through 8th New Jersey, all of these units received US-regulation clothing and were issued with "state muskets, altered from flintlocks to percussion."[31] On September 8, the War Department authorized the organization of a rifle regiment, plus an additional company of artillery. Designated the 9th New Jersey,

Enlisting in the Garibaldi Guards—a volunteer militia company recruited in Phillipsburg, by the Delaware River, in Warren County, New Jersey—before the end of April 1861, Thomas Leonard was mustered into Co. D, 1st New Jersey Infantry (three years) on May 22, 1861. He was killed at Salem Heights, Virginia, on May 3, 1863. He wears an example of the uniform provided by the state, which was made by the firms of N. Perry & Co. and Halsey, Hunter & Co., of Newark, New Jersey. The cloth for these uniforms was supplied by the mills at Bloomfield and Baskenridge owned by David Oakes. Typical of what the New Jersey Quartermaster Department supplied, his coat is embellished around the base of the collar, shoulder straps, and cuffs with light-blue trim. The two small buttons decorating the cuff fronts may have been a distinctive feature of his company or the whole regiment. Note the numeral "1" attached to his cap front. *Sixth-plate ambrotype, Paul Mehney collection*

the former wore green trim on their uniforms, rather than the customary infantry sky blue, and were armed with "new model Springfield rifle-muskets."[32] Each man of this regiment was presented with "an oil-silk Havelock cap cover" from "the ladies of Princeton."[33] In addition, a special corps called the Olden Legion was raised by private subscription, which later became the 10th New Jersey. Recruited in Camden, New Jersey, the West Jersey Zouaves became Co. H of this regiment and were described as wearing "a handsome Zouave uniform" on November 20, 1861.[34] Finally, two batteries of light artillery and the 1st New Jersey Cavalry, originally known as "Halsted's Independent Cavalry," were recruited before the end of the year.

New Jersey Order of Battle, 1861

New Jersey Foot Militia ("Three-months' Service")

1st Regiment (1st Regiment, Newark Brigade, Active Militia)

2nd Regiment (2nd Regiment, Hudson Brigade, Active Militia)

3rd Regiment

4th Regiment

Volunteer Infantry

1st Regiment

2nd Regiment

3rd Regiment

4th Regiment

5th Regiment (merged into 7th Regiment)

6th Regiment (merged into 8th Regiment)

7th Regiment

8th Regiment

9th Regiment (Rifle Regiment)

10th Regiment (Olden Legion)

Volunteer Infantry

1st Regiment (Halsted's Independent Cavalry)

Volunteer Artillery

Battery A, 1st New Jersey Light Artillery

Battery B, 1st New Jersey Light Artillery

CHAPTER 4:

DELAWARE

The second-smallest state in the Union and one of four "border," or slave, states that did not secede, Delaware was somewhat reluctant to respond to the presidential call for one regiment of "infantry or riflemen" for three months' service issued on April 15, 1861. Indeed, Democrat and pro-Southern Gov. William Burton replied ten days after that date that there was "no organized militia in the State nor any law authorizing such organization," and he took no active part in the formation of regiments for the Union.[1] However, Gen. Henry du Pont, a West Point graduate and senior partner of Du Pont—the largest supplier of gunpowder to the Union army during the Civil War—was nominally the state adjutant general and assumed leadership in the mobilization of the military resources of Delaware.

The nucleus of the 1st Delaware Volunteer Militia (three months) was formed around the military companies already in existence in Wilmington, including the Delaware Blues, Columbia Rifles, and National Guards. The volunteers enlisting from these units wore whatever uniform clothing they already had, whether it was full dress or fatigue uniform. Meanwhile, the women of Delaware made blue flannel shirts, underclothes, blankets, and haversacks for all the volunteer companies preparing for service. The work began in Wilmington on April 26, at the Presbyterian, St. Paul's, Second Baptist, and Central Churches, and continued until the beginning of June 1861. By May 28, the Volunteers' Sewing Society had produced 150 shirts for each of the five encamped companies of the regiment.[2]

The poorly tailored uniforms worn by these two volunteers of the Delaware Blues (Co. A), 1st Delaware Infantry (three months), are very apparent. Their coats are devoid of trim, although they have a single small button attached to either side of the collar. The man at right has a large patch pocket on his left breast. He also has a small metal letter "A" attached to the front of his cap. They are armed with M1842 muskets and are equipped with plain shoulder slings supporting cartridge boxes, with 1839-pattern plates fastening their waist belts. Companies A and B of the Delaware Blues were organized prior to September 1860 as Bell and Everett Political Clubs. *Military and Historical Imagebank*

Some of the companies forming elsewhere in the state were more quickly provided for than those in Wilmington. Organized at Camden, in Kent County, the company commanded by Capt. James Green (Co. D) thanked "the patriotic ladies of St. Paul's M.E. Church, for their invaluable services in making up … uniform and clothing" on May 18, 1861. The citizens of Smyrna provided similar aid to the company led by Capt. Samuel H. Jenkins (Co. H).[3] Frustrated by the lack of provision for the Wilmington companies, the *Republican* of May 20 stated, "If the Legislature is not to be convened, and the City Council decline to act, we suggest the calling of a public meeting and the appointment of a committee to raise the money and take the matter in charge."[4]

Volunteer work continued, and as each unit received some vestige of uniform it was ordered to report to "Camp Brandywine," on the grounds of the Agricultural Society near Wilmington. There the men elected Col. Henry H. Lockwood—professor of mathematics and instructor of infantry tactics at the US Naval Academy, Annapolis, Maryland—as their commanding officer, and the 1st Delaware Volunteer Militia (three months' service) was mustered-in

Worn by Pvt. John Crozier, who enlisted in the Wilmington Rifles (Co. E), 1st Delaware Volunteers (three months), this dark-blue satinet frock coat was made by the ladies of Wilmington and has a small state button on each side of the standing collar, which is trimmed with light-blue twill tape. Note the large patch pocket on the left breast and the gap in the spacing of buttons where the waist belt plate would have rested. Crozier was born in Pennsylvania in 1839 and was resident at Wilmington, Delaware, where he worked as a blacksmith. *Don Troiani collection*

company by company from May 2 through May 20, 1861. Attached to the command of Maj. Gen. John Dix, Department of the Potomac, and assigned to duty guarding the line of the Philadelphia, Wilmington, and Baltimore Railroad, companies A, B, D, and E, 1st Delaware, departed for duty without full uniforms on May 28, and the remainder of the regiment followed on June 9, 1861.

Still without uniforms by June 2, a member of the Wilmington Rifles (Co. E) reported from "Camp Dare," by the Bush River, Maryland, that the "men begin to ask for their uniforms and overcoats." He also noted that havelocks had been received, and recorded a novel use for the flannel body bandages issued as a preventative treatment for diarrhea, stating, "Some of the men wear the red flannel bands, designed for another part of the body, around their caps and on the outside of their garments, thus displaying a taste for martial colors not unbecoming a soldier."[5]

With the exception of Companies H and I, the 1st Delaware (three months' service) finally received poorly made, dark-blue uniforms consisting of "coats, pantaloons, shoes, caps" on June 14 and 15, 1861, on which occasion a member of the Wilmington Rifles reported that the "boys" were "strutting about in their 'sojer' clothes."[6] A letter from Camp Milligan dated June 23 stated, "The men have received their uniforms; it is made of dark blue cassinet, with trimmings of light blue, making a very fine appearance when worn upon parades, drills or guard duties, being seldom worn at other times."[7]

During the same period, another volunteer at "Camp Dare" recorded, "The long-looked for uniforms . . . are a pretty hard set of garments, very few fitting in anything like a decent manner, and reflecting but little credit on the tailor who cut them out. Some pants are too short, some too long, some too narrow in the waist, some too wide.—The coats have equally as many faults, some having no shape at all."[8] On July 1, yet another volunteer wrote, "The uniforms furnished to the company are of the most indifferent description, and will not outlast a summer campaign."[9] Regarding overcoats, each company had received thirty-two "stout, durable" garments for use on guard duty by June 9, 1861.[10]

Clearly not proud of his appearance, a member of the Sussex Volunteers (Co. G) wrote on June 29, "Very little attention is paid to dress down here, there being no ladies to dress for. We are indifferent as to style; it is a matter of no moment whether we black our boots or not, or have on a collar, which we now regard as superfluous; we can wear our blue flannel shirts without either coat or vest, and have no apprehension of the ladies criticizing our appearance. We fit ourselves for the camp, not the parlor."[11] On August 14, 1861—its last day of "bloodless though active campaign" guarding the railroad in Maryland—the 1st Delaware paraded for roll call with "clean uniforms, brightened arms, polished ornaments, and gleeful faces." Whether these were new uniforms or those received in mid-June is not known.[12]

Although hoping to be armed with rifles, the 1st Delaware was issued with M1842 muskets and conversions. Possibly drilling with rifles from the state armory before enlistment, a member of the Wilmington Rifles reported on June 17, 1861, "The drill of Co. E has been changed from the rifle to the musket, which comes rather awkward to our well-drilled riflemen; but, give us enough to eat, and we are happy with any drill."[13]

Recruited between September 10 and October 19, 1861, the 1st Delaware Volunteers (three years' service) were commanded by Col. John W. Andrews and were composed of many members of the three months' regiment that reenlisted for three years. Andrews had served as major in that unit. Companies A and B of the new regiment were reported on September 23 to be "costumed *a la* Zouave, blue uniform, red trimmings, fatigue caps and leggings." En route for Fortress Monroe aboard the transport ship *Patapsco* during October, they were described as wearing the "picturesque Zouave dress, white and dark blankets, sheepskin leggings, black knapsacks" and "were prominent by the light of the lamp in the cabin, and by the light of the moon on deck."[14]

Reported to be "'harnessed up' in Uncle Sam's best on September 23, 1861," the remainder of this regiment received a uniform that was based on US army regulations, consisting of "blue cloth pants, frock-coat, and blouse (or fatigue coat), high black felt hats, with rim gracefully looped up on the left side and secured by a brass shield; they are also adorned in front by a brass bugle, and encircled with a light blue cord and tassels."[15] By October 21, Col. Andrews had secured "brass shoulder-scales and white gloves for the men, required the officers to provide themselves with epaulets and the regulation felt hat and plumes, and had furnished Drum-Major Dooley with the tallest and most gorgeous of shakos, with trimmings to match."[16]

The 2nd Delaware Volunteers were organized at Wilmington from June 12 through October 7, 1861, and were ordered to Baltimore, Maryland, in October 1861, where they were attached to Dix's Command until June 1862. Made from materials considered to be "vastly superior to the clothing of most of the three months volunteers," the uniform received by this regiment consisted of "army blue jacket and dark blue pantaloons." It was armed with "U.S. muskets, new and in good order."[17] With the ranks filled in both three-year regiments, the War Department granted permission for a third regiment, which began organization at Camden from December 30, 1861.[18] The 3rd Delaware Volunteers were issued US-regulation infantry clothing.

Organized into three provisional regiments and used as a semiofficial home guard to enforce loyalty to the Union cause, the volunteer militia of Delaware continued to be uniformed and armed via volunteer contribution. Commanded by Capt. Robert Andrews, the City Guard of Wilmington wore "a navy blue

One of four brothers who served in Co. E, 1st Delaware Volunteers (three years), Thomas P. Carey enlisted on September 10, 1861, and was killed in action at Gettysburg on July 3, 1863. He wears an example of the federal-style frock coat issued to his regiment in September 1861. *Courtesy of the Delaware Public Archives*

frock coat, collar and cuffs braided with red material, and brass scales on shoulders; pants of same material, with red cord down the outer seam of the leg; U.S. Army fatigue cap, with metallic letters 'C.G.' encircled in a wreath, in front."[19] Parading through the streets of the city on July 20, the Delaware Light Dragoons wore "dark-blue pants and jacket, trimmed with Orange, and black hat with red, white and blue rosette on the side."[20] On May 25, 1861, the Red Lion Mounted Guards received a "Blue uniform; short, single-breasted frock-coat; fatigue cap; sword and revolver in belt."[21] During the same month, the Cadets of St. Mary's College, in Wilmington, paraded "equipped as riflemen with Zouave caps, blue frock coat, with gilt buttons, trimmed with gold lace."[22]

Concerning arms issued to the volunteer militia, Vincent C. Gilpin—pro-Union mayor of Wilmington—had by August 12, 1861, distributed "636 rifles and muskets" held at the armory at Wilmington, as follows: "Home Guards, Capt. Sturgis, 100 muskets; City Guards, Capt. Andrews, 100 muskets; Union Guards, Capt. Wisdom, 60 muskets; Brandywine Village Guards, Capt. Febiger, 100 muskets; Brandywine Home Guards, Capt. L. DuPont, 50 muskets; Home Guards, Capt. C. I. DuPont, 50 muskets; Capt. Tybout, 100 muskets; Capt. Porter, 30 muskets; Capt. Henry, 20 muskets; Capt. Biddle, 26 rifles." Weapons remaining on hand in care of the mayor consisted of "Muskets, 80, Rifles, 12, pistols, 15."[23]

Delaware Order of Battle, 1861

Delaware Volunteer Militia ("Three-months' Service")

1st Infantry Regiment

Volunteer Infantry

2nd Regiment

3rd Regiment

OUR UNION,
God's greatest Blessing on Earth.

CHAPTER 5:
MARYLAND

The presidential call for three-month troops in April 1861 required the border state of Maryland to provide four regiments of militia infantry or riflemen with the assurance that they would be used only in-state, or for the defense of Washington, DC. However, these units were never raised. As Frederick Todd and colleagues stated in *American Military Equipage*, Vol. 2, *State Forces*, the impotency of the Baltimore regiments, the unorganized condition of the county militia commands, and the uncertain allegiance of both precluded this.[1] As a result, the process was so delayed that the three-month term was abolished before the required four regiments could be organized and put in the field. Also, most of their weapons were seized by federal authorities, backed by a proclamation by Gov. Thomas H. Hicks on June 7, 1861.[2]

As tensions rose between loyalist and secessionist factions in Baltimore, an ordinance passed by Mayor George W. Brown prohibited the display of flags or banners except on the buildings and vessels of the federal government. On May 1, 1861, the *Baltimore Clipper* commented, "For a period the flags, banners and emblems of secession and treason were in our streets as thick as blackberries. They soon began, however, to disappear, and the time-honored flag of our country to take their place."[3] Some Unionists in Baltimore distinguished themselves by wearing "Union" badges with "the stars and stripes painted on white satin" and the word "Union" printed in large type under the flag.[4]

Although the Maryland Militia (MM) regiments were disbanded in April 1861, and many of the militiamen migrated south to join the Confederacy, some individual companies remained loyal to the Union. One such corps was the Baltimore City Guard. Having left the 53rd Regiment MM in 1858, they obtained a charter as an independent corps and expanded into a battalion. Toward the end of 1860, its loyal members joined the 1st Light Artillery MM to become Co. D of that regiment.[5] Originally formed in 1833, the City Guard wore a full dress consisting of bearskins, described as being "taller than those of the Grenadier Guards" and "dark blue tailcoats laced with gold, and light blue pants."[6] Other volunteer militia companies that remained true to the Union included the Home Guards, of Talbot County; Union Defenders; Eagle Artillery; Zouave Cadets;

A farmer in Frederick County, Maryland, Charles A. Gilson enlisted at Emmetsburg on August 27, 1861, and was mustered-in for three years at Frederick as a private in Co. C (Capt. Horner's cavalry company), 1st Regiment, Potomac Home Brigade, on September 9, 1861. Unusual for a Union trooper, he provided his own horse and equipment on enlistment, for which he received forty cents a day. Serving throughout 1862–63, he was mustered-out at Harper's Ferry on February 13, 1864, and reenlisted the next day in the same unit, being promoted to corporal by November. He was honorably discharged on June 28, 1865, on which occasion he retained a Colt revolver and saber belt for which he was charged from pay due. In this early war image, his uniform includes a nine-button sack coat with shoulder straps. He holds a Sharps carbine and has a holstered revolver. His equipment consists of a carbine sling, waist belt, and cap pouch. *Carte de visite, Gil Barrett collection*

Independent Riflemen; and most of the United Guards, of Frederick County.[7]

Formed at Easton during June 1860, the Home Guards of Talbot County were attached to the 4th Regiment MM and wore a dress uniform consisting of "white pants, blue cap with white plume, tipped with red, and blue frock coat trimmed with gold lace and gold gilt buttons."[8] On July 12, this company received their arms, which were of "the Minnie patent [US Rifle Musket M1855], burnished barrels, and in every way nicely finished."[9] Established by 1858, the Independent Riflemen, 16th Regiment MM, wore "a dark green frock coat, of strict military cut, single breasted, with three rows of regulation R[iflemen] buttons on the breast, and trimmed with gold lace *au regle*."[10] During February 1859, this company acquired "fifty of the new Rifle, model of 55, with Maynard improvement on the lock, and sabre attachment together with full accoutrements."[11] Regarded as "all Union men," a "strong detachment" of the Independent Riflemen was ordered out to guard the railroad bridge over the Monocacy River on May 13, 1861.[12] The United Guards were formed by members of the United Volunteer Fire Company, of Frederick, in March 1858, on which occasion their uniform was described as "nearly the same as that of the Fire Company, with fatigue cap, &c."[13]

Baltimore became the rallying point for newly forming companies in 1861. On April 23, the *American and Commercial Advertiser* reported that Brig. Gen. Charles C. Egerton, commanding the uniformed volunteers of the Maryland Militia, had "received by letters and personal applications, offers of regular military organizations from almost *every* county in the State—the companies being fully uniformed and equipped, and ready for service."[14] Two days later, the same journal stated, "The work of organizing military companies is being prosecuted throughout the city and in the suburbs with quiet vigor and industry. The greater portion of those already formed . . . have adopted as their uniform the neat and simple grey woollen shirt, with black trowsers and glazed fatigue cap." This column continued, "The tailors of our city are said to be literally overrun with orders for uniforms, the overwhelming demand for which has given a decided impetus to that department of the trade. A great number of these orders are from the adjoining counties, where additional companies are being rapidly formed."[15]

Loyal Unionists continued to form Home Guard companies throughout the remainder of the year. On September 13, 1861, the Home Guards of "the 13th, 14th and 18th wards [of Baltimore] marched to their armory, the Western Station house, and after getting their muskets paraded through the different streets in the western part of the city." According to the *Baltimore Clipper*, "They attracted a great deal of attention and looked well.—Their uniforms consist of black pants, grey shirt, and cap to match, and the letter of the company on the front, and a leather belt."[16] When presented with "a beautiful American flag" on October 4, 1861, Co. I, 1st Regiment Home Guard, wore "grey shirts, black pants and blue caps" and were armed with "new muskets," which were probably M1861 Springfield rifle muskets.[17]

Issued on May 3, 1861, the next presidential call to Maryland was for four three-year regiments, all of which received US-regulation clothing. Recruiting for the 1st Maryland Volunteers, or 1st Independent Volunteers, began within days. A "U.S. Rendezvous" for recruits was established at the National Hotel on Camden Street, Baltimore, where regular army officer Capt. John C. McConnell had enrolled about 250 men by the tenth of the month.[18] McConnell initially commanded Co. A, 1st Maryland, but vacated his appointment on August 5, 1861, to accept promotion as colonel of the 3rd Maryland Volunteers. Recruited in the 13th District of Baltimore County by Capt. Francis G. F. Waltemeyer, the Home Guards became Co. B.[19] The National Hotel was fired upon and stoned by secessionists on May 13, 1861, but the police prevented the spread of any further violence. Following this, three companies of these recruits were ordered to Fort McHenry by May 17 for "the purpose of being uniformed."[20] On May 20, these troops were ordered to the military encampment near the Relay House; they were still "very poorly clothed" but "in good spirits."[21]

The National Hotel continued to be used to accommodate federal recruits, and on May 16, 1861, the Union Rifles, commanded by Capt. John W. Wilson, were temporarily quartered there, later being mustered-in as Co. G, 1st Maryland.[22] According to the *Clipper*, the organization of the 1st Maryland was complete by May 23, 1861, and on June 11, Mexican War veteran John R. Kenly was appointed its colonel.[23]

By June 21, 1861, Co. H, 1st Maryland, had received "100 white Havelocks" from Mrs. Frederick Schley, of

Frederick City.[24] In a letter to the *Baltimore Clipper* dated September 16, 1861, a member of this regiment identified only as "Dos" wrote that the citizens of Shepherdstown, Virginia, were surprised to see the "U.S." on their belts when several companies of the 1st Maryland entered the town, having driven Confederate troops out.[25]

The organization of the 2nd Maryland, or 2nd Independent Volunteers, was also authorized on May 3, and recruitment had begun by June 10, 1861, under the supervision of Brig. Gen. James Cooper, with Capt. J. P. Creager—who was subsequently appointed colonel of the 1st Maryland Cavalry—as "General Recruiting Officer."[26] Within twenty-four hours, the ranks of Co. A were filled and Capt. Henry Howard marched them off to Camp Carroll, near Mount Clare station, where the "Maryland Division" was being formed.[27] Nine days later they were joined by Co. C, which was described as "ununiformed" [*sic*] when it left Baltimore.[28] Recruited by Capt. William E. Conoway, Co. G, 2nd Maryland, was proposed to be a "Zouave Company."[29] Mexican War veteran John Sommer was appointed to command this regiment on September 21, 1861. The 2nd Maryland was still waiting for "full equipments" by September 14, 1861.[30] After a flag presentation to Co. H of this regiment, a correspondent of the *Clipper* observed "a marked improvement in its appearance" since Lt. Col. J. Eugene Duryea had "assumed command over it."[31] This regiment received "the balance of their equipments" on October 7, 1861.[32] On December 31, 1861, the *Clipper* reported that the 2nd Maryland had "recently been supplied with new uniforms and hats."[33]

Promoted to lieutenant colonel, John McConnell began to recruit the 3rd Maryland in Baltimore on July 31, 1861.[34] Volunteering for this regiment was slow, and its organization was finally completed in May 1862, when four companies of the 1st Virginia Union Volunteers, consisting of refugees from Jefferson and Berkeley Counties, Virginia, were combined with the understrength Baltimore Light Infantry and members of the 4th Maryland, or German Rifles, which also failed to complete its organization.[35] Recruits for the Baltimore Light Infantry had received "superior uniforms" on November 21, 1861.[36]

The 5th Maryland was originally recruited for state defense as the "Public Guard Regiment" at Camp Hoffman, Baltimore, on August 30, 1861. Commanded by Col. William Louis Schley, it was initially assigned "to do duty along the lines of the Railroads and property of the General Government."[37] On October 28, 1861, this regiment voted unanimously to be designated the 5th Maryland, and to go out of the state, which it eventually did on March 11, 1862. By the former date it had also received half its clothing, with the remainder expected "within a few days," and was armed with "Minie rifled muskets."[38] By November 18, 1861, the 5th Maryland had been supplied with "two suits of uniform, including the regulation hats and caps," which indicates they received dress and fatigue uniforms.[39] Two days later, Capt. Uriah Garber reported a deserter from the Steuben Guard (Co. G), Public Guard Regiment, as wearing "dark dress, [and a] military cap."[40] The Public Guard Regiment paraded through the streets of Baltimore in "new uniforms" on December 5, 1861, and by mid-January 1862 had been armed with "the Austrian rifled musket."[41]

Efforts to recruit a Maryland Home Brigade began on July 19, 1861, when Secretary of War Simon Cameron authorized ex-governor and representative Francis Thomas to enlist four regiments of "loyal citizens" for home defense along the shores of the upper Potomac.[42] Called into service on August 10, 1861, the 1st Regiment of this brigade, under Col. William P. Maulsby Sr., was initially a mixed command composed of infantry, including the Frederick Zouave Cadets, plus one company of cavalry.[43]

Also known as the Allegany County Regiment, the 2nd Regiment, Potomac Home Brigade, was organized at Cumberland under Col. Thomas Johns from August to October 1861.[44] According to a report in the *Civilian & Telegraph*, of Cumberland, dated September 5, "Col. Thos. Johns and Ex-Governor Thomas left for Washington city, via Bedford, Penn., for the purpose of receiving arms, uniforms and equipment for the entire regiment, when the entire corps will take the field for active duty."[45] On September 19, the same journal stated, "The tents and necessary camp equipage of the Allegany county Regiment, arrived here on yesterday, from Hopewell. The uniforms and clothing will be on the last of the week. The Regiment will at once go into Camp, and be relieved from their unpleasant and unhealthy quarters in pened [*sic*] up rooms."[46] Most of this regiment had been uniformed and equipped by October 5, since five days later the *Civilian &*

WANTED
FOR THE UNITED STATES ARMY,
ONE THOUSAND
ABLE BODIED MEN,
Between the ages of eighteen and forty-five years. Term of service—Three years, unless sooner discharged. Pay—Twenty dollars per month. Apply at the Recruiting Office, 112 Baltimore street, over the "Patriot" office.
Capt. J. C. McCONNELL,
my11-tf Recruiting Officer.

Aided by this notice in the *Baltimore Clipper*, recruiting for the 1st Maryland Volunteers was begun in Baltimore by Capt. John C. McConnell during May 1861, with a recruiting office at 112 Baltimore Street—"over the 'Patriot' office"—and accommodation for volunteers being provided at the National Hotel on Camden Street. Recruits were offered $20 per month, which was $7 above that paid to other volunteers. *Author's collection*

Twenty-one-year-old Franklin T. Porter enlisted in Co. E, Purnell Legion, Maryland Infantry, in Cecil County, Maryland, on September 7, 1861, and was mustered-in for three years at Pikesville, Baltimore County, six days later. He was detailed for guard duty at Camp Dix, Cockeysville, Maryland, during March–April, 1862 and later in the year was reported sick in the US General Hospital near Sharpsburg from September 19, 1862, following his regiment's involvement at Antietam. Back with his unit by January 1863, he served with the Army of the Potomac during Grant's Overland Campaign until mustered-out near Petersburg, Virginia, on October 24, 1864. Photographed after enlistment, holding a Union flag, he wears a frock coat with low-cut collar, cap with waterproof cover, and cavalry gauntlets and boots. *Carte de visite by Marken's Gallery, Frederick, Maryland; Gil Barrett collection*

Telegraph reported that "with the exception of one full company and part of another," most of the regiment paraded in "full uniform" and the "men appeared highly pleased with their new uniforms."[47]

Organization of the 3rd Regiment, Potomac Home Brigade, was begun at Cumberland, Maryland, on October 31, 1861. Recruitment was slow, and by August 1862 the ranks of only five companies had been filled. As a result, this regiment was supplemented with the three companies of the 4th Regiment, Potomac Home Brigade, which failed to complete its organization.[48]

The 1st Regiment Eastern Shore Home Guard was authorized for three years' service as an infantry regiment under Col. James Wallace on August 16, 1861, to protect the shore of Maryland east of the Chesapeake Bay and to prevent food supplies from reaching the Western Shore.[49] Organization of the 2nd Regiment Eastern Shore Home Guard began at Camp Vickers on September 14, 1861, with Col. Edward Wilkins, of Chestertown, in command. On October 19, the *Kent News* reported, "During the past few days the uniforms, arms, and equipments have been received and distributed to the men. The uniforms are of army blue cloth, well made, warm, and quite neat in appearance. The army shoe is particularly a noticeable article. Made of the very best leather, heavy but coarse, sewed, and soles projecting a little from the upper, they are remarkably elastic and easy to the feet."[50] The six companies of this regiment were on duty in the lower part of the Eastern Shore by February 1862.

Postmaster at Baltimore, William H. Purnell was authorized by the War Department to raise a regiment of three years' men for "Home Service" on the Eastern Shore of Maryland on August 21, 1861.[51] Originally known as the Maryland Border Legion, what became the Purnell Legion was a mixed command consisting of ten companies of infantry, four companies of cavalry, and two companies of artillery—the latter including the Gist Artillery. Volunteers for its ranks were advised that "Clothing, Uniforms, Horses, Arms, Equipments" were to be "on a footing with the Regular Army."[52] Recruits for Infantry Co. H were promised "Sharp's Breech-Loading Rifles" and "Clothing . . . as in the Regular Army."[53] On October 5, 1861, this regiment received uniforms consisting of "blue pants, dark blue fatigue coat, felt hat, of the regular army pattern, and heavy blue overcoat."[54] When deployed to Salisbury, Maryland, in December 1861, the 2nd and 3rd Light Artillery companies of Purnell's Legion were described as consisting of "twelve brass guns, and the horses numbering near two hundred, ordinance [*sic*] and baggage wagons constituted quite a long and imposing train."[55]

The 1st Regiment Maryland Independent Volunteer Cavalry, originally known as the Maryland Dragoons, began organizing under the command of Col. J. P. Creager on August 6, 1861. Enlisting for three years, volunteers were promised "complete suits of clothing . . . horses, arms and complete equipments" but had not been equipped by September 21, 1861. Two days later, recruits were promised a "Horse, sabre, pistol holster and revolvers."[56] Organized in August 1861 by Henry A. Cole, of Frederick, Maryland, as a mounted company attached to the 1st Regiment, Potomac Home Brigade, "Cole's Cavalry," or the "Cole Rangers," received twenty-nine "U.S. rifles" taken from Southern sympathizers at New Market, Maryland, for "guard service" until "their own arms should be furnished."[57] Combined with the cavalry companies originally attached to the other three Potomac Home Brigade regiments, this unit expanded into the 1st Battalion, Potomac Home Brigade Cavalry, in 1862.

Maryland Order of Battle, 1861

Volunteer Infantry

1st Regiment (1st Independent Volunteers)

2nd Regiment (2nd Independent Volunteers)

3rd Regiment

4th Regiment (German Rifles) (failed to complete organization)

5th Regiment (Public Guard)

Volunteer Cavalry

1st Regiment Independent Volunteer Cavalry (Maryland Dragoons)

Cole's Cavalry Battalion (Cole Rangers)

Home Guard

1st Potomac Home Brigade

2nd Potomac Home Brigade (Allegany County Regiment)

3rd Potomac Home Brigade

4th Potomac Home Brigade

1st Eastern Shore Home Guard

2nd Eastern Shore Home Guard

Purnell Legion (mixed command)

CHAPTER 6:
DISTRICT OF COLUMBIA

The president called out the local District of Columbia Militia (DCM) for three months on April 9, 1861, although they were not mustered-in until the following day. A composite sixty-man company of the Washington Light Infantry Battalion, commanded by Col. James Y. Davis, was mustered-in on April 15, being the first Northern militia to enter active federal service. Thirty-three companies of infantry and riflemen, plus two troops of cavalry, were sworn into federal service. The cavalry consisted of the President's Mounted Guard and Georgetown Mounted Guard. The latter company was uniformed in a "dark blue coat with brass buttons, light blue pants with buff stripe, and regulation hat" when they escorted the carriage carrying president-elect Abraham Lincoln to his inauguration on March 4, 1861.[1]

Having done much to prevent prosecessionist paramilitary groups from seizing the federal capital, Mexican War veteran and regular army officer Charles P. Stone was assigned to command as inspector general of the District of Columbia militia, with the rank of colonel, on April 16, 1861. As a result of General Order No. 3, dated May 3, 1861, the DC militia was organized into eight battalions.

The First Battalion consisted of the Anderson Rifles, Carrington Home Guard, Potomac Light Guard, and Andrew Johnson Guards. During the George Washington birthday parade on February 22, 1861, the *National Republican* observed that the Anderson Rifles, Co. A, wore "dark pants with red stripe, gray hunting coats trimmed with red, and fatigue caps."[2] For the inauguration of President Lincoln ten days later, Companies A and B, Anderson Rifles, were reported wearing "a dark gray coat and pants, with red trimmings on the coat and red stripe on the pantaloons, and a fatigue cap to correspond."[3] On February 22, 1861, the Carrington Home Guards wore "dark pants with red stripe, army overcoats, and fatigue caps." Parading for the inauguration of President Lincoln on March 4, 1861, they wore "army great coats, black pants with red seam stripe, and neat fatigue caps."[4]

The tentative identification of these enlisted men—plus musician—as being members of the Washington Light Guard, 4th Battalion, District of Columbia, is based on the red tops seen on their chasseur-pattern gray fatigue caps. Note these volunteers also have white webbing accoutrement belts hung over their stacked muskets, one of which has a small guide marker flag attached. *Michael J. McAfee collection*

Of the 2nd Battalion, the Henderson Guard wore "a dark blue frock coat, similar to the new army regulation coat, light blue pants and artillery facings and glazed fatigue cap." The remainder of this unit consisted of four companies of the Union Regiment. On March 4, three of these companies paraded with Co. A in "new grey coats and pants," and Co. C similarly dressed in "grey frock coats and pants, and orange facings, and glazed fatigued caps." Co. B wore "regular army overcoats, glazed fatigue caps, and black pants with red facings."[5]

The 3rd Battalion was composed of the National Rifles, Slemmer Guards, Cameron Guards, and Co. F of the Union Regiment. Formed in 1859, most of the original membership of the National Rifles consisted of Marylanders—including its commander, Capt. F. B. Schaeffer—who were Southern sympathizers. Forced to flee across the Potomac River to Alexandria, Virginia, in April 1861, they organized the Beaureguard Rifles at Phoenix Hall, Alexandria, on May 1. Meanwhile, the National Rifles were reorganized under 1st Lt. John R. Smead, 2nd US Artillery, and were mustered into federal service on April 15, 1861. This company was assigned to guard duty onboard

The pencil inscription "Brothers Smedburg" on this *carte de visite* identifies these two volunteers. The man seated is Charles G. Smedburg, who belonged to Sixth Company, 7th NYSM, and who was later commissioned in the 14th Infantry and died in service. The man standing was his brother William Renwick Smedburg, who enlisted in the National Rifles, Third Battalion, District of Columbia Militia. He wears the gray frock coat, trousers, and forage cap trimmed with red adopted by his unit in 1859. He is armed with an M1855 rifle with sword bayonet and has matching accouterments, including an 1855-pattern rifle belt with two-piece, interlocking, cast brass plate and frog for a bayonet. This photograph was taken in May 1861, following the reorganization of the National Rifles and while the 7th NYSM was helping guard the nation's capital. *Todd D.C. album, Anne S. K. Brown Military Collection, Brown University*

the steamer *St Nicholas* and was stationed at the Telegraph Office in Washington, DC, on April 19, 1861. During a visit to Pennsylvania in September 1860, the National Rifles were variously described as wearing "a gray coat and pants with scarlet trimmings, high hat and pompoon" and "[gray] frock coat and pants trimmed with red, blue cadet cap, with red pompon, and rifles with sabre bayonet."[6]

The 4th Battalion consisted of Co. A of the Washington Light Infantry Battalion, the Washington Light Guard, and the District Union Rifles, plus the Washington Zouaves, commanded by Capt. J. Tyler Powell, which were attached to the Washington Light Infantry Battalion during March 1861 as Co. E. The Washington Light Guard had "gray pants, and coats with mixed red and orange lacings, and gray fatigue caps with red tops."[7] Organized at the beginning of March 1861 and drilled for several days by Elmer Ellsworth, the Washington Zouaves adopted a uniform consisting of a "dark blue Zouave jacket,

Standing at center and right, two unidentified officers of the National Rifles pose with three enlisted men of the 7th NYSM. A pencil inscription beneath this image states "Jenkins asleep" and presumably refers to the man seated at left. *Todd D.C. album, Anne S. K. Brown Military Collection, Brown University*

trimmed with buff . . . having a row of bell buttons around the collar, light-blue pantaloons, with buff stripe down the seam, tea-green shirt, with fancy bosom, buckskin leggings, and cap after the pattern of the [Washington] Light Infantry."[8] On May 2, the *Evening Star* reported, "This fine corps has been kept under a cloud since they were drafted into service, by reason of their not all being provided with company uniforms. Their uniforms were promised long since by the firm engaged to make them. They now expect them when they get them."[9] An undress uniform was acquired, and by May 1 the Zouaves paraded in "overcoats, making quite a creditable appearance."[10] By mid-June 1861, some of this battalion was stationed at Camp Jim Davis, where they manned nearly completed breastworks containing seven large cannon guarding the Chain Bridge across the Potomac River.[11]

The 5th Battalion contained the Metropolitan Rifles, Jackson Guards Sappers and Miners, Constitutional Guards, and two companies of the Putnam Rifles. The Metropolitan Rifles, commanded by Capt. W. H. Nalley, wore "neat gray jackets and fatigue caps" that were more fully described as "a glazed fatigue cap, gray jacket with gold-lace trimmings, and black pantaloons with gold stripe." On May 29, 1861, this company paraded in new gray caps provided by their commanding officer.[12] The Putnam Rifles were uniformed in "gray coat with orange facings, black pants with orange stripes, and glazed fatigue cap."[13]

Commanded by Col. James A. Tait, the 6th Battalion was composed of Companies A, C, E, and F of the prewar National Guard Battalion, which adopted a gray-trimmed red uniform in May 1860.[14] This unit paraded in "beautiful uniforms" with Pioneer Gwinn Harris in "full uniform and cap, towering full eight feet in height" at their head during the anniversary parade on February 22, 1861.[15] Elements of the 6th Battalion were stationed as "a special guard" near the platform from which Lincoln delivered his inaugural address on March 4, 1861.[16] On June 7, Co. E received "110 fine havelocks" made by "the ladies of the Ninth street Methodist Church."[17]

The 7th Battalion contained the City Guards, Mechanics Union Rifles, Co. D of the Washington Light Infantry (Howitzer Corps), and Co. C of the Union Regiment. Composed of "young mechanics employed on the capital extension work," the Mechanics Union Rifles paraded in "blue fatigue blouse, fatigue cap, and dark blue pants, with gold stripe" in March 1861.[18] Of the 8th Battalion, the Washington Rifles were posted on "several prominent buildings on the avenue, in squads, to overlook the [inaugural] procession as it passed" on March 4, 1861.[19]

Organized in northwestern Washington, the 1st Georgetown Volunteer Battalion included the Potomac Light Infantry, who wore a "frock coat and pants, of dark blue, the pants with light blue stripe, and a fatigue cap in unison with the whole." The Scott Rifles donned a "dark blue jacket with orange trimmings, black pants with buff stripe and red cord, and dark blue cap with gold band and the figure 8 in front." The District of Columbia Rifles wore "bright blue coats and pants, the former with red trimmings, and the latter with red stripes, and neat fatigue caps."[20]

Mustered-in from July to October 1861 under Col. James A. Tait—late commander of the 5th Battalion, DCM—the 1st Regiment DC Infantry—was assigned to guarding the Washington Branch, Baltimore & Ohio Rail Road, in November 1861. The 2nd Regiment DC Infantry began to organize in November 1861. Both of these regiments wore US-regulation uniforms.

District of Columbia Order of Battle, 1861

District of Columbia Volunteer Militia ("Three-months' Service")

Washington Light Infantry Battalion

President's Mounted Guard

Georgetown Mounted Guard

1st Battalion

2nd Battalion

3rd Battalion

4th Battalion

5th Battalion

6th Battalion

7th Battalion

7th Battalion

1st Georgetown Volunteer Battalion

Volunteer Infantry

1st Regiment

2nd Regiment

GLOSSARY

basque: A tight-fitting jacket worn by some *vivandières*.

bersaglieri: A corps of the Italian army originally created by Gen. Alessandro La Marmora on June 18, 1836, to serve in the Army of the Kingdom of Sardinia.

blouse: Loose-fitting midlength coat worn for fatigue or undress occasions. Also known as the "sack coat," it was the fatigue wear of the US Army since 1858.

bodice: Female attire consisting of a tight-fitting vest covering the neck to the waist.

breeches: Tight trousers fastened just below the knee.

brogans: Any stout, coarse shoes of the period. Also called bootees.

cadet gray: A bluish-gray cloth commonly used for uniforms.

chasseurs: A term applied to units that were uniformed, armed, and drilled similarly to the *chasseurs à pied* (foot chasseurs) of the French army. They wore low-crowned caps, short-skirted jackets, full trousers gathered below the knee, and gaiters.

dress cap: Cap with a tall, stiffened crown based either on the 1851 pattern with band of branch service color or the 1854 pattern, with a thin welt of branch service color above the band. Usually topped either with a worsted pompon or fountain plume.

drop-front trousers: Sailor's trousers with a large flap at the front, usually fastened by six buttons.

duck: A cheap, durable linen canvas material sometimes used for fatigue clothing and tents. Also used for sailor's clothing.

fatigue uniform: Designed for fatigue duties, but often worn for field service under arms.

fez: A brimless, soft headdress of Middle Eastern origin—usually red—worn by Zouave-style units. Often little more than a skull cap; all had a tassel hanging from the top.

firemen's shirt: A heavy woolen shirt usually dyed either red or dark blue, and generally a pullover pattern with a double-breasted opening in front. Common undress for volunteer fire companies and adopted by military companies, especially if organized from the former.

flannel: A soft woolen cloth of loose texture usually used for shirts and blouses, or sack coats.

frock: Outer garment for service wear for a seaman, consisting of a loose shirt with wide "sailor's" collar.

frock coat: Single- or double-breasted coat with skirts the same length before and behind, falling to at least midway between the top of the thigh and bend of the knee, and sometimes as low as the knee.

Garibaldi shirt: Red woolen shirt copied from that worn by troops who fought under Garibaldi during the Italian Wars of Unification in 1849, 1859, and 1860.

glazed hat: Brimmed straw hat, also called a "Sennit" hat, with a black-painted canvas cover that has been rubberized with India rubber or gutta percha.

greaves: Also known as *jambières*. Leg cuffs worn with French-influenced uniforms. Usually made of russet leather and worn over gaiters.

grosgrain: Stiff silk trim with distinct transverse ribs used on some dress uniforms.

Hardee hat: Regulation felt hat introduced for the US Army in 1855 for cavalry, supposedly by (then) Maj. William J. Hardee. The name also applied to the very similar 1858-pattern dress hat. Also called the "Jefferson Davis" or "Kossuth" hat.

havelock: A white cotton or linen covering for a cap, with a flap hanging over the wearer's neck as protection against the sun. Named for Maj. Gen. Henry Havelock of the Indian army.

havelock hat: Felt hat with adjustable brim.

hunting shirt: A loose-fitting overshirt, often with fringes on the sleeves and hem, usually worn as a fatigue uniform and based on that worn by the Continental army during the Revolutionary War.

jean: A twilled cotton cloth used for summer clothing and cheaper uniforms.

Kossuth hat: Brimmed felt hat, closely resembling the US Army 1858-pattern dress hat. Sometimes contemporaneously referred to as a "cockade hat."

leggins: High gaiters reaching from the ankle to the knee.

logwood: Violet or purple dye produced from the heartwood of the logwood tree.

mazarine blue: A deep, purplish blue.

merino: A soft woolen material made from the fleece of merino sheep—generally used for shirts.

Minié musket: A shoulder arm, such as the US Springfield rifle-musket, that could fire a cylindro-conoidal ball which could be loaded at the muzzle and expand when fired, so as to engage with the rifling in the barrel.

National Guard–style cap: A dress cap with patent leather band and top of the type worn by the 7th NYSM or "National Guard."

pantaloons, or pants: Tight-fitting trousers extending from waist to ankle, sometimes with straps passing under the instep.

pea jacket: A double-breasted, calf-length woolen overcoat.

peg-top trousers: Trousers cut very wide at the hips and narrow at the ankles. Mainly confined to French-style uniforms.

placket: Double layers of fabric that hold the buttons and buttonholes in a shirt front.

polka-style skirts: Short skirts of a coat or jacket with slits let in both sides.

pompon, or pompoon: Spherical or spheroidal, colored, worsted ornament affixed on top in the front of a dress cap.

roundabout: Short and usually tight-fitting, waist-length, and tailless jacket.

Russian knot: Shoulder straps formed from twisted gold cord, terminating with a trefoil at the shoulder seam.

satinet: A fabric woven with a cotton warp and woolen weft, giving a satin-like finish.

shako: See National Guard–style cap.

shoddy: Cloth made of yarn obtained by tearing refuse woolen rags to shreds, with some new wool added. Hence, any low-grade or worthless cloth made to look like a superior article.

shoulder knot: A strap of twisted lace forming a trefoil at shoulder seam.

tailcoat: A single- or double-breasted coat cut squarely across the front at waist level, with two skirts or tails hanging down in the rear.

tombeau: Circle on each side of the front of a Zouave jacket, formed by the lace or tape trim descending from a trefoil.

Turcos: North African infantry units of the French army whose full title was Tirailleurs Algerians. They wore a light-blue Zouave-style uniform trimmed in yellow.

vivandière, or cantinière: French name for women attached to a regiment as canteen carriers.

voltigeur: Synonymous with chasseur, a light infantry corps.

wamus: A rough, loose-fitting overshirt or frock.

wings: A strap with short bullion fringe at the seam of the shoulder.

worsted: High-quality type of wool yarn. The name derives from Worstead, a village in the English county of Norfolk.

Zouaves: Militia and volunteer soldiers wearing variations of the Middle Eastern–style Zouave uniform and trained in the peculiar drill adapted in the US after 1859, on the basis of that of the Corps of Zouaves of the French army.

BIBLIOGRAPHY

General Sources

Books

Bazelon, Bruce S., and William F. McGuinn. *A Directory of American Military Goods Dealers & Makers, 1785–1885.* Manassas, VA: REF Typesetting & Publishing, 1987.

Campbell, J. Duncan, and Michael J. O'Donnell. *American Military Headgear Insignia*. Alexandria, VA: O'Donnell, 2004.

Coates, Earl J., and John D. McAulay. *Civil War Sharps Carbines & Rifles*. Gettysburg, PA: Thomas, 1996.

Dornbusch, C. E., comp. *Military Bibliography of the Civil War*. Vol. 1, *Regimental Publications and Personal Narratives: Northern States*. New York: New York Public Library, 1961–1962.

Elting, John R., and Michael J. McAfee, eds. *Military Uniforms in America*. Vol. 3, *Long Endure: The Civil War Period, 1852–1867*. Novato, CA: Presidio, 1982.

Hewett, Janet B., Jocelyn Pinson, and Julia H. Nichols, eds. *Supplement to the Official Records of the Union and Confederate Armies*. 100 vols. Wilmington, NC: Broadfoot, 1995–1999.

Langellier, John P. *Army Blue: The Uniform of Uncle Sam's Regulars, 1848–1873*. Atglen, PA: Schiffer Military History, 1998.

Langellier, John P., and C. Paul Loane. *Army Headgear, 1812–1872*. Atglen, PA: Schiffer Military History, 2002.

McAulay, John D. *Rifles of the U.S. Army, 1861–1906*. Lincoln, RI: Andrew Mowbray, 2003.

O'Donnell, Michael J., and J. Duncan Campbell. *American Military Belt Plates*. 2nd ed. Alexandria, VA: O'Donnell, 2000.

Scott, Robert N. *The War of the Rebellion: A Compilation of the Official Records of the Union and Confederate Armies*. 128 vols. Washington. DC: Government Printing Office, 1880–1901.

Tice, Warren K. *Uniform Buttons of the United States, 1776–1865*. Gettysburg, PA: Thomas, 1997.

Todd, Frederick P., George C. Woodbridge, Lee A. Wallace Jr., and Michael J. McAfee. *American Military Equipage, 1851–1872*. Vol. 1, *A Description by Word and Picture of What the American Soldier, Sailor, and Marine of These Years Wore and Carried, with Emphasis on the American Civil War*. Providence, RI: Company of Military Historians, 1974.

Todd, Frederick P., George C. Woodbridge, Lee A. Wallace Jr., and Michael J. McAfee. *American Military Equipage, 1851–1872*. Vol. 1, *A Description by Word and Picture of What the American Soldier, Sailor, and Marine of These Years Wore and Carried, with Emphasis on the American Civil War*. Providence, RI: Company of Military Historians, 1977.

Todd, Frederick P., George C. Woodbridge, Lee A. Wallace Jr., Michael J. McAfee, and Maria P. Todd Damerel. *American Military Equipage, 1851–1872*. Vol. 2, *State Forces*. New York: Chatham Square, 1983.

Troiani, Don, Earl J. Coates, and Michael J. McAfee. *Don Troiani's Regiments & Uniforms of the Civil War*. Mechanicsburg, PA: Stackpole Books, 2002.

Wilson, Mark R., *The Business of Civil War: Military Mobilization and the State, 1861–1865*. Baltimore: Johns Hopkins University Press, 2006.

Journals & Magazines

Military Collector & Historian. A quarterly journal published by the Company of Military Collectors and Historians (1951–1961) and by the Company of Military Historians (1962–).

Military Images: Photographic History of the U.S. Soldier and Sailor, 1839–1920. A bimonthly magazine founded by Harry Roach, 1979–.

North South Trader Civil War: The Magazine for Collectors & Historians. A quarterly magazine founded by William S. Mussenden, published by Stephen W. Sylvia, 1973–.

Pennsylvania

Primary Sources

The Erie City Directory, 1861–62. Erie, PA: H. W. Hulbert, 1861.

McElroy's Philadelphia City Directory for 1861. Philadelphia: E. C. & J. Biddle, 1861.

National Archives: Record Group 92, entry 2194, book 3; Record Group 94, Regimental Books, 62nd Pennsylvania Infantry. US Patent Office, patent No. 2896. 33.900, Washington, DC.

Newspapers

Allentown, Pennsylvania, *Lehigh Register*

Altoona, Pennsylvania, *Altoona Tribune*

Baltimore, *Baltimore American and Commercial Advertiser*

Baltimore, *Baltimore Clipper*

Bellafonte, Pennsylvania, *Centre Democrat*

Bellafonte, Pennsylvania, *Central Press*

Bloomsburg, Pennsylvania, *Columbia Democrat & Bloomsburg General Advertiser*

Boston, *Boston Evening Transcript*

Clearfield, Pennsylvania, *Raftsman's Journal*

Columbia, Pennsylvania, *Columbia Spy*

Ebensburg, Pennsylvania, *Democrat and Sentinel*

Ebensburg, Pennsylvania, *The Alleghanian*

Gettysburg, Pennsylvania, *The Compiler*

Gloucester, Massachusetts, *Cape Ann Light and Gloucester Telegraph*

Harrisburg, Pennsylvania, *Daily Patriot and Union*

Harrisburg, Pennsylvania, *Pennsylvania Daily Telegraph*
Lowell, Massachusetts, *Lowell Daily Courier*
New York, *Irish American Weekly*
New York, *New York Herald*
Philadelphia, Pennsylvania, *North American and United States Gazette*
Philadelphia, *Philadelphia Inquirer*
Philadelphia, *Public Ledger*
Philadelphia, *The Press*
Pittsburgh, Pennsylvania, *Pittsburgh Daily Gazette & Commercial Journal*
Pottsville, Pennsylvania, *Miners' Journal & Pottsville General Advisor*
Providence, Rhode Island, *Providence Daily Evening News*
Trenton, New Jersey, *Daily State Gazette & Republican*
Washington, DC, *Evening Star*
Washington, DC, *National Republican*
Wellsboro, Pennsylvania, *The Agitator*
Wheeling, Virginia, *Daily Intelligencer*

Secondary Sources

Banes, Charles H. *History of the Philadelphia Brigade*. Philadelphia: J. B. Lippincott, 1876.

Bates, Samuel P. *History of the Pennsylvania Volunteers, 1861–1865*. Vol. 1. Harrisburg, PA: B. Singerly, 1869.

Elting, John R., and Michael J. McAfee, eds. *Military Uniforms in America*. Vol. 3, *Long Endure: The Civil War Period, 1852–1867*. Novato, CA: Presidio, 1982.

Fleming, George T. *My High School Days*. Pittsburgh, PA: Wm. G. Johnston, 1904.

Galloway, G. Norton. *The Ninety-Fifth Pennsylvania Volunteers (Gosline's Pennsylvania Zouaves), in the Sixth Corps*. Philadelphia: Collins, 1884.

Hennessey, James, and H. Michael Madaus. "72nd Regiment, Pennsylvania Volunteer Infantry, 1861–1864, '3rd California Regiment,' 'Baxter's Fire Zouaves.'" *Military Collector & Historian* 32, no. 2 (1980): 71–75.

Judson, A. M. *History of the Eighty-Third Regiment Pennsylvania Volunteers*. Erie, PA: B. F. H. Lynn, 1865.

Latta, James W. *History of the First Regiment Infantry, National Guard of Pennsylvania (Grey Reserves), 1861–1911*. Philadelphia: J. B. Lippincott, 1912.

McAfee, Michael J. "Uniforms & History: 72nd Regiment, Pennsylvania Volunteer Infantry (Baxter's Philadelphia Fire Zouaves)." *Military Images* 11, no. 6 (May–June 1990): 27.

McAfee, Michael J. "Uniforms & History: The 83rd Pennsylvania Volunteer Infantry, 1861–1862." *Military Images* 12, no. 1 (July–August 1990): 27–29.

McAfee, Michael J. "Uniforms & History: The Anderson Troop." *Military Images* 12, no. 2 (September–October 1990): 29.

McAfee, Michael J. "Uniforms & History: 'Gosline's Pennsylvania Zouaves' (95th Infantry Regt.)." *Military Images* 16, no. 4 (January–February 1995): 32–33.

McAfee, Michael J. "Uniforms & History: Brave Lancers; Sixth Regiment Pennsylvania Volunteer Cavalry (Rush's Lancers), 1861–1865." *Military Images* 19, no. 6 (May–June 1998): 32.

McAfee, Michael J. "Uniforms & History: 'Like a Regiment of Quakers.'" *Military Images* 33, no. 3 (Summer 2015): 57.

McDermott, Andrew W. *A Brief History of the 69th Regiment Pennsylvania Veteran Volunteers*. Philadelphia: D. J. Gallagher, 1889.

Miller, John. *A Twentieth Century History of Erie County, Pennsylvania: A Narrative Account of Its Historic Progress, Its People, and Its Principal Interests*. Chicago: Lewis, 1909.

Prowell, George Reeser. *History of the Eighty-Seventh Regiment, Pennsylvania Volunteers*. York, PA: Press of the York Daily, 1903.

Rauscher, Frank. *Music on the March, 1862–'65, with the Army of the Potomac, 114th Regt. P. V., Collis' Zouaves*. Philadelphia: Wm. F. Fell, 1892.

Ray, Frederick E., Jr., and John R. Elting. "23rd Regiment Pennsylvania Infantry (Birney Zouaves)." *Military Collector & Historian* 14, no. 1 (1962): 17.

Sturcke, Roger David, and Michael J. Winey. "1st Infantry Regiment (Gray Reserves) Reserve Brigade, Philadelphia Militia, 1861." *Military Collector & Historian* 34, no. 2 (1982): 70–71.

Taylor, Frank H. *Philadelphia in the Civil War 1861–1865*. Philadelphia: City of Philadelphia, 1913.

Thompson, Barry L., and John L. Marsh. "The Raftsmen's Guard, April/May 1861." *Military Collector & Historian* 26, no. 3 (1974): 168–169.

Thomson, O. R. Howard. *History of the Bucktails: Kane Rifle Regiment of the Pennsylvania Reserve Corps*. Philadelphia: Electric Printing, 1906.

Todd, Frederick P., and Harry C. Larter. "6th Pennsylvania Cavalry (Rush's Lancers), 1862." *Military Collector & Historian* 6, no. 4 (1954): 102.

Troiani, Don, Earl J. Coates, and Michael J. McAfee. *Don Troiani's Regiments & Uniforms of the Civil War*. Mechanicsburg, PA: Stackpole Books, 2002.

Vanderslice, Catherine H., ed. *The Civil War Letters of George Washington Beidelman*. Richmond, VA: Pamplin Historical Park, 2002.

Woodbridge, George C., Frederick E. Ray Jr., and John R. Elting. "42nd Regiment, Pennsylvania Volunteer Infantry ("The Bucktails"), 1861–1865." *Military Collector & Historian* 14, no. 3 (1962): 88–89.

Wray, William J. *History of the Twenty Third Pennsylvania Volunteer Infantry—Birney's Zouaves: Three Months and Three Years Service*. Philadelphia: Compiled by the Secretary by Order of the Survivors Association, 1904.

New York

Primary Sources

Adjutant General. *General Regulations for the Military Forces of the State of New-York, 1858*. Albany, NY: Weed, Parsons, 1858.

The Albany Directory for the Year 1861. Albany, NY: Adams, Sampson, 1861.

Alfred Davenport Letterbook. MS Coll., New-York Historical Society.

By-Laws of the "New-York Zouaves" (Independent Corps). New York: L. H. Frank, 1860.

Communication from the Governor Transmitting the Report of the Board of State Officers Named in the Act of April 16, 1861, Entitled, "An Act to Authorise the Embodying and Equipment of a Volunteer Militia and to Provide for the Public Defence." State of New York. No. 15. In Assembly, January 9, 1862.

"Letter from Devlin, Hudson & Co. [Clothing Goods, New York City], to Col. Duryee, May 8, 1861." Todd files, Anne S. K. Brown Coll., Brown University, Providence, RI.

Letter from James Albert Hudson, "Headquarters 1st New York Vol. (Late Lincoln) Cavalry, Camp Kearney, near Alexandria, Va., February 3d 1862."

Murphy, William D. *Biographical Sketches of the State Officers and Members of the Legislature of the State of New York, in 1861.* New York: William D. Murphy, 1861.

New York (State) Bureau of Military Statistics. *3rd Annual Report of the Bureau of Military Statistics.* Albany, NY: Bureau of Military Statistics, 1866.

"Report of the Board of Officers named in the Act to Authorize the Embodying and Equipping of a Volunteer Militia and to Provide for the Public Defence," State of New York. No. 15. In Assembly, January 9, 1862.

Newspapers

Albany, New York, *Albany Evening Journal*

Albany, New York, *Atlas and Argus*

Baltimore, *Baltimore Clipper*

Binghamton, New York, *Broome Republican*

Brockport, New York, *Brockport Republican*

Buffalo, New York, *Buffalo Daily Courier*

Burlington, Vermont, *Burlington Free Press*

Charleston, South Carolina, *Charleston Daily Courier*

Hartford, Connecticut, *Hartford Weekly Times*

Indianapolis, Indiana, *Indianapolis Daily Sentinel*

Lewiston, Maine, *Lewiston Daily Evening Journal*

Lowell, Massachusetts, *Lowell Daily Courier*

Madison, Wisconsin, *Wisconsin Daily Patriot*

Malone, New York, *Frontier Palladium*

New York City, *Evening Post*

New York City, *Harper's Weekly*

New York City, *Irish American Weekly*

New York City, *Morning Courier and New-York Enquirer*

New York City, *New York Commercial Advertiser*

New York City, *New York Daily News*

New York City, *New-York Daily Tribune*

New York City, *New York Herald*

New York City, *New York Morning Express*

New York City, *New-York Times*

Odensburgh, New York, *St. Lawrence Republican and Odensburgh Weekly Journal*

Oswego, New York, *Oswego Commercial Times*

Philadelphia, *Philadelphia Inquirer*

Pittsburgh, Pennsylvania, *Pittsburgh Gazette and Commercial Journal*

Providence, Rhode Island, *Providence Daily Post*

Providence, Rhode Island, *Providence Evening Press*

Rochester, New York, *Rochester Evening Express*

Syracuse, New York, *Syracuse Daily Courier and Union*

Syracuse, New York, *Syracuse Daily Standard*

Trenton, New Jersey, *Daily State Gazette & Republican*

Troy, New York, *Troy Daily Whig*

Utica, New York, *Utica Daily Observer*

Utica, New York, *Utica Morning Herald and Daily Gazette*

Washington, DC, *Evening Star*

Washington, DC, *National Republican*

Westfield, New York, *Westfield Republican*

Wilmington, Delaware, *Delaware State Journal and Statesman*

Secondary Sources

Archambault, Alan H., Anthony F. Gero, Philip G. Maples, and Roger David Sturcke. "8th Regiment, New York Volunteer Cavalry (Rochester Regiment); "22nd Regiment, New York Volunteer Cavalry (Rochester Cavalry), 1861–1865." *Military Collector & Historian* 47, no. 4 (1995): 178–179.

Balace, Francis R., and John R. Elting "Les Enfants Perdus, 1861–1864." *Military Collector & Historian* 22, no. 1 (1970): 26–27.

Bilby, Joseph, "Blue Bonnets over the Border: The 79th New York Highlanders in the Civil War," *Military Images* 6, no. 1 (July–August 1984): 5–15.

Brooks Brothers. *A Chronicle Recording One Hundred Twenty-Five Years: A Compendium of Historical Facts & Random Reminiscences Abridged to Encompass in the Form of a Hand Book the Course of the Century and a Quarter Which Has Elapsed since the Founding of Brooks Brothers' Business in 1818.* New York: Brooks Brothers, 1943.

Carr, Joseph B. "Operations of 1861 about Fort Monroe." In *Battles and Leaders of the Civil War.* Vol. 2. Edited by Robert Underwood Johnson & Clarence Clough Buel, 144–152. New York: Thomas Yoseloff, 1956.

Cavanagh, Michael. *Memoirs of Gen. Thomas Francis Meagher.* Worcester, MA: Messenger, 1892.

Chapman, Frederick T., and Frederick P. Todd. "69th Regiment, N.Y.S.M., at the First Battle of Bull Run, 21 July 1861." *Military Collector & Historian* 29, no. 3 (Fall 1977): 121.

Cheney, Newell. *History of the Ninth Regiment, New York Volunteer Cavalry.* New York: Poland Center, 1901.

Cowtan, Charles W. *Services of the 10th New York Volunteers (National Zouaves) in the War of the Rebellion.* New York: Charles W. Ludwig, 1882.

Davenport, Alfred. *Camp and Field Life of the Fifth New York Volunteer Infantry (Duryee Zouaves).* New York: Dick & Fitzgerald, 1879.

Field, Ron, and Roger Sturcke. "41st New York Volunteer Infantry Regiment (DeKalb Regiment, or 2nd Yaeger Regiment, 1861–1865." *Military Collector & Historian* 39, no. 2 (Summer 1987): 76–77.

Floyd, Sergeant Fred C. *History of the Fortieth (Mozart) Regiment, New York Volunteers.* Boston: F. H. Gilson, 1909.

Graham, Lt. Matthew J. *The Ninth Regiment New York Volunteers (Hawkins' Zouaves), Being a History of the Regiment and Veteran Association from 1860 to 1900.* New York: E. P. Coby, 1900.

Grube, Harry T., and George C. Woodbridge. "14th Regiment New York State Militia, 1861–1864." *Military Collector & Historian* 10, no. 3 (Fall 1958): 80–82.

Harrington, Peter. "Colonel Hawkins' Uniform." *Military Collector & Historian* 35, no. 4 (Winter 1983): 188.

Hennessey, James. "Uniforms of the Fifth New York Volunteer Infantry: 'Duryee Zouaves' 1861–1863." *Journal of the Confederate Historical Society of Great Britain* 15, no. 3 (Autumn 1987).

History of the 71st N.Y.N.G. New York: Veterans Association, 71st N.Y.N.G., 1919.

The History of the Fighting Fourteenth. Published in Commemoration of the Fiftieth Anniversary of the Muster of the Regiment into the United States Service, 1911.

The History of a Volunteer Regiment . . . Sixth Regiment New York Infantry. New York: Veteran Volunteer Publishing, 1891.

Jacques, John W., *Three Years' Campaign of the Ninth, N.Y.S.M., during the Southern Rebellion.* New York: Hilton, 1865.

Johnson, Raymond S., Richard P. Ugino, Anthony F. Gero, and Roger David Sturcke. "21st New York Volunteer Infantry Regiment (1st Buffalo Regiment), 1861–1863." *Military Collector & Historian* 47, no. 2 (Summer 1995): 84–85.

Johnson, Raymond S., Anthony F. Gero, Philip G. Maples, and Roger David Sturcke. "13th, 19th, and 24th New York Volunteer Infantry Regiments, Contract Uniforms, 1861." *Military Collector & Historian* 40, no. 1 (Spring 1988): 22–23.

Johnson, Robert Underwood, and Clarence Clough Buel, eds. *Battles and Leaders of the Civil War.* Vol. 2. New York: Thomas Yoseloff, 1956.

Lord, Francis A., and Robert L. Miller. "Hawkins Zouaves: Uniform Addenda." *Military Collector & Historian* 13, no. 4 (Winter 1961): 128.

McAfee, Michael J. "Uniforms and History: 9th New York Volunteer Infantry (Hawkins' Zouaves) 1861–1863." *Military Images* 10, no. 2 (September–October 1988): 25–26.

McAfee, Michael J. "Uniforms and History: 22nd Regiment National Guard State of New York." *Military Images* 10, no. 3 (November–December 1988): 28.

McAfee, Michael J. "Uniforms & History: 79th Regiment, New York State Militia." *Military Images* 11, no. 2 (September–October 1989): 28–29.

McAfee, Michael J. "Uniforms & History: 69th Regiment, New York State Militia—'the National Cadets'—1861." *Military Images* 11, no. 5 (March–April 1990): 26–27.

McAfee, Michael J. "Uniforms & History: 9th Regiment, New York State Militia." *Military Images* 12, no. 5 (March–April 1991): 28–29.

McAfee, Michael J. "Uniforms & History: 62nd Regiment, New York Volunteer Infantry, "Anderson's Zouaves." *Military Images* 12, no. 6 (May–June 1991): 31.

McAfee, Michael J., "Uniforms & History: 14th Regiment, New York State Militia '14th Brooklyn'–84th New York Volunteers." *Military Images* 13, no. 4 (January–February 1992): 26–27.

McAfee, Michael J. "Uniforms & History: The Seventh Regiment New York State Militia." *Military Images* 13, no. 5 (March–April 1992): 30–31.

McAfee, Michael J. "Uniforms & History: 13th Regiment, New York State Militia." *Military Images* 13, no. 6 (May–June 1992): 6.

McAfee, Michael J. "Billy Reb and Johnny Yank." *Military Images* 15, no. 4 (January–February 1994): 16–22.

McAfee, Michael J. "Uniforms & History: 8th New York Volunteer Infantry ('1st German Rifles')." *Military Images* 16, no. 5 (March–April 1995): 31.

McAfee, Michael J. "Uniforms & History: Musicians of the Tenth Legion, 56th Regt., New York Volunteers." *Military Images* 17, no. 3 (November–December 1995): 28–29.

McAfee, Michael J. "Uniforms & History: *Les Enfants Perdus*—the 'Lost Children' of the Independent Battalion, New York Volunteer Infantry, 1862–1864." *Military Images* 18, no. 3 (November–December 1996): 32–33.

McAfee, Michael J. "Uniforms & History: "The Polish Legion —Company C, 31st New York Volunteers." *Military Images* 18, no. 6 (May–June 1997): 36–37.

McAfee, Michael J. "Uniforms and History—'the Lafayette Guard.'" *Military Images* 20, no. 2 (September–October 1998): 40–41.

McAfee, Michael J. "Uniforms & History: 20th New York Volunteer Infantry, the United Turner Rifles." *Military Images* 20, no. 6 (May–June 1999): 44–45.

McAfee, Michael J. "Uniforms & History: 65th New York Volunteer Infantry—1st U.S. Chasseurs." *Military Images* 21, no. 1 (July–August 1999): 39.

McAfee, Michael J. "Uniforms & History: First Regiment, New York Marine Artillery 1861–1863." *Military Images* 22, no. 6 (May–June 2001): 31–32.

McAfee, Michael J. "Uniforms & History: 5th New York, 'the Red Devils.'" *Military Images* 23, no. 5 (February–March 2002): 36–37.

McAfee, Michael J. "Uniforms & History: The 71st Regiment, New York State Militia, "the American Guard." *Military Images* 25, no. 6 (May–June 2004): 34–35.

McAfee, Michael J. "Uniforms & History: The 44th Regiment, N.Y.S. Volunteer Infantry—'Ellsworth's Avengers.'" *Military Images* 26, no. 1 (July–August 2004): 33–34.

McAfee, Michael J. "Uniforms & History: The First Regiment of Mounted Rifles, New York Volunteers." *Military Images* 26, no. 5 (March–April 2005): 32.

McAfee, Michael J. "Uniforms & History: The Fifth Regiment, New York Volunteer Infantry (Revisited)." *Military Images* 27, no. 3 (November–December 2005): 42–44.

McAfee, Michael J. "Uniforms & History: The Twentieth Regiment, New York State Militia, 1861." *Military Images* 28, no. 2 (September–October 2006): 22–25.

McAfee, Michael J. "Uniforms & History: First Regiment of Cavalry, New York State Volunteers." *Military Images* 30, no. 2 (September–October 2008): 42–43.

McAfee, Michael J. "69th New York State Militia Addendum." *Military Collector & Historian* 63, no. 1 (Spring 2011): 30.

McAfee, Michael J. "Uniforms & History: "Just before the Battle . . . (the 8th Regiment, New York State Militia at Bull Run)." *Military Images* 31, no. 1 (July–August 2011): 28–29.

McAfee, Michael J., and Roger David Sturcke. "6th Regiment New York Volunteer Infantry ("Wilson's Zouaves") 1861–1863." *Military Collector & Historian* 27, no. 1 (Spring 1975): 24–29.

McBarron, H. Charles, Jr., and Frederick P. Todd. "12th Regiment, New York State Militia, 1861–1869." *Military Collector & Historian* 4, no. 4 (December 1952): 93–94.

McBarron, H. Charles, Jr., and Frederick P. Todd. "3rd Regiment, New York State Militia (Hussars), 1850–1860." *Military Collector & Historian* 10, no. 4 (Winter 1958): 26–27.

McBarron, H. Charles, Jr., and Robert E. Mulligan. "Albany Burgesses Corps, 1849–1861." *Military Collector & Historian* 22, no. 1 (Spring 1970): 20–21.

Mills, J. Harrison, *Chronicles of the 21st Regiment New York Volunteer Infantry*. Buffalo, NY: Gies, 1863, reprinted 1887.

Morris, Gouverneur. *The History of a Volunteer Regiment . . . Sixth Regiment New York Infantry*. New York: Veteran Volunteer Publishing, 1891.

Osborne, Seward R. "This Hand for Our Country." *Military Collector & Historian* 42, no. 4 (Winter 1990): 122–124.

Preston, N. D. *History of the Tenth Regiment of Cavalry, New York Volunteers*. New York: D. Appleton, 1892.

Schoenfeld, Martin. "The 14th Brooklyn." *Military Images* 9, no. 2 (September–October 1987): 24–25.

Severin, John P., and Frederick P. Todd. "71st Regiment (the American Guard) N.Y.S.M., 1857–1861." *Military Collector & Historian* 6, no. 3 (September 1954): 72–73.

Severin, John P., and Frederick P. Todd. "79th Regiment, New York State Militia, 1860–1861." *Military Collector & Historian* 8, no. 1 (Spring 1956): 20.

Severin, John P., and Frederick P. Todd. "9th New York Volunteer Infantry Regiment (Hawkins' Zouaves), 1861–1863." *Military Collector & Historian* 8, no. 3 (Fall 1956): 76.

Southwick, Thomas Paine. *A Duryee Zouave*. Washington, DC: Acme, 1930.

Sturcke, Roger David. "62nd Regiment, New York Volunteer Infantry (Anderson's Zouaves), 1861–1865." *Military Collector & Historian* 35, no. 1 (Spring 1983): 32–33.

Sturcke, Roger David, and William D. Mohr. "20th New York Volunteer Infantry Regiment (United Turner Rifles), 1861–1863." *Military Collector & Historian* 34, no. 3 (Fall 1982): 120–121.

Sturcke, Roger David, and Frederick P. Todd. "13th Regiment, New York State Militia (National Greys), 1861–1865." *Military Collector & Historian* 25, no. 3 (Fall 1973): 148–149.

Swinton, William. *History of the Seventh Regiment, National Guard, State of New York, during the War of the Rebellion*. New York and Boston: Fields, Osgood, 1870.

Synder, Charles M. "The 24th Infantry: First to Answer the Call in Oswego County, New York in the Civil War." *Oswego County Historical Society Yearbook*, 1962.

Todd, Frederick P. "8th Regiment, New York State Militia (Washington Grays) circa 1850–1870." *Military Collector & Historian* 5, no. 4 (December 1953): 101.

Todd, Frederick P., and George C. Woodbridge. "44th New York Volunteer Infantry Regiment (People's Ellsworth Regiment), 1861–1864." *Military Collector & Historian* 11, no. 1 (Spring 1959): 10.

Todd, Frederick P., and George C. Woodbridge. "39th New York Volunteer Infantry Regiment (Garibaldi Guard), 1861–1862." *Military Collector & Historian* 11, no. 3 (Fall 1959): 85.

Todd, Frederick P., George C. Woodbridge, Lee A. Wallace Jr., Michael J. McAfee, and Maria P. Todd Damerel. *American Military Equipage, 1851–1872*. Vol. 2, *State Forces*. New York: Chatham Square, 1983.

Todd, William. *The Seventy-Ninth Highlanders, New York Volunteers, in the War of the Rebellion*. New York: Brandow, Barton, 1886.

Vail, Enos B., *Reminiscences of a Boy in the Civil War*. Brooklyn, NY: Enos B. Vail, 1915.

Warren, Richard A., and Roger David Sturcke. "11th New York Volunteer Infantry (Ellsworth's First New York Fire Zouaves), First Uniform, 1861." *Military Collector & Historian* 39, no. 4 (Winter 1987): 174.

Warren, Richard A., and Roger David Sturcke. "11th New York Volunteer Infantry (Ellsworth's First New York Fire Zouaves), Second Uniform, 1861–1862." *Military Collector & Historian* 39, no. 4 (Winter 1987): 174.

Wingate, General George W. *History of the Twenty Second Regiment of the National Guard of the State of New York*. New York: Edwin W. Dayton, 1896.

New Jersey

Primary Sources

Annual Report of the Quartermaster General of the State of New Jersey for the Year 1861. Jersey City, NJ: John H. Lyon, 1862.

Newspapers

Atlantic City, New Jersey, *Atlantic Democrat*
Camden, New Jersey, *Camden Democrat*
Camden, New Jersey, *West Jersey Press*
Newark, New Jersey, *Centinel of Freedom*
Newark, New Jersey, *Newark Daily Advertiser*
New York City, *Irish American Weekly*
New York City, *New York Herald*
Philadelphia, *Philadelphia Inquirer*
Trenton, New Jersey, *Daily State Gazette & Republican*

Washington, DC, *Daily National Intelligencer*
Washington, DC, *Evening News*
Washington, DC, *Evening Star*
Wilmington, Delaware, *Delaware State Journal and Statesman*

Secondary Sources

Baquet, Camille. *History of the First Brigade, New Jersey Volunteers*. Trenton, NJ: State of New Jersey, 1910.
Pynne, Henry R. *The History of the First New Jersey Cavalry (Sixteenth Regiment, New Jersey Volunteers)*. Trenton, NJ: J. A. Beecher, 1871.
Todd, Frederick P., George C. Woodbridge, Lee A. Wallace Jr., Michael J. McAfee, and Maria P. Todd Damerel. *American Military Equipage, 1851–1872*. Vol. 2, *State Forces*. New York: Chatham Square, 1983.

Delaware

Primary Sources

Newspapers

Milford, Delaware, *Peninsula News and Advertiser*
Philadelphia, *Philadelphia Inquirer*
Wilmington, Delaware, *Delaware Republican*
Wilmington, Delaware, *Delaware State Journal and Statesman*

Secondary Sources

Seville, William P. *History of the First Regiment, Delaware Volunteers, from the Commencement of the Three Months Service to the Final Muster-Out at the Close of the Rebellion*. Wilmington, DE: Historical Society of Delaware, 1884.

Maryland

Primary Sources

Newspapers

Baltimore, *Baltimore American and Commercial Advertiser*
Baltimore, *Baltimore Clipper*
Baltimore, *Baltimore Sun*
Baltimore, *Daily Exchange*
Boston, *Boston Evening Transcript*
Chestertown, Maryland, *Kent News*
Cumberland, Maryland, *Civilian & Telegraph*
Easton, Maryland, *Easton Star*
Elkton, Maryland, *Cecil Whig*
Frederick, Maryland, *Examiner*
Washington, DC, *Evening Star*

Secondary Sources

Hewett, Janet B., Jocelyn Pinson, and Julia H. Nichols, eds. *Supplement to the Official Records of the Union and Confederate Armies*. 100 vols. Wilmington, NC: Broadfoot, 1995–1999. Part II, Record of Events, Vol. 26 (Serial No. 38).
Hunt, Roger D. *Colonels in Blue: Union Army Colonels of the Civil War; The Mid-Atlantic States; Pennsylvania, New Jersey, Maryland, Delaware, and the District of Columbia*. Mechanicsburg, PA: Stackpole Books, 2007.
Scharf, J. Thomas. *History of Western Maryland: Being a History of Frederick, Montgomery, Carroll, Washington, Allegany, and Garrett Counties*. Vol. 1. Philadelphia: Louis H. Everts, 1882.
Todd, Frederick P., George C. Woodbridge, Lee A. Wallace Jr., Michael J. McAfee, and Maria P. Todd Damerel. *American Military Equipage, 1851–1872*. Vol. 2, *State Forces*. New York: Chatham Square, 1983.

District of Columbia

Primary Sources

Newspapers

Washington, DC, *Evening Star*
Washington, DC, *National Republican*

Secondary Sources

McAfee, Michael J. "Uniforms & History: The National Rifles —District of Columbia Militia; 'A Matter of Loyalty." *Military Images* 19, no. 3 (November–December 1997): 31–32.
Stone, Charles P. "Washington on the Eve of the War." In *Battles and Leaders of the Civil War*. Vol. 1, *From Sumter to Shiloh*. Edited by Robert Underwood Johnson and Clarence Clough Buel, 7–25. New York: Thomas Yoseloff, 1956.

ENDNOTES

Introduction

1 "From Annapolis to Washington," *Lowell Daily Courier*, May 3, 1861, 2:2; "Arrival and Departure of Troops for United States Service," *Baltimore American and Commercial*, April 19, 1861, 1:9.

2 "Arrival of Troops," *National Republican*, April 19, 1861, 3:1. According to an 1859 newspaper report, the Allen Rifles had a dress uniform of "dark blue cloth, that of the Rifles trimmed with gold." See "Military Visitors," *Lehigh Register*, November 2, 1859, 2:6—citing *Reading Gazette and Democrat*. Formed in 1859, the National Light Infantry had acquired a dress cap of "the same style as the National Guards of Philadelphia." See "The Fourth," *Miners' Journal & Pottsville General Advisor*, July 9, 1859, 2:5.

3 "War Correspondence," *Miners' Journal & Pottsville General Advisor*, April 27, 1861, 2:6.

4 Although the Allen Rifles had acquired "Sharp's Rifles, mounted with sword bayonets" in January 1860, it is not known if they carried these to Washington, DC, in 1861. See "Local Affairs," *Lehigh Register*, January 25, 1860, 2:5.

5 Organized in Philadelphia by Col. W. F. Small on April 15–16, 1861, and consisting of two undersized regiments of unarmed volunteers without uniforms, the Washington Brigade accompanied the 6th Massachusetts to Baltimore but returned to Philadelphia when confronted by the secessionist mob. Following this it was disbanded, and elements of the two regiments formed the 26th and 27th Pennsylvania, respectively.

6 See "Gray Uniforms Prohibited," *Boston Herald*, August 22, 1861, 4:1.

7 "Proposals for Army Cloths," *North America and United States Gazette*, November 13, 1861, 2:3.

8 The various references to the regular US uniform that follow refer either to a full dress consisting of a nine-button dark-blue frock coat with sky-blue trim, sky-blue trousers, and black felt Hardee hat, or an undress composed of a four-button dark-blue blouse or sack coat, sky-blue trousers, and dark-blue forage cap. Cavalry and light artillery wore a twelve-button jacket with yellow or scarlet trim, respectively. For a comprehensive understanding of this, see John P. Langelier, *Army Blue: The Uniform of Uncle Sam's Regulars, 1843–1873* (Atglen, PA: Schiffer Military History, 1998).

Chapter 1: Pennsylvania

1 "The Military at Harrisburg," *Centre Democrat*, April 26, 1861, 3:5.

2 "The City: The Departure of 1st Artillery Regiment, *The Press*, May 9, 1861, 2:8.

3 See Samuel P. Bates, *History of the Pennsylvania Volunteers, 1861–1865*, vol. 1 (Harrisburg, PA: B. Singerly, 1869), 159; and "The Returning Volunteers," *Philadelphia Inquirer*, July 26, 1861, 8:3.

4 Before the war, Edmund Baudin was the foreman at Miskey, Archer & Warner, makers of brass gas light fittings, and built "the grand stairway at the new Capitol extension." See "The City," *The Press*, April 17, 1861, 2:8.

5 "Inspection of a French Military Company," *The Press*, April 7, 1860, 2:7. For other reports based on this original description, see "Queer Parade," *Daily Dispatch* (Richmond, VA), April 12, 1860, 1:6; and *Daily Chronicle & Sentinel* (Augusta, GA), April 17, 1860, 1:1.

6 "Pic Nic and Drill of the Philadelphia Zouaves," *Philadelphia Inquirer*, August 7, 1860, 8:1.

7 See "Military Parades," *The Press*, April 10, 1860, 2:7; and "The Pennsylvania Regiments in Maryland, from the Baltimore Sun Yesterday," *Philadelphia Inquirer*, May 17, 1861, 2:2.

8 "Head-Quarters, 8th Reg't M.V.M., Camp Essex (Relay House), June 4, '61," *Cape Ann Light and Gloucester Telegraph*, June 12, 1861, 2:3.

9 "Birthday of Lafayette," *New York Herald*, August 21, 1860, 8:1. When the 18th Pennsylvania returned to Philadelphia upon the expiry of its three-month period of service, the *Philadelphia Inquirer* of July 25, 1861, reported, "An old acquaintance of our citizens also arrived last evening—the French vivandiere, with her husband, who joined Col. Lewis' regiment. The soldiers praise the contents of her little keg, and consider them far better than that which is usually obtained elsewhere."

10 "Washington's Birth Day in the Capital City," *Pennsylvania Daily Telegraph*, February 22, 1861, 4:3.

11 "The National Guard," *The Press*, April 26, 1861, 2:6. This regiment complained about receiving inferior arms, which were reported to be "of the old pattern of 1824—flint-locks altered to percussion" that had "ugly vents in them." See "Movements of the Military," *The Press*, May 7, 1861, 2:1.

12 "Our Baltimore Letter," *Philadelphia Inquirer*, July 20, 1861, 4:6. Members of the National Guards reenlisted for three years in the 90th Pennsylvania Volunteers.

13 See "Military Movements," *Baltimore American and Commercial Advertiser*, May 16, 1861, 1:3; and "War Movements—Military Camp of Gen. Cadwalader," *Baltimore American and Commercial Advertiser*, May 18, 1861, 1:3.

14 "Monument Dedication," *Lehigh Register*, April 25, 1855, 2:3.

15 *Pittsburgh Daily Gazette and Advertiser*, June 7, 1858, 3:5. On December 7, 1860 (1:1), the *Philadelphia Inquirer* reported that the Scott Legion was "having prepared for them a new uniform" to consist of "a blue frock coat, blue pants, and a cap similar to the 'fatigue' worn by the Washington Greys." There is no evidence that this uniform was acquired.

16 "Scott Legion Regiment," *Philadelphia Inquirer*, May 18, 1861, 5:1. A Pittsburgh company of the 7th Pennsylvania (three months) was also called "the Scott Legion."

17 "The City: Military Movements; Departure of the Scott Legion," *The Press*, May 30, 1861, 2:6. Another report observed that they wore "the regular United States uniform of sky-blue cloth roundabout and gray pantaloons, the same as worn by them in the Mexican war." See "The City: Military Movements," *The Press*, May 16, 1861, 2:8.

18 "The City: Military and Naval Matters," *The Press*, May 18, 1861, 1:8. According to Bates's *History of Pennsylvania Volunteers*, 1:185–186, the Scott Legion was "clothed in the old United States blue jacket and pants, of so excellent a quality that the men did not require re-clothing during their term of service. This uniform was secured by the personal exertions of General Patterson, for which he had a great partiality, being the pattern worn in Mexico."

19 "The Departure of the Scott Legion," *The Press*, May 25, 1861, 3:2.

20 "The Military Clothing Department," *The Press*, June 17, 1861, 3:2. Tailors and clothiers Daniel H. Rockhill and Franklin S. Wilson had established a "Ready Made Clothing" firm at the Old Franklin Hall, 199 Chestnut Street, Philadelphia, by August 1847. By 1856, they had moved to the "Brown Stone Clothing Hall" at 603 and 605 Chestnut, where they were still located in 1861. See "Out Again," *Philadelphia Inquirer*, August 4, 1847, 2:7; "Clothing at Wholesale," *Philadelphia Inquirer*, August 6, 1856, 2:9; and *McElroy's Philadelphia City Directory for 1861* (Philadelphia: E. C. & J. Biddle, 1861), 841.

21 "The City. War Preparations," *The Press*, April 27, 1861, 2:8.

22 See "Military Movements," *The Press*, January 7, 1861, 2:2; and "The City—Return of Ballier's Regiment," *The Press*, July 29, 1861, 3:2. Battalion and then regimental commander Col. John F. Ballier commanded the Lafayette Rifles before the war—see "The City—Funeral of the Mexican Volunteers," *The Press*, January 18, 1858, 2:7.

23 "Formation of a New Regiment," *Philadelphia Inquirer*, February 25, 1861, 2:4.

24 See "Military Celebration of the Day," *Public Ledger*, February 24, 1851, 2:2; and "The City," *The Press*, April 28, 1861, 2:8.

25 See "The City Troop," *North American and United States Gazette*, August 13, 1861, 2:1; "Local Intelligence," *Philadelphia Inquirer*, May 29, 1861, 2:4; and "Local Intelligence—the Philadelphia City Troop at Home," *Philadelphia Inquirer*, August 15, 1861, 8:3.

26 See "The City: Arrival of Col. Robert Anderson," *The Press*, May 13, 1861, 2:7; and "City Military Affairs," *Philadelphia Inquirer*, May 24, 1861, 3:1.

27 "Military," *Philadelphia Inquirer*, July 12, 1861, 8:5; and "A Philadelphia Merchant Troop," *Baltimore Clipper*, June 11, 1861, 2:3.

28 "Model Uniforms," *Philadelphia Inquirer*, May 31, 1861, 5:2.

29 "Local Intelligence: City Military Affairs," *Philadelphia Inquirer*, May 4, 1861, 7:1; "Parade of the Reserves—Handsome Display," *Philadelphia Inquirer*, May 28, 1861, 2:5; and James W. Latta, *History of the First Regiment Infantry, National Guard of Pennsylvania (Grey Reserves) 1861–1911* (Philadelphia & London: J. B. Lippincott), 1912, 15. See also Roger D. Sturcke and Michael J. Winey, "1st Infantry Regiment (Gray Reserves) Reserve Brigade, Philadelphia Militia, 1861," *Military Collector & Historian* 34, no. 2 (Summer 1982): 70–71; and Michael J. McAfee, "Uniforms & History: 'Like a Regiment of Quakers,'" *Military Images* 23, no. 3 (Summer 2015): 57.

30 "Independent Rangers," *The Press*, June 1, 1861, 2:7.

31 *Philadelphia Inquirer*, June 22, 1861, 3:4. Benjamin Bullock & Sons, 16 South Front Street, advertised their "Cadet Cloth" as manufactured at "their own

Mills, near Conshohocken, Montgomery county, Pa.," which they described as "very superior both in color and texture, being of a pure indigo blue, and manufactured expressly for army clothing." See *The Press*, May 10, 1861, 3:2 & 5. The companies of the infantry battalion, 4th Regiment, Reserve Brigade, consisted of the Kenderton Life Guards, Butler Guards, Germantown Guards, Holmesburg Guards, and Rising Sun Guards.

32 See "City Military Affairs," *Philadelphia Inquirer*, July 18, 1861, 8:1.

33 *Philadelphia Inquirer*, June 22, 1861, 3:4.

34 See "A Corps of Gymnasts," *Philadelphia Inquirer*, April 27, 1861, 2:3; "The Gymnast Zouaves," *Philadelphia Inquirer*, June 10, 1861, 2:6; "Local Intelligence," *Philadelphia Inquirer*, July 4, 1861, 8:2; and "Military Matters," *Philadelphia Inquirer*, July 8, 1861, 8:5. Born in Hanover ca. 1830, Louis Hildebrand was listed as a "Teacher of Gymnastics" in the 1860 census and was reported to have "served in the Zouaves in Europe." He commanded Co. B of the 23rd Pennsylvania (three years).

35 "Public Safety—the Philadelphia Troops," *The Press*, April 22, 1861, 3:1.

36 *Philadelphia Inquirer*, June 22, 1861, 3:4.

37 See "Home Guards Headquarters, Philadelphia, April 22, 1861," *The Press*, April 22, 1861, 3:4; and "Headquarters Home Guard, City of Philadelphia," *The Press*, April 24, 1861, 3:6. The style of cap adopted by the Home Guards was advertised in the same issue of *The Press* as available from Chas. Laing & Co., Sixth & Chestnut Streets, Philadelphia.

38 See "The New Zouaves," *Daily Pittsburgh Gazette*, August 21, 1860, 3:1; and "The Zouaves," *Daily Pittsburgh Gazette*, August 24, 1860, 3:1. The United States Zouave Cadets, Co. B, was recruited in Pittsburgh during May/June 1861. See "Cadets from Pittsburg," *Philadelphia Inquirer*, June 7, 1861, 5:3.

39 "Celebrations of the Twenty-Second," *Daily Pittsburgh Gazette*, February 23, 1861, 3:3.

40 See "The War!!!," *The Press*, April 22, 1861, 2:5; and "The United States Zouaves," *The Press*, June 24, 1861, 3:1. For the Pittsburgh Zouaves, see George T. Fleming, *My High School Days* (Pittsburgh, PA: Wm. G. Johnston, 1904), 139–141. According to the *Pittsburgh Post Gazette* of April 9, 1861, they wore "baggy pantaloons and jaunty red sashes."

41 See "A Zouave Military Company," *The Alleghanian*, August 30, 1860, 3:2; and *Democrat and Sentinel*, September 5, 1860, 2:3.

42 See "Military Intelligence," *Daily Pittsburgh Gazette*, November 3, 1860, 3:1; "Washington's Birthday in the Capital," *Pennsylvania Daily Telegraph*, February 22, 1861, 4:3; and "The 22nd in Harrisburg," *Daily Patriot and Union*, February 23, 1861, 3:3.

43 "Camp Scott, at York," *Philadelphia Inquirer*, May 2, 1861, 2:2.

44 See "The Harrisburg Rifles," *Pennsylvania Daily Telegraph*, May 24, 1861, 3:1; "Zouave Cadets," *Pennsylvania Daily Telegraph*, June 10, 1861, 3:1; and "The First City Zouaves," *Pennsylvania Daily Telegraph*, June 13, 1861, 3:1.

45 George Reeser Prowell, *History of the Eighty-Seventh Regiment, Pennsylvania Volunteers* (York, PA: Press of the York Daily, 1903), 3.

46 "Ellsworth Zouaves," *The Compiler*, June 24, 1861, 3:1—citing the *Hanover Citizen*. The "Solferno Zouaves" is an inaccurate reference to the Zouaves of the French Imperial Guard. Formed during the Crimean War of 1854–56, this regiment wore red fezzes with yellow tassels, blue jackets and vests trimmed with red tape, full red trousers, and white canvas gaiters, over which were leather greaves. Expanded into three regiments, these French Zouaves fought at Solferino, in northern Italy, during 1859.

47 *The Compiler*, September 2, 1861, 3:5. See image of a Gettysburg Zouave in the collection of the Rochester Museum & Science Center.

48 John Miller, *A Twentieth Century History of Erie County* (Chicago: Lewis, 1909), p. 674. For John Gensheimer, see *The Erie City Directory—1861–62* (Erie, PA: H. W. Hulbert, 1861), 58.

49 "Regiment Disbanded," *Pennsylvania Daily Telegraph*, July 2, 1861, 3:1.

50 "Departure of the Twenty-First Regiment," *The Press*, May 27, 1861, 2:8.

51 "City Military Affairs," *Philadelphia Inquirer*, May 27, 1861, 2:5.

52 "More Pennsylvania Troops," *Evening Star*, June 19, 1861, 3:3. Commanded by Col. Max Einstein, this regiment was misidentified as the 24th Pennsylvania in this report. Another report referred to "the vivandieres with their jaunty little hats." See *The Press*, June 17, 1861, 3:1.

53 "Volunteers of Schuylkill County," *Miners' Journal & Pottsville General Advisor*, April 27, 1861, 2:1.

54 "The Home Guards," *Altoona Tribune*, May 9, 1861, 2:3.

55 *Altoona Tribune*, July 12, 1860, 3:4.

56 See *Pennsylvania Daily Telegraph*, April 29, 1861, 3:1; and "Arrival of Troops," *Daily Patriot and Union*, April 23, 1861, 3:2.

57 See *Columbia Democrat and Bloomsburg General Advertiser*, May 11, 1861, 2:5—citing *Lock Haven Watchman*; "More Troops Arriving at Harrisburg," *Philadelphia Inquirer*, May 3, 1861, 1:4; and O. R. Howard Thomson, *History of the Bucktails: Kane Rifle Regiment of the Pennsylvania Reserve Corps* (Philadelphia: Electric Printing, 1906), 11.

58 "The Northern Tier in Motion," *Pennsylvania Daily Telegraph*, May 2, 1861, 3:2.

59 "Arrival Extraordinary—the Raftsmen's Guards," *Daily Pittsburgh Gazette*, May 25, 1861, 3:1. See also Barry L. Thompson and John L. Marsh, "The Raftsmen's Guard, April/May 1861," *Military Collector & Historian* 26, no. 3 (Fall 1974): 168–170; and George C. Woodbridge, Frederick Ray Jr., and John R. Elting, "42nd Regiment, Pennsylvania Volunteer Infantry ('the Bucktails'), 1861–1865," *Military Collector & Historian* 14, no. 3 (Fall 1962): 88–89.

60 "From Camp Curtin: News from the Tioga Boys . . . Harrisburg, June 10, 1861," *The Agitator*, June 19, 1861, 1:4. On May 25, 1861, the *Warren Mail* (2:3) of that date commented that "busy fingers [of the local womenfolk] had provided in a very short space of time the neat uniform" worn by the Raftsmen's Guards.

61 "The Raftsmen Rangers," *Raftsman's Journal*, May 15, 1861, 3:1.

62 "The Scotch Rifle Company," *The Press*, May 23, 1861, 2:7.

63 "The War Feeling in Philadelphia," *Philadelphia Inquirer*, April 20, 1861, 4:4.

64 "The War Feeling in Philadelphia," *Philadelphia Inquirer*, April 20, 1861, 4:4; and "Local Intelligence," *Philadelphia Inquirer*, April 22, 1861, 2:5.

65 The Girard House was a hotel leased by Presbury, Sykes, and Chadwick, who transferred the lease to Stevens, of the Continental Hotel, for £30,000 and moved to Nashville, Tennessee. See *Philadelphia Inquirer*, February 15, 1861, 8.

66 "The State Clothing Establishment," *Philadelphia Inquirer*, May 8, 1861, 2:6.

67 See "The City," *The Press*, April 24, 1861, 2:7; and *The Press*, April 28, 1861, 2:8.

68 "Local Intelligence," *Philadelphia Inquirer*, April 30, 1861, 2:5.

69 "Local Intelligence. Movement of Troops," *Philadelphia Inquirer*, April 27, 1861, 2:3.

70 "City Military Affairs," *Philadelphia Inquirer*, May 10, 1861, 2:6; and "City Military Affairs," *Philadelphia Inquirer*, May 14, 1861, 2:6. In the western part of the state, Brig. Gen. James S. Negley, commanding the 18th Division, Pennsylvania Militia, was charged with organizing and arming the volunteers with headquarters at the Girard House, on Smithfield Street in Pittsburgh. For this purpose, about 12,000 "stand of arms" were transferred to the city hall from the Allegheny Arsenal at Lawrenceville by April 24, 1861. See "The War Excitement," *Pittsburgh Daily Gazette*, April 18, 1861, 3:1; and "Latest News from Head-Quarters," *Pittsburgh Daily Gazette*, April 23, 1861, 3:2.

71 "Proposals for Supplies," *Pennsylvania Daily Telegraph*, May 2, 1861, 2:6.

72 "The Quartermaster's Department," *Philadelphia Inquirer*, May 23, 1861, 5:2. Clothiers Strauss & Goldman were at 306 Market Street, Philadelphia; Bartalott & Blynn were wholesale hat and cap merchants at 111 North Third Street, Philadelphia; and Sullender & Pascall were at 8 South Street off Sixth Avenue in Philadelphia—see *M'Elroy's Philadelphia City Directory, 1861*, pp. 960, 43, and 965. Charles Lacroix Pascal was born in Philadelphia in 1818, the son of John Pascal (1784–1856), a tavern keeper born in France. The 1860 census lists him as age forty and a "Hatter master" with a personal estate of $4,000.

73 See "Army Supplies," *Pennsylvania Daily Telegraph*, May 24, 1861, 2:5.

74 See letter from R. Phillips to Martha Hummel, Shamokin Dam, Snyder County, Pennsylvania, dated June 3, 1861.

75 "More Arrivals of Volunteers," *Evening Star*, April 29, 1861, 2:1.

76 "Letter from Washington," *Pittsburgh Daily Gazette*, May 3, 1861, 1:4.

77 "Scene in the Baltimore Depot—the Schuylkill Regiment," *The Press*, April 24, 1861, 3:1.

78 See "Letter from Camp Curtin, Harrisburg, May 3, 1861," *Philadelphia Inquirer*, May 4, 1861, 1:6; and "Letter from Camp Curtin, Harrisburg, May 1, 1861," *Philadelphia Inquirer*, May 4, 1861, 2:1.

79 "The Camp at West Chester," *Philadelphia Inquirer*, May 7, 1861, 8:1.

80 "From Camp Scott," *Pennsylvania Daily Telegraph*, May 4, 1861, 3:3.

81 For receipt of uniforms, see "The Pennsylvania Regiment," *Evening Star*, May 8, 1861, 2:2. According to a brief report in the *Advertiser*, of Lebanon, Pennsylvania, of May 15, 1861 (2:1), John Killinger, representative for the 10th District, Pennsylvania, was involved in forwarding this clothing. For the extract from the Minersville Artillerists letter, see "Letters from Our Volunteers," *Miners' Journal & Pottsville General Advisor*, May 18, 1861, 2:6.

82 See "Our Camp Correspondence: Camp Slifer at Chambersburg . . . May 9th, 1861," *Philadelphia Inquirer*, May 11, 1861, 8:2; and "Letter from Camp Slifer," *Pennsylvania Daily Telegraph*, May 29, 1861, 2:4.

83 Bates, *History of the Pennsylvania Volunteers, 1861–1865*, 1:97.

84 "Our Army Correspondence . . . Camp Scott, May 14, 1861," *Columbia Spy*, May 18, 1861, 2:3.

85 See "Correspondence of the Compiler. Camp Scott, York, May 3, 1861," *The Compiler*, May 13, 1861, 2:3—letter from "Bageney"; and "Local Items," *The Compiler*, May 22, 1861, 2:6.

86 "Letters from Camp Cameron, Friday, June 21, 1861," *The Compiler*, July 1, 1861, 2:2.

87 "Army Correspondence, Camp Scott, York, Pa., May 21," *Central Press*, May 30, 1861, 2:7.

88 "Letter from the Rhode Island Regiment," *Providence Daily Evening News*, May 16, 1861, 2:2. This was a probable reference to the 4th or 5th Pennsylvania.

89 "Letter from Washington—May 18, 1861," *Pittsburgh Daily Gazette*, May 22, 1861, 1:4.

90 "Letter from Washington—May 21, 1861," *Pittsburgh Daily Gazette*, May 25, 1861, 2:1.

91 "Letter from Havre-de-Grace," *The Press*, June 6, 1861, 1:1.

92 "Our Army Correspondence," *Pittsburgh Daily Gazette*, May 16, 1861, 1:5.

93 "Our Army Correspondence," *Pittsburgh Daily Gazette*, May 29, 1861, 3:2.

94 "The Soldiers' Clothing and Shoes—Who Furnished Them?," *Philadelphia Inquirer*, May 18, 1861, 8:1–2.

95 "Caps of Many Colors," *Philadelphia Inquirer*, May 30, 1861, 1:6. Not everyone in the 1st Pennsylvania was disappointed with the clothing received. Quartermaster A. J. Camblos wrote to Col. Robert L. Martin, Girard House, stating that "both officers and men have expressed their satisfaction at the quality and quantity of clothing distributed among them, not one of whom would exchange them for the uniforms furnished by the United States." Minds may have been changed shortly afterward. See "Quartermaster's Supplies," *The Press*, May 7, 1861, 2:8.

96 "Army Correspondence: Quarters, Company H, 4th Reg. Pa. Vol. at Washington, DC, May 11," *Democratic Watchman*, May 30, 1861, 2:4.

97 "The Pennsylvania Regiments," *Philadelphia Inquirer*, May 28, 1861, 8:4; and "B. Haywood, Esq.—Our Volunteers," *Miners' Journal & Pottsville General Advisor*, June 1, 1861, 2:2. Benjamin Haywood was the proprietor of iron-rolling mills and a prominent citizen of Schuylkill County, and Jacob Fry Jr. was an ex-representative and auditor general of Pennsylvania. For Col. Roberts's arrival, see "Letter from Washington—May 21, 1861," *Pittsburgh Daily Gazette*, May 25, 1861, 2:1.

98 "Our Baltimore Letter," *Philadelphia Inquirer*, June 10, 1861, 4:6.

99 "Our Baltimore Letter," *Philadelphia Inquirer*, July 20, 1861, 4:6.

100 "The Army Clothing Frauds," *Pittsburgh Daily Gazette*, June 15, 1861, 3:1. This group consisted of A. [Ashra] & A. [Abraham] Frowenfeld, and L. [Louis] & J. [Joseph] Morganstern, plus Emanuel Frowenfeld and Maurice Frowenfeld. See "The Army Frauds," *Pittsburgh Daily Gazette*, June 25, 1861, 3:1, for reference to the mill of Joseph Lee and Alfred Slade.

101 "The Army Clothing Frauds," *Pittsburgh Daily Gazette*, June 17, 1861, 3:1. See also *Daily State Gazette & Republican*, June 22, 1861, 2:2.

102 See "The Clothing Fraud Case," *Philadelphia Inquirer*, July 3, 1861, 5:1–2; and "The Alleged Clothing Fraud Case—Acquittal of Messrs. L. & J. Morganstern, and A. & A. Frowenfeld," *Pittsburgh Daily Gazette*, April 3, 1862, 3:3.

103 "The Quartermaster's Department," *Philadelphia Inquirer*, May 23, 1861, 5:2.

104 "Special Order, No. 1," *Pennsylvania Daily Telegraph*, May 29, 1861, 3:6.

105 "Inspection of Troops," *Philadelphia Inquirer*, June 17, 1861, 1:4.

106 "Army Correspondence," *Central Press*, June 28, 1861, 2:5.

107 "Local Intelligence," *Philadelphia Inquirer*, June 19, 1861, 8:1. On a later date, the same journal advised that this uniform was "made of cadet cloth." See "Military Matters," *Philadelphia Inquirer*, July 8, 1861, 8:5.

108 "Military Matters," *Philadelphia Inquirer*, August 3, 1861, 8:3; and "City Affairs," *North American and United States Gazette*, July 29, 1861, 1:7.

109 "Military Matters," *The Press*, June 19, 3:1.

110 "Our Camp Wayne Letter, Head-Quarters, Camp Wayne, West Chester, June 7," *Philadelphia Inquirer*, June 8, 1861, 1:5.

111 "Camp Wayne, West Chester, July 5, 1861," *The Compiler*, July 15, 1861, 2:6.

112 H. N. Minnigh, *History of Co. K, 1st (Inft.) Penn'a Reserves: "The Boys Who Fought at Home"* (Duncansville, PA: "Home Print" Publisher), 6; see also "Distribution of Clothing at Camp Wayne," *Philadelphia Inquirer*, July 3, 1861, 5:2.

113 See "Our Army Correspondence," *Columbia Spy*, June 29, 1861, 2:6; and "Letter from Camp Washington . . . July 3, 1861," *Philadelphia Inquirer*, July 5, 1861, 2:2.

114 "Our Army Correspondence," *Columbia Spy*, July 13, 1861, 2:5–6. The "light blue army cloth" may have been "gray cadet cassimere" purchased by the state at $1.10 per yard in late April or early May and not used on the three-month volunteers. See "What Became of the Cassimere?," *Pittsburgh Daily Gazette*, May 22, 1861, 2:2.

115 See "Our Camp Wayne Letter," *Philadelphia Inquirer*, June 8, 1861, 1:5; and "The Camp at West Chester," *Philadelphia Inquirer*, July 13, 1861, 4:3.

116 "Military Affairs," *Philadelphia Inquirer*, July 11, 1861, 8:5.

117 "From the Tioga Boys . . . Camp Biddle, near the Line, Greencastle, Franklin Co. Pa., July 17, 1861," *The Agitator*, July 24, 1861, 2:4.

118 "Editor's Correspondence . . . June 27, 1861," *Columbia Democrat*, June 29, 1861, 2:6.

119 See "Military Movements," *Columbia Democrat*, August 12, 1861, 8:2. For the uniform of the 23rd Pennsylvania (Birney's Zouaves), see Frederick Ray Jr. and John R. Elting, "Military Uniforms in America: 23rd Regiment Pennsylvania Infantry (Birney Zouaves)," *Military Collector & Historian* 14, no. 1 (Spring 1962): 17, 19. Reporting on the early organization of the 23rd Pennsylvania, the *North American*, of Philadelphia, stated, "The flank companies of the new regiment, and probably the whole body, will be equipped in dark blue Zouave dress, with light blue vests and tasteful caps." See "City Affairs," *North American and United States Gazette*, July 29, 1861, 1:7.

120 "Col. D. B. Birney's Zouave Regiment," *The Press*, September 28, 1861, 3:4.

121 William J. Wray, *History of the Twenty-Third Pennsylvania Volunteer Infantry—Birney's Zouaves* (Philadelphia: Compiled by the Secretary by Order of the Survivors Association, 1904), 131.

122 "Miscellaneous," *The Press*, September 6, 1861, 2:3.

123 See Wray, *History of the Twenty-Third Pennsylvania*, 34.

124 National Archives, Record Group 92, entry 2194, book 3; and Record Group 94, Regimental Books, 62nd Pennsylvania Infantry—see *Don Troiani's Regiments & Uniforms of the Civil War* (Mechanicsburg, PA: Stackpole Books, 2002), 27 and 36. A nine-month regiment called the Scott Legion and designated the 154th Pennsylvania was recruited in November/December 1862, but before commissions had been issued to the field officers, seven of its companies were detailed for special duty, and only three companies remained together. These performed provost duty in Philadelphia without field or staff officers, except assistant surgeon. They were mustered out of service on September 29 and October 21, 1863. See "Another Nine-Months Regiment Accepted," *The Press*, November 4, 1862, 4:2.

125 "Military Matters," *The Press*, July 10, 1861, 3:1; and "Military Matters," *Philadelphia Inquirer*, July 8, 1861, 8:5.

126 See Frank H. Taylor, *Philadelphia in the Civil War, 1861–1865* (Philadelphia: City of Philadelphia, 1913), 86; and James Hennessey and H. Michael Madaus, "72nd Regiment, Pennsylvania Volunteer Infantry, 1861–1864, '3rd California Regiment,' 'Baxter's Fire Zouaves,'" *Military Collector & Historian* 32, no. 2 (Summer 1980): 74–75.

127 "Letter from Fort Schuyler . . . N.Y., May 30, 1861," *Philadelphia Inquirer*, June 3, 1861, 2:2. A report in the *Commercial Advertiser* of New York City dated April 25, 1861 (1:4), stated, "The uniforms seized by the police at No. 3, Dey street, have been transferred to the Quartermaster-General of the New York state militia, and will adorn our own instead of rebel troops. The goods seized were as follows: 769 coats and 266 pair pants, and cloth already cut ready for making, for 130 coats and 55 pair pants. The material is a fine mixed satinet. The uniforms were trimmed with red cord. One lot of this cord was also seized."

128 Catherine H. Vanderslice, ed., *The Civil War Letters of George Washington Beidelman* (Richmond, VA: Pamplin Historical Park, 2002), 29.

129 Andrew W. McDermott, *A Brief History of the 69th Regiment Pennsylvania Veteran Volunteers* (Philadelphia: D. J. Gallagher, 1889), 6. Of the 24th Pennsylvania (three months), a New York correspondent visited their encampment at Charlestown, Virginia, on July 19, 1861, and reported "many of the brave fellows . . . without shoes or pants; in fact, many of them were out in their drawers." See "The Pennsylvanians," *Irish American Weekly*, August 3, 1861, 3:1. An Irish company called the National Guards from Wilmington, Delaware, formed Co. H of this regiment, according to "The Philadelphia 'Irish Brigade,'" *Irish American Weekly*, August 17, 1861, 2:7.

130 "Colonel E. D. Baker's Brigade," *Philadelphia Inquirer*, August 31, 1861, 8:4.

131 "Colonel Owen's Irish Regiment," *The Press*, September 9, 1861, 2:8. See also "Independent Company," *The Press*, September 17, 1861, 1:5.

132 See "Independent Zouave Company," *The Press*, September 17, 1861, 1:5; "The Second Company of Independent Zouaves," *Philadelphia Inquirer*, October 19, 1861, 8:4. For the Tiger Zouaves, see "Col. E. D. Baker's Brigade," *Philadelphia Inquirer*, September 20, 1861, 8:4. According to a report in *Philadelphia Press* of October 28, 1861 (p. 2), the Reville Zouaves were "named by the lamented Baker in honor of a gentleman who has influenced the recruiting of several companies of the California Brigade." This might have been Adam Reville, listed as a "produce dealer" in the 1861 *Philadelphia City Directory*, p. 820.

133 "Local Affairs: Manufacturing Operations in Philadelphia," *Public Ledger*, September 2, 1861, 1:2. See Michael J. McAfee, "Uniforms & History: 72nd Regiment, Pennsylvania Volunteer Infantry (Baxter's Philadelphia Fire Zouaves)," *Military Images* 11, no. 6 (May–June 1990): 27. Fire companies that contributed recruits to the 72nd Pennsylvania included the Hope Hose Company—see "The Hope Hose and the Zouaves," *Philadelphia Inquirer*, September 30, 1861, 3:5.

134 Charles H. Banes, *History of the Philadelphia Brigade* (Philadelphia: J. B. Lippincott, 1876), 11–12.

135 "A Daughter of the Regiment," *Pennsylvania Daily Telegraph*, October 26, 1861, 7:1.

136 "Colonel Power's Regiment," *Philadelphia Inquirer*, September 4, 1861, 1:6. For a description of the second Zouave uniform worn by this regiment, see Mike Stiles, Roger David Sturcke, and Harry T. Grube, "Military Uniforms in America: 76th Pennsylvania Volunteer Infantry Regiment (Keystone Zouaves) 1861–1865," *Military Collector & Historian* 32, no. 4 (Winter 1980): 170–171. John M. Power originally commanded the 3rd Pennsylvania (three months) Volunteers.

137 "Camp Cameron, near Harrisburg, September 23d, 1861," *Altoona Tribune*, September 26, 1861, 2:4.

138 "Letter from a Wheeling Boy in South Carolina, Beaufort, February 4, 1862," *Daily Intelligencer*, February 18, 1862, 1:4.

139 "Departure of Gosline's Zouaves," *Philadelphia Inquirer*, October 14, 1861, 8:3.

140 "Regiments in Process of Formation," *Philadelphia Inquirer*, August 13, 1861, 8:3.

141 G. Norton Galloway, *The Ninety-Fifth Pennsylvania Volunteers (Gosline's Pennsylvania Zouaves) in the Sixth Corps* (Philadelphia: Collins, 1884), 8. See also Michael J. McAfee, "Uniforms & History: 'Gosline's Pennsylvania Zouaves' (95th Infantry Regt.)," *Military Images* 16, no. 4 (January–February 1995): 32–33.

142 "Letter from Federal Hill," *Philadelphia Inquirer*, July 25, 1861, 4:4.

143 "Military Affairs," *Philadelphia Inquirer*, August 15, 1861, 8:3.

144 "Recruiting," *Philadelphia Inquirer*, August 2, 1861, 8:3.

145 "Regiments in Process of Formation," *Philadelphia Inquirer*, August 13, 1861, 8:3.

146 Frank Rauscher, *Music on the March, 1862–'65, with the Army of the Potomac, 114th Regt. P. V., Collis' Zouaves* (Philadelphia: Wm. F. Fell, 1892), 12.

147 See "A Compliment to Massachusetts Soldiers," *Boston Evening Transcript*, November 23, 1861, 4:1.

148 A. M. Judson, *History of the Eighty-Third Regiment Pennsylvania Volunteers* (Erie, PA: B. F. H. Lynn, 1865), 25. See also "83rd Pennsylvania Volunteer Infantry Regiment, 1861–1862," in *Military Uniforms in America. Long Endure: The Civil War Period, 1852–1867*, ed. John R. Elting (Novato, CA: Presidio, 1982), 72–73; and Michael J. McAfee, "Uniforms & History: The 83rd Pennsylvania Volunteer Infantry, 1861–1862," *Military Images* 12, no. 1 (July–August 1990): 27–29.

149 "Anderson's Body Guard," *Altoona Tribune*, November 28, 1861, 3:1.

150 "Rush's Regiment of Lancers," *Philadelphia Press*, December 11, 1861, 2:7. See also Frederick P. Todd and Harry C. Larter, "6th Pennsylvania Cavalry (Rush's Lancers), 1862," *Military Collector & Historian* 6, no. 4, (December 1954): 101–102; Michael J. McAfee, "Uniforms & History: The Anderson Troop," *Military Images* 12, no. 2 (September–October 1990): 29; and Michael J. McAfee, "Uniforms & History: Brave Lancers; Sixth Regiment Pennsylvania Volunteer Cavalry (Rush's Lancers), 1861–1865," *Military Images* 19, no. 6 (May–June 1998): 32–33.

151 "New Regiment: Philadelphia Light Cavalry, Colonel Richard Henry Rush," *Philadelphia Inquirer*, August 26, 1861, 5:3.

152 United States Patent Office. Patent No. 2896. 33.900.

153 "Rush's Regiment of Lancers," *Philadelphia Press*, December 11, 1861, 2:7.

Chapter 2: New York

1 See Adjutant General, *General Regulations for the Military Forces of the State of New-York, 1858* (Albany, NY: Weed, Parsons, 1858), 250–276.

2 For a description of the full dress of the 5th NYSM, see "Our Welcome to the Prince," *New York Herald*, October 12, 1860, 4:3. Also see Frederick P. Todd, George C. Woodbridge, Lee A. Wallace Jr., and Michael J. McAfee, *American Military Equipage, 1851–1872*, vol. 2, *State Forces* (New York: Chatham Square, 1983, 1035 (hereafter, Todd et al., vol. 2, *State Forces*); and "Encampment of the Fifth Regiment on the Battery," *New York Herald*, April 26, 1861, 3:2.

3 "The Sixth Regiment," *New York Herald*, April 21, 1861, 4:5; and "Our Welcome to the Prince," *New York Herald*, October 12, 1860, 4:2.

4 "The Military Display," *New York Herald*, October 12, 1860, 4:2.

5 See "Arrival of the New York Seventh Regiment," *Evening Star*, April 25, 1861, 3:1. At a meeting of the Committee of the Board of Aldermen of New York City to arrange for the equipping of volunteers, future Union general Daniel Sickles advised that the 7th NYSM fatigue uniform cost "$24 per man, and the 71st Regiment $27 per man. The regular uniform of the New York State Militia would cost about $24." See "Equipment of a New York Brigade," *Morning Courier and New-York Enquirer*, April 25, 1861, 4:4.

6 "William Swinton, *History of the Seventh Regiment, National Guard, State of New York, during the War of the Rebellion* (New York & Boston: Fields, Osgood, 1870), 184–185. See also Michael J. McAfee, "Uniforms & History: The Seventh Regiment New York State Militia," *Military Images* 13, no. 5 (March–April 1992): 30–31. William Henry Aspinwall was a partner in Howland & Aspinwall, owners of the fastest clipper ships in the world, such as the *Rainbow* and the *Sea Witch*. He also owned the Pacific Mail Steamship Company during the Gold Rush of 1849. Regarding the white cross belts worn by the 7th NYSM, an unidentified member of the regiment wrote in his journal on May 27, 1861, "Today we received new cross belts. On the march from Annapolis, the men of our company cut the cross belts at the halting place so as to be free and easy in case of an attack and we have since been without them—the white cross belts and shining brass plates present a beautiful appearance on parade but they are unfit for active service. It requires a great deal of time to keep them in order. They compact the chest and shoulders, and are an admirable mark to fire at in an engagement." "Journal of a Recruit in the 7th Regiment," p. 19, the Gilder Lehrman Institute of American History, GLC06563.

7 "More Troops—Arrival of the New York Eight Regiment," *Evening Star*, May 18, 1861, 3:2. See also Frederick P. Todd, "8th Regiment, New York State Militia (Washington Grays) circa 1850–1870," *Military Collector & Historian* 5, no. 4 (December 1953): 101, 103; and Michael J. McAfee, "Uniforms & History: "Just Before the Battle . . . (the 8th Regiment, New York State Militia at Bull Run)," *Military Images* 31, no. 1 (July–August 2011): 28–29.

8 See "More Arrivals of Military," *National Republican*, April 29, 1861, 3:1; "Our Welcome to the Prince," *New York Herald*, October 12, 1860, 4:3; and "Departure of the Twelfth Regiment," *New York Herald*, April 22, 1861, 1:6.

9 "Departure of the Twelfth Regiment," *New York Herald*, April 22, 1861, 1:6.

10 "The New York Twelfth Regiment," *Evening Star*, May 11, 1861, 3:1.

11 "The Twelfth Regiment in Franklin Square," *National Republican*, May 9, 1861, 3:2. See also H. Charles McBarron Jr. and Frederick P. Todd, "12th Regiment, New York State Militia, 1861–1869," *Military Collector & Historian* 4, no. 4 (December 1952): 96, 98.

12 See Roger Sturcke and Frederick P. Todd, "13th Regiment, New York State Militia (National Greys), 1861–1865," *Military Collector & Historian* 25, no. 3 (Fall 1973): 146, 148–149; and Michael J. McAfee, "Uniforms & History: 13th Regiment, New York State Militia," *Military Images* 13, no. 6 (May–June 1992): 6.

13 "Our War Correspondent . . . Annapolis, Md., May 12, 1861," *New York Morning Express*, May 15, 1861, 4:2. The following day, the *Morning Courier* reported that the Committee of the Common Council had supplied "254 overcoats, 249 jackets and pantaloons, underclothing, shoes, and stockings. Also 400 equipments, 209 knapsacks, 500 canteens, and 500 haversacks." See "Military Affairs in Brooklyn," *Morning Courier and New-York Enquirer*, May 13, 1861, 3:3.

14 See "Thirteenth Regiment," *New York Tribune*, April 24, 1861, 8:2; and "Our War Correspondent . . . Annapolis, Md., May 12, 1861," *New York Morning Express*, May 15, 1861, 4:2. The mention of "Daddy Lambert" is a probably reference to Daniel Lambert, an eighteenth-/early-nineteenth-century English goalkeeper who was famous for his unusually large size.

15 See "Our Welcome to the Prince," *New York Herald*, October 12, 1860, 4:1; "Return of the Twenty-Eighth (Brooklyn) Regiment," *New York Herald*, July 29, 1861, 5:1; and Todd et al., vol. 2, *State Forces*, 1041. See also Frederick T. Chapman and Frederick P. Todd, "69th Regiment, N.Y.S.M., at the First Battle of Bull Run, 21 July 1861," *Military Collector & Historian* 29, no. 3 (Fall 1977): 121; see also Michael J. McAfee, "69th New York State Militia Addendum," *Military Collector & Historian*. 63, no. 1 (Spring 2011): 30; and Michael J. McAfee, "Uniforms & History: 69th Regiment, New York State Militia—'the National Cadets'—1861," *Military Images* 11, no. 5 (March–April 1990): 26–27.

16 "Departure of Meagher's Irish Zouaves," *New York Herald*, May 23, 1861, 8:1. The Phoenix Zouaves were originally attached to the "First Regiment of the Phoenix Brigade," which was described in Meagher's memoirs as "the Military portion of the Fenian Brotherhood" of New York. In a report on the reception of the 69th NYSM on return to the city on July 27, 1861, the *Herald* referred to the Phoenix Brigade as wearing "full green uniform, bright with lace and gold fringe." See "Home Again: Return of the Sixty-Ninth Regiment," *New York Herald*, July 28, 1861, 1:5.

17 "Reinforcements for the New York Regiments," *National Republican*, May 24, 1861, 3:2. A member of the Irish Zouaves mentioned in a letter written on July 22, 1861, that his company suffered more than any in the regiment at First Bull Run "on account of their red jackets." See *Irish American Weekly*, August 3, 1861, 2:4.

18 See "Military Movements in New York," *New York Herald*, April 22, 1861, 2:1; and "The Sixty-Ninth," *Evening Star*, May 4, 1861, 2:1.

19 "Letters from the Sixty-Ninth," *Irish American Weekly*, June 15, 1861, 2:3. Wife of Irish-born Judge Charles P. Daly, of New York, Lydig Daly plus "a number of ladies associated with her" supplied the 69th New York State Militia with 1,200 linen havelocks. See "Havelocks for the Sixty-Ninth," *Evening Star*, May 22, 1861, 3:1.

20 "Letters from the Sixty-Ninth," *Irish American Weekly*, June 15, 1861, 2:4.

21 "Letters from the 69th—Fort Corcoran, Arlington Heights, Va., July 3, 1861" (Correspondence of the *New York Express*), July 13, 1861, 2:3.

22 "The Last Days of the 69th in Virginia," *Irish American Weekly*, August 3, 1861, 2:2.

23 "The War for the Union," *Irish American Weekly*, July 27, 1861, 2:6. Earlier, during engagement at Blackburn's Ford on July 19, 1861, the 69th NYSM had shown the same éclat. The *Irish American Weekly* published a letter from Col. Michael Corcoran dated July 19, stating, "Off, then, went the boys—cheering heartily, and bounding with excitement—and as we neared the scene of action, off went their blankets, their coats, their canteens, and every stitch almost they had." See "Letters from the 69th . . . Headquarters 69th Regt., N.Y.S.M. Centerville, Fairfax Co., Near Bull's Run, Virginia, July 19th, 1861," *Irish American Weekly*, July 27, 1861, 2:8.

24 "Arrival of the Sixty-Ninth Regiment," *Atlas and Argus*, July 29, 1861, 3:1.

25 See "The New Military Road—Arrival of the Seventy-First Regiment of New York," *Evening Star*, April 27, 1861, 2:1; and "More Arrivals of Military," *National Republican*, April 29, 1861, 3:1.

26 "The Arrivals This Morning," *Evening Star*, April 27, 1861, 2:2.

27 "For Our Country and for Glory," *New York Herald*, April 22, 1861, 1:4.

28 *History of the 71st N.Y.N.G.* (Veterans Association 71st N.Y.N.G., 1919), 160.

29 *History of the 71st N.Y.N.G.*, 213. The fatigue dress had been worn since at least 1857, during which year the *Newburgh News* of June 18 reported the 71st wearing "close fitting jackets of blue, relieved by the white cross belts," in lieu of their new dress uniform not being ready. See *History of the 71st N.Y.N.G.*, 29. For further reference to the 71st NYSM, see John P. Severin and Frederick P. Todd, "71st Regiment (the American Guard) N.Y.S.M., 1857–1861," *Military Collector & Historian* 6, no. 3 (September 1954): 72–73; and Michael J. McAfee, "Uniforms & History: The 71st Regiment, New York State Militia—the American Guard," *Military Images* 25, no. 6 (May–June 2004): 34–35.

30 Enos B. Vail, *Reminiscences of a Boy in the Civil War* (Brooklyn, NY: Enos B. Vail, 1915), 19. See also Seward R. Osborne, "This Hand for Our Country," *Military Collector & Historian* 42, no. 4 (Winter 1990): 122–124; and Michael J. McAfee, "Uniforms & History: The Twentieth Regiment, New York State Militia, 1861," *Military Images* 28, no. 2 (September–October 2006): 22–25.

31 "Patterson Park Encampment," *Baltimore Clipper*, July 1, 1861, 1:7.

32 See "War Preparations," *Commercial Advertiser*, April 29, 1861, 3:4; "Letter from 'Personne,' Annapolis, Md., May 27, 1861," *Charleston Daily Courier*, June 3, 1861, 1:5; and "Miscellaneous War News," *New York Tribune*, May 1, 1861, 8:3.

33 See "City News—the Fourth," *Albany Evening Journal*, July 5, 1861, 2:5; "Another Company off for Washington," *Atlas and Argus*, April 30, 1861, 3:2; and "The Notes of War: The Albany Burgess Corps," *Morning Courier and New-York Enquirer*, May 2, 1861, 4:6. Also see H. Charles McBarron Jr. and Robert E. Mulligan, "Albany Burgesses Corps, 1849–1861," *Military Collector & Historian* 22, no. 1 (Spring 1970): 20–22.

34 "The War. Departure of the Twenty-Fifth Regiment," *Atlas and Argus*, April 23, 1861, 3:3.

35 "Twenty-Fifth Regiment—Letter from Captain John Gray, of the Worth Guards. Washington, D.C., May 3d, 1861," *Albany Evening Journal*, May 7, 1861, 2:4. After the 25th's return home, Albany hatter W. Frothingham claimed he was owed $200 for "caps furnished the regiment." At a meeting of the officers, it was agreed that "on the day of departure for Washington, and while at rest on Broadway, each member of the regiment was approached from behind, their caps taken from their head and another—a new one—placed in its stead." See *Atlas and Argus*, August 24, 1861, 3:1. William Frothingham sold hats and caps at 444 Broadway, Albany.

36 "The Citizen Soldiers at Washington," *Atlas and Argus*, May 13, 1861, 2:2.

37 "Clothing for the Twenty Fifth Regiment," *Atlas and Argus*, May 16, 1861, 3:1. Rowland Davis, C. G. Craft, and George P. Wilson were tailors and clothiers at 465 Broadway, Albany. See *The Albany Directory for the Year 1861*, p. 40.

38 See "The Gift of the Common Council to the Twenty-Fifth," *Atlas and Argus*, June 7, 1861, 3:2.

39 "Return of the Twenty-Fifth Regiment, of Albany," *New York Herald*, July 29, 1861, 5:1; and "The Twenty-Fifth at Home —Their Reception by the People—an Immense Turnout," *Atlas and Argus*, July 29, 1861, 2:3.

40 Gen. George W. Wingate, *History of the Twenty Second Regiment of the National Guard of the State of New York* (New York: Edwin W. Dayton, 1896), 19; and Michael J. McAfee, "Uniforms and History: 22nd Regiment National Guard State of New York," *Military Images* 10, no. 3 (November–December 1988): 28. In a letter written from New York City to her sisters abroad, Abby Howland Woolsey described meeting a relative or friend who had enlisted in the Union Grays: "You should see Charley in his Home Guard martial array. It is a sight to strike awe into feeble sisters—a grey tight-fitting coat, with red cuffs and collar edged with white cord, and a red and grey cap trimmed with white braid." See Georgeanna Woolsey Bacon and Eliza Woolsey Howland, *Letters of a Family during the War for the Union, 1861–1865*, vol. 1 (Printed for private distribution, 1899), 88.

41 "*Communication from the Governor Transmitting the Report of the Board of State Officers Named in the Act of April 16, 1861, Entitled, 'An Act to Authorise the Embodying and Equipment of a Volunteer Militia and to Provide for the Public Defence,'*" State of New York. No. 15. In Assembly, January 9, 1862, 13. Hereafter, see *Communication from the Governor*.

42 See *Communication from the Governor*, 27; "The Quartermaster General's Department," *Albany Evening Journal*, April 24, 1861, 2:4; and "The Military Cap Contract," *New York Herald*, June 20, 1861, 5:4. Also see Todd et al., vol. 2, *State Forces*, 1018. Founded in 1818 by Henry Sands Brooks, the firm of Brooks Brothers was owned by his four sons, Elisha, Daniel H., John, and Edward L., by 1861 and was at 464 Broadway—see Brooks Brothers, *A Chronicle Recording One Hundred Twenty-Five Years . . .* (New York: Brooks Brothers, 1943). Joshua G. Cottrell was a thirty-six-year-old hatter from England. With his son Edgar, he claimed to have "the largest stock of Hats and Caps . . . ever offered in Albany." See "Hats, Caps and Straw Goods," *Albany Evening Journal*, May 18, 1861, 2:8. Merchant tailor Joseph H. McDonald was resident at Westchester, New York. See the *Commercial Advertiser*, May 14, 1861, 3:9, for a report of McDonald delivering 6,000 military caps, which added, "This is the first contract promptly filled." Thomas Murphy and Warner A. Childs advertised as dealers in "hats & straw goods & furs" at 50 Day and 90 Murray, New York City. G. A. Woolverton & Co. were listed as "Manufacturers and Jobbers" of "Boots and Shoes" at 459 Broadway, Albany, in 1861.

43 "Mr. Dorsheimer and the Contractors," *New York Times*, June 9, 1861, 8:4. An earlier report of this statement is to be found in "The Military Board—the Contracts for Blankets and Clothing: Letter from Mr. Dorsheimer. Albany, June 1st, 1861," *Atlas and Argus*, June 6, 1861, 2:5.

44 Todd et al., vol. 2, *State Forces*, 1018; see also *Communication from the Governor*, 49–50.

45 "Local Military Movements—Uniforms for the New-York State Troops—Delivery Day," *New York Times*, May 10, 1861, 5:1.

46 Quoted in Raymond S. Johnson, Anthony F. Gero, Philip G. Maples, and Roger David Sturcke, "13th, 19th, and 24th New York Volunteer Infantry Regiments, Contract Uniforms, 1861," *Military Collector & Historian* 40, no. 1 (Spring 1988): 23.

47 "The Volunteer Uniforms," *Syracuse Daily Courier and Union*, May 30, 1861, 2:2.

48 *Report of the Board of Officers Named in the Act to Authorize the Embodying and Equipping of a Volunteer Militia and to Provide for the Public Defence*, State of New York. No. 15. In Assembly, January 9, 1862. See also "The Alleged Clothing Frauds," *New York Tribune*, August 17, 1861, 5:6 and 8:1–2.

49 "The Military Cap Contract," *New York Herald*, June 20, 1861, 5:4. Thomas Murphy and Warner A. Childs, of 50 Day & 19 Murray Streets, New York, supplied "hats & straw goods and furs." Isaac and Lewis J. Phillips sold caps at 64 Broadway and 19 New Street, New York. Both of these firms continued to contract for army caps throughout the war.

50 See "Local Military Movements," *New York Times*, May 13, 1861, 8:4; "Local Military Matters," *New York Tribune*, May 13, 1861, 8:3; and "Colonel Allen's First Regiment: Their Departure Today," *New York Herald*, May 25, 1861, 8:4.

51 "Troops Quartered Up Town," *New York Herald*, May 12, 1861, 5:1. On the basis of photographic evidence, the field and staff officers of this regiment wore dark-blue frock coats, company-grade officers wore gray nine-button coats with shorter sack-coat-length skirts, and enlisted men had round jackets with shoulder straps and an eight-button front. See Michael J. McAfee, "Billy Reb and Johnny Yank," *Military Images* 15, no. 4 (January–February 1994): 16–17.

52 "New Caps," *Troy Daily Whig*, May 3, 1861, 3:4.

53 "Camp Willard," *Troy Daily Whig*, May 18, 1861, 3:4. An earlier inaccurate report in the same journal dated May 14 (3:3) stated, "The uniforms will be worn for the first time on Wednesday morning. They consist of sky-blue pantaloons, a blue round-about covering the hips, and a blue fatigue cap, with oil-skin cover to be used when necessary."

54 "Local Military Matters," *New York Tribune*, May 20, 1861, 8:4.

55 Joseph B. Carr, "Operations of 1861 about Fort Monroe," in *Battles and Leaders of the Civil War*, vol. 2, ed. Robert Underwood Johnson and Clarence Clough Buel (New York: Thomas Yoseloff, 1956), 145.

56 "Return of the Volunteers," *Troy Daily Whig*, July 11, 1861, 3:3.

57 "Not Complimentary," *Troy Daily Whig*, July 10, 1861, 3:5. Regarding the knapsacks, the *Whig* of July 9, 1861 (3:4), included a letter from H. J. Raymond previously published in the *New York Times*, which stated, "The lot of knapsacks sent from New York for Col. Carr's regiment, have been condemned as unfit for

use. I do not know who made them, but they are the flimsiest and most worthless things of the kind I ever saw. They are pasted together instead of being sewed, and pull apart upon the slightest provocation. I do not believe they would sustain their own weight when filled. It is an outrage which should be punished with the utmost severity, to attempt to palm off such trash upon the troops of the State."

58 "The Scott Life Guard," *New York Herald*, May 31, 1861, 5:3. A contradictory report states that at least Co. K of the 28th New York received "a uniform consisting of a grey overcoat with cape and gilt buttons; dark blue jacket, trimmed with gilt buttons; and blue pants." See "Our Volunteers—Industrial School Barracks, Albany, May 22 1861," *St. Lawrence Republican*, May 28, 1861 2:6.

59 "The Brooklyn Boys Arrive," *Evening Star*, May 6, 1861, 3:1.

60 "Our Troops at Elmira—Their Condition, Wants, etc.," *Oswego Commercial Times*, May 27, 1861, 3:1.

61 "War Correspondence of the Standard," *Syracuse Daily Standard*, May 25, 1861, 3:4.

62 See "War Correspondence of the Standard," *Syracuse Daily Standard*, May 23, 1861, 3:3; and "Volunteers on a Visit," *Syracuse Daily Courier and Union*, May 24, 1861, 2:1. A further report in the *Daily Standard* of the same date stated, "The men are attired in their new uniforms except the hats, which we understand have not yet been distributed. The grey overcoats . . . look comfortable and neat."

63 "The Uniforms," *Syracuse Daily Courier and Union*, May 27, 1861, 2:3. When the 12th New York reached Washington on May 30, it was reported to be wearing a uniform of "Austrian grey"—see "More Troops," *Evening Star*, May 31, 1861, 3:3.

64 "A Letter from Camp Onondaga," *Atlas and Argus*, June 27, 1861, 3:1.

65 See "The Camp at Elmira," *Utica Morning Herald and Daily Gazette*, May 27, 1861, 2:7; and "More Troops," *Evening Star*, May 31, 1861, 3:3. See also Raymond S. Johnson, Anthony F. Gero, Philip G. Maples, and Roger David Sturcke, "13th, 19th, and 24th New York Volunteer Infantry Regiments, Contract Uniforms, 1861," *Military Collector & Historian* 40, no. 1 (Spring 1988): 22–23. Prior to receipt of regimental clothing, several of the companies of the 13th New York wore colorful uniforms. The Rochester Light Guard (Co. A) began to receive a new Zouave uniform prior to departure for Elmira. On April 29, the *Express* stated, "All of the new uniforms of the company which are completed were filled, and the company made a very fine appearance." See "The Zouave Drill," *Rochester Evening Express*, April 29, 1861, 2:1. This was later reported as consisting of "cottonade pants, gray shirt and plaid cap. The legs of the pants are a fraction too tight, perhaps, and would not hold more than a bushel of spices. Altogether it looks exceedingly well, and is decidedly Zouave." See "Our Volunteers at Elmira, Editorial Correspondence of the Evening Express: In Barracks No. 3, Quinby Regiment, Elmira, May 17th, 1861," *Rochester Evening Express*, May 20, 1861, 2:3–4. The Volunteer Rangers were described as wearing Zouave-style dress of "red flannel shirts and canton flannel drawers," plus heads "bound or covered with white handkerchiefs." See "The Departure of the Volunteer Regiment," *Rochester Evening Express*, May 3, 1861, 2:1; and "Visit of the Light Guard to Elmira—What They Did, What They Saw, and How They Were Treated," *Rochester Evening Express*, May 17, 1861, 2:1. The company commanded by Capt. H. B. Williams (Co. H) was presented with red shirts made by the ladies of the First Presbyterian Church. See "The Work of the Ladies," *Rochester Evening Express*, April 29, 1861, 3:2. Of the other companies of this regiment, a correspondent of the *Express* commented, "I long to see our noble fellows—many of whom are now arrayed in coats of many colors, ragged pants, soleless shoes, and every imaginable variety of old hat. . . . I have seen bare toes peeping out imploringly from torn and antiquated shoes, that would disgrace the most irreclaimable of 'rags.' Others have not changed their underclothing since leaving home. They received from their supply committee, one shirt, one pair drawers, ditto shoes, apiece, with the expectation that they would get their 'change' on arrival at Elmira, and for which they are still awaiting." See "Our Volunteers at Elmira, Editorial Correspondence of the Evening Express: In Barracks No. 3, Quinby Regiment, Elmira, May 17th, 1861," *Rochester Evening Express*, May 20, 1861, 2:3–4.

66 See Cat. # 1014 / Accession # 27.80. For previous reference to the uniform worn by Brownell, see Raymond S. Johnson, Anthony F. Gero, Philip G. Maples, and Roger David Sturcke, "13th, 19th, and 24th New York Volunteer Infantry Regiments, Contract Uniforms, 1861," *Military Collector & Historian* 40, no. 1 (Spring 1988): 22, 23.

67 "Operations of the New York Military Board," *New York Herald*, June 6, 1861, 8:4, citing Rochester *Union*, June 4.

68 See "Letters from the Seat of the War . . . [from a Regular Correspondent] Washington, DC, June 5, 1861," *Rochester Evening Express*, June 7, 1861, 2:4; and "A Letter from a Private in the 13th Regiment," *Albany Evening Journal*, June 12, 1861, 2:4. According to the *Rochester Evening Express*, May 29, 1861 (2:4), "expert tailor" W. Roberts, of Elmira, was employed to alter the uniforms of three companies of the 13th New York.

69 "Letter from Captain Adolph Nolte [Translated for the *Express* from the Observer by K. P. G.], Arlington Hights [*sic*], June 5th, 1860 [*sic*]," *Rochester Evening Express*, June 15, 1861, 2:2.

70 "Army Uniforms," *Rochester Evening Express*, June 28, 1861, 2:2. According to a report in the *Brockport Republican* of August 22, 1861 (3:1), new uniforms had been in Washington for three weeks, and "the State authorities" had "repeatedly written to the proper officers," but they had not responded.

71 "Arrival of the Nineteenth New York Regiment," *Evening Star*, May 8, 1861, 3:1.

72 "Review of the Cayuga Regiment," *National Republican*, June 15, 1861, 3:3.

73 "Field and Camp Life, Number IV," *Commercial Advertiser*, April 22, 1861, 4:3.

74 Todd et al., vol. 2, *State Forces*, 1018–19; cited from Charlie Caulkins, *Camp Sketches of Life in the Old Nineteenth* (Auburn, 1862).

75 See "Uniforms for the Seventy Fourth Regiment," *Buffalo Daily Courier*, May 7, 1861, 3:1; "The Uniforms Sold to the State," *Buffalo Daily Courier*, May 13, 1861, 3:1; "The Uniforms," *Buffalo Daily Courier*, May 11, 1861, 3:3; "From the Buffalo Regiment," *Buffalo Daily Courier*, May 18, 1861, 3:2; "The Volunteer Uniforms," *Syracuse Daily Courier and Union*, May 30, 1861, 2:2; "The Buffalo Regiment," *Buffalo Daily Courier*, June 5, 1861, 3:2; and "The Regiments at Elmira," *Utica Morning Herald and Daily Gazette*, June 8, 1861, 2:6. Tailors Anthony & Gabriel Arnoux were at 521 Broadway, New York City. See also Raymond S. Johnson, Rick P. Ugino, Anthony F. Gero, and Roger David Sturcke, "21st New York Volunteer Infantry Regiment (1st Buffalo Regiment), 1861–1863," *Military Collector & Historian* 47, no. 2 (Summer 1995): 84–85.

76 J. Harrison Mills, *Chronicles of the 21st Regiment New York Volunteer Infantry* (Buffalo, NY: Gies, 1863, reprinted 1887), 45.

77 "Letter from Elmira . . . June 19th, 1861, Union Regt., Barracks No. 4," *Rochester Evening Express*, June 22, 1861, 2:2.

78 "Military Movements in the City," *National Republican*, June 20, 1861, 3:3. Also see Johnson et al., "21st New York Volunteer Infantry Regiment (1st Buffalo Regiment), 1861–1863," 84–85.

79 Dr. Charles M. Synder, "The 24th Infantry: First to Answer the Call in Oswego County, New York in the Civil War," *Oswego County Historical Society Yearbook*, 1962, 21. The uniforms received by the 24th New York were quickly condemned, since on June 9, 1861, the *Oswego Commercial Times* published a letter from Elmira Barracks stating, "Everything here now goes on like clockwork. Our men are all perfectly contented on account of the Military Board condemning the old rubbish that has been furnished the volunteers. It seems that the Board knew nothing as regards what kind of clothing was provided." See "Letter from Elmira, Elmira Barracks, No. 4, June 8, '61," *Oswego Commercial Times*, June 9, 1861, 3:2.

80 "Arrival of the Twenty-Sixth New York Regiment," *Evening Star*, June 22, 1861, 3:2.

81 See "From the Fourteenth Regiment, Camp Douglas, Washington, June 23," *Utica Daily Observer*, June 26, 1861, 2:5; and "From the 26th Regiment," *Utica Daily Observer*, July 9, 1861, 2:5. When these uniforms were first issued at the beginning of June 1861, they were described as an "awful disgraceful gray and no gray, red and no red, and all other colors of gray ever heard of, without fit." See "The Regiments at Elmira," *Utica Morning Herald and Daily Gazette*, June 8, 1861, 2:6.

82 "Local Military Matters," *New York Tribune*, May 20, 1861, 8:4 and 5.

83 See "The Military Spirit," *Syracuse Daily Courier and Union*, April 20, 1861, 2:2; and "The Military Spirit of Our City," *Syracuse Daily Courier and Union*, April 22, 1861, 2:4. According to the same journal, dated April 29, 1861 (2:4), a second company of Syracuse Zouaves under Capt. Samuel E. Thompson enlisted in the 14th New York, but it is uncertain whether they wore a Zouave-style uniform. This company was formed by an amalgamation of the Young American Reserve Guards and "the remaining members" of Zouave Company A. See *Syracuse Daily Standard*, May 18, 1861, 2:2.

84 See "From Our Volunteers," *Utica Daily Observer*, May 27, 1861. 2:5; an undated news clipping titled "Banner Presentation to the Fourteenth Regiment at Albany, Yesterday," probably from *Utica Morning Herald & Daily Gazette*, May 25, 1861, 2:5; and "Arrival of the Fourteenth (Oneida) New York Regiment," *Evening Star*, June 20, 1861, 3:3.

85 See "Military Affairs in Baltimore," *Baltimore Clipper*, May 22, 1861, 1:2; and "Letter from Volunteer: Camp Sprague, Washington, May 22, 1861," *Providence Daily Post*, May 25, 1861, 2:2. Thaddeus P. Mott had served under Scott and Taylor in the Mexican War, with Garibaldi in 1849, and in the US Navy during the 1850s. Rising to the rank of lieutenant colonel of cavalry during the Civil War, he served as a major general in the Egyptian army in the 1870s.

86 "Letters from the Seat of War . . . Camp Lincoln, Arlington Hights [*sic*], June 14th, 1861," *Rochester Evening Express*, June 18, 1861, 2:2.

87 "The City and Vicinity," *Rochester Evening Express*, August 20, 1861, 2:1.

88 *Utica Morning Herald and Daily Gazette*, August 1861, 2.

89 See *Communications from the Governor*, 120; as well as "The State Military Department—Bids for Articles in the Quartermaster's Department," *Albany Evening Journal*, May 20, 1861, 2:4; "Clothing for the Volunteers—Contracts Awarded," *Albany Evening Journal*, May 25, 1861, 1:7; and "Additional Uniforms," *Albany Evening Journal*, June 13, 1861, 2:3. Founded by Daniel Devlin in 1843, the clothing and uniform-making firm of Devlin, Hudson & Co. was situated at 259 and 459 Broadway. Belgian-born Wilhelm Seligman was listed at 32 Vesey. Francis B. Baldwin was a clothing dealer at 70 Bowery from 1860 to 1864. Clothier Palmer P. Kellogg was at 53 Franklin Square, Utica, in 1859. The latter produced "1,003 pants, 1,026 overcoats, and 500 jackets" of "army-colored cloth, strong and durable, of good cut, and well made"—see "Additional Uniforms," *Utica Daily Observer*, June 14, 1861, 2:4. While it is believed that all of the jackets made via the May contracts were dark blue, those produced by Kellogg may have been light blue. Describing this clothing, a report published in the *Utica Morning Herald* on June 6, 1861 (2:5), stated, "The color is the light army blue, and the goods are all wool, heavy and strong. The pantaloons are stayed to give additional strength to the seams. The overcoats are lined with red flannel, of wool warp, and all the trimmings are of good quality. The buttons bear the coat of arms of our State."

90 "Enfield Rifles for the New York Volunteers," *New York Herald*, June 23, 1861, 5:2.

91 See "The State Military Department—Clothing for the Volunteers—Contracts Awarded," *Albany Evening Journal*, May 25, 1861, 1:7. Thomas Murphy and Warner A. Childs sold "hats & straw goods, and furs" at 50 Day and 19 Murray, New York City. According to a report in the *Atlas and Argus*, of Albany, June 22, 1861 (2:5), this firm was not cap manufacturers, but speculators. Acquiring the contract at $11.40 per dozen caps, they subcontracted the work to J. L. & J. Phillips, of New York City, to furnish them the caps for $7 per dozen, making the net gain of $4.40 on each dozen caps. Roswell S. Benedict and William A. Hall of 21 or 23 Park Row supplied 3,500 pairs of shoes in 1861. Suppliers of clothing and equipment Cronin, Hurxthal & Sears, of 118 and 120 Duane Street, New York City, advertised in the *New York Times* on May 4, 1861, that they had "on hand 8000 pairs grey and white blankets," plus "genuine mackinaw blankets."

92 "The 16th Regiment at Albany," *Frontier Palladium*, June 20, 1861, 2:2, 3; and "More Troops," *Evening Star*, June 29, 1861, 3:1.

93 "Uniformed," *Atlas and Argus*, June 16, 1861, 3:1. Parker & O'Brien were merchant tailors at 481 Broadway in Albany, while Carpenter & Kirk were merchant tailors at 556 Broadway, house at 146 N. Pearl. See *The Albany Directory for the Year 1861* (Albany, NY: Adams, Sampson, 1861), 28 & 110.

94 "Quartermaster Griswold," *Syracuse Daily Courier and Union*, June 20, 1861, 2:1.

95 "Letter from Camp Onondaga," *Syracuse Daily Courier and Union*, July 2, 1861, 2:3.

96 "The Troops," *Evening Star*, June 24, 1861, 3:2.

97 See "Still They Come," *Delaware State Journal and Statesman*, June 21, 1861, 2:6. This regiment was incorrectly reported as the 11th New York Volunteers on this occasion. For the flag reference, see "More Troops," *Evening Star*, June 21, 1861, 3:2.

98 "Oswego Regiment," *Syracuse Daily Courier and Union*, June 27, 1861, 2:1. Also see "A Correspondent of the Syracuse Journal, Writing from Elmira Last Thursday, Says: The Oswego Regiment To-day Received Uniforms for Three Companies, and It Is Expected That This Evening Will Reveal to the Gaze of Both the Oswego and Union Regiments [27th New York] Enough Army Blue to Well and Properly Clothe Every Man." "The Twenty-Fourth," *Oswego Commercial Times*, June 24, 1861, 3:1.

99 See "Letter from Elmira June 19th, 1861, Union Regt., Barracks No. 4," *Rochester Evening Express*, June 22, 1861, 2:2; and "Military Stampede at Elmira—Return of Captain Wanzer's Company," *Rochester Evening Express*, July 1, 1861, 2:1. Earlier, on June 3, 1861, an unnamed corporal of the 27th New York wrote, "We are anxious to know what kind of uniforms we are to have; whether one coat is to be large enough for three men or one. I fear there will be trouble if we do not get something better than those furnished to the Quinby regiment [13th New York]. . . . I understand we are to have a dark blue frock, light blue pants, and a light blue overcoat." See "Letter from a Corporal in Capt. Wanzer's Company, Elmira, June 3, 1861, Barracks No. 5," *Rochester Evening Express*, June 6, 1861, 2:2. See also "The City and Vicinity," *Rochester Evening Express*, August 15, 1861, 2:1. In a letter about the performance of the 27th New York at Bull Run published in the *Express* on August 21, 1861, Capt. George G. Wanzer, commanding the Independent Zouaves (Co. E), stated, "Before leaving our camp, Sunday morning, several of us line officers came to the sensible conclusion of leaving our coats and vests behind, in our trunks, which we did, it being very warm, and the less we had on, the better." The 27th New York may also have received federal-issue clothing, since on August 11, 1861, a correspondent of the *Evening Express* visited its encampment near Alexandria, Virginia, and observed that it had a "new uniform."

100 "Condition of the Union Regiment," *Broome Republican*, August 14, 1861, 2:6.

101 "Arrival of the Twenty-Eighth Regiment from Albany," *New York Herald*, June 26, 1861, 4:6. Also see "Uniformed," *Atlas and Argus*, June 16, 1861, 3:1.

102 "Uniformed," *Troy Daily Whig*, June 24, 1861, 3:4. See also "Arrival of Col. Frisby's Thirtieth Regiment from Albany—Their Departure for Washington," *New York Herald*, June 29, 1861, 5:1. Organized among the Washington Engine Company No. 4 of Lansingburgh, Rennselaer County, New York, Co. A of this regiment uniformed themselves in "red shirts and black pants" before reporting for duty at Albany—see "Company A, Thirtieth Regiment," *Troy Daily Whig*, July 13, 1861, 3:4.

103 "The Troops," *Evening Star*, June 24, 1861, 3:2. By August 16, 1861, the 37th New York Volunteers were reported to be "in need of shoes and hats, especially." See "37th Regiment, New York Volunteers: Bellevue, Alexandria, Virginia," *Irish American Weekly*, August 24, 1861, 2:7.

104 "Troops en Route for Washington: Departure of the Second Life Guard Regiment," *New York Herald*, June 20, 1861, 8:2.

105 "From the 33d Regiment, Col. Taylor," *Rochester Evening Express*, August 22, 1861, 2:1.

106 See "Troops for Washington: Departure of the Twenty-Ninth New York Regiment," *New York Herald*, June 22, 1861, 4:6; and "The Twenty-Ninth Regiment," *New York Herald*, June 4, 1861, 8:3. On June 17, 1861, the *Atlas and Argus* (2:3) reported that the uniforms of the 29th New York were of "regulation pattern U.S. army, and are neatly and thoroughly made of apparently excellent material and well fitting."

107 "The City: Military Matters," *The Press*, June 24, 1861, 3:1. Of German immigrant stock, William Backhouse Astor had a strong interest supporting a regiment of German-speaking volunteers.

108 "Local Military Movements," *New York Times*, July 2, 1861, 8:2.

109 Mills, *Chronicles of the 21st Regiment*, 103.

110 "From the 13th Regiment, Fort Bennett, August 19," *Rochester Evening Express*, August 23, 1861, 2:2. Earlier, in a letter dated July 5, 1861, an officer of the 13th New York wrote, "We have received some shirts, nice blue ones." "From the Quinby Regiment," *Rochester Evening Express*, July 10, 1861, 2:3.

111 "Interesting Letter from the 13th Regiment, Correspondence of the Evening Express, Fort Bennett, Aug. 19th 1861," *Rochester Evening Express*, August 24, 1861, 2:3.

112 "From the 13th Regiment, Correspondence of the Evening Express, Fort Bennett, Va., Aug. 19th 1861," *Rochester Evening Express*, August 29, 1861, 2:2.

113 "From the 13th Regiment," *Rochester Evening Express*, September 17, 1861, 2:1.

114 "Local Military Matters," *New York Tribune*, May 13, 1861, 8:3. On May 18, 1861 (7:4), the same journal added, "The uniform of the staff is the national grey, with green facings and red caps." See also Michael J. McAfee, "Uniforms & History: 8th New York Volunteer Infantry ('1st German Rifles')," *Military Images* 16, no. 5 (March–April 1995): 31, 36. A conflicting description was published in the *Baltimore American and Commercial Advertiser* of May 29, 1861 (1:3), stating that this regiment had "grey coats and pantaloons, trimmed with red, and a light overcoat of the same color."

115 "More Troops," *Delaware State Journal and Statesman*, May 31, 1861, 2:4.

116 "War Movements Here and Elsewhere . . . the Germans," *New York Morning Express*, May 18, 1861, 4:3. On this occasion the 20th New York "retained the cloaks furnished, which were of a better quality."

117 See "Departure of the Twentieth Regiment, German Turners," *New York Herald*, June 14, 1861, 8:3; and "Twentieth Regiment—United Turner Rifles," *New York Herald*, June 8, 1861, 5:2. See also Michael J. McAfee, "Uniforms & History: 20th New York Volunteer Infantry, the United Turner Rifles," *Military Images* 20, no. 6 (May–June 1999): 44–45; and Roger David Sturcke and William D. Mohr, "20th New York Volunteer Infantry Regiment (United Turner Rifles), 1861–1863," *Military Collector & Historian* 34, no. 3 (Fall 1982): 120–121. The Turner societies, or turnvereins, began at a gathering near Berlin in 1811. Their role was to foster nationalism and patriotism through a program of disciplined physical training and gymnastics. The name "Turner" seems to come from the German *turnen* ("to perform gymnastics"), an adaptation of the French *tourner*, meaning "to turn." Turner societies sprouted up throughout the German-speaking territories until their radical espousal of German unity and representative government led authorities to suppress them in the 1830s. When the "48-ers" immigrated to the US, turnvereins blossomed quickly and

soon became a strong voice in the German community for political, social, and religious reform. Many local turnvereins also had associated military organizations called Turner Rifles or "Turner Schützen." Their dual purpose was marksmanship and protection of the society members in the often-violent environment where they lived.

118 "Important from Fort Monroe," *New York Times*, December 5, 1861, 4:6.

119 See Michael J. McAfee, "Uniforms & History: "The Polish Legion—Company C, 31st New York Volunteers," *Military Images* 18, no. 6 (May–June 1997): 36–37.

120 "More Troops," *Evening Star*, June 26, 1861, 3:2; "Local Affairs," *Baltimore Clipper*, June 26, 1861, 1:6; and "Military Movements in the City—Arrival of the New York Thirty-First," *National Republican*, June 26, 1861, 3:1.

121 "The Polish Legion," *New York Herald*, May 2, 1861, 5:3.

122 "The Sixty-Ninth Regiment," *Baltimore Clipper*, November 20, 1861, 1:6. A report in the *Irish American Weekly* of November 30, 1861 (2:6), mentioned that on the day of departure from Fort Schuyler, on November 18, the 69th New York Volunteers received uniforms that "were put on with the nicest attention to fit and figure." The previous day each man had been issued "a knapsack and haversack, belts . . . [&] canteens." The reporter added, "It was almost dark before the muskets were all served out."

123 "The Great Union Feeling," *New York Times*, April 24, 1861, 8:5; and "City and County Affairs," *New York Times*, May 10, 1861, 5:3.

124 Situated on Broadway and Grand and Broadway and Warren Streets, Devlin, Hudson & Co. advertised "Military Clothing of all descriptions" in the *New York Commercial Advertiser* dated April 22, 1861, 2:6. Clothing merchant William Seligman & Co. was listed at Vesey and Church, while the Seamless Clothing Company was at 342 Broadway.

125 "Local Military Movements," *New York Times*, May 24, 1861, 8:3. Not all were happy with the Zouave attire of the 5th New York. On May 20, 1861, the *New York Tribune* reported, "They are to discard their inelegant, not to say uncouth, Zouave uniform for the more becoming one worn by the State Militia"—see "Local Military Matters," *New York Tribune*, May 20, 1861, 8:4.

126 "Letter from New York," *Burlington Free Press*, May 31, 1861, 2:4.

127 Thomas Paine Southwick, *A Duryee Zouave*, 31.

128 "Alfred Davenport Letterbook." MS Coll., New York Historical Society. Letter from Fort Schuyler dated May 7, 1861. This information is provided courtesy of James Hennessey. See James Hennessey, "Uniforms of the Fifth New York Volunteer Infantry: 'Duryee Zouaves' 1861–1863," *Journal of the Confederate Historical Society of Great Britain* 15, no. 366 (Autumn 1987): 71.

129 See "Letter from Devlin, Hudson & Co. [Clothing Goods, New York City], to Col. Duryee, May 8, 1861" in Todd files, Anne S. K. Brown Coll., Brown University, RI; and National Archives, Record Group 94, Regimental Papers—courtesy of James Hennessey.

130 Alfred Davenport, *Camp and Field Life of the Fifth New York Volunteer Infantry (Duryee Zouaves)* (New York: Dick & Fitzgerald, 1879), 92. See also Michael J. McAfee, "Uniforms & History: 5th New York, 'the Red Devils,'" *Military Images* 23, no. 5 (February–March 2002): 36–37; and Michael J. McAfee, "Uniforms & History: The Fifth Regiment, New York Volunteer Infantry (Revisited)," *Military Images* 27, no. 3 (November–December 2005): 42–44.

131 "Letter from Col. Warren to Col. Vinton, January 8, 1862," in Todd files; and National Archives, Record Group 94, Regimental Papers—courtesy of James Hennessey.

132 "Wilson's Fighting Men," *Harper's Weekly* 15, no. 229 (May 18, 1861): 309, 311.

133 "A Visit to 'Billy Wilson's' Reg't," *Wisconsin Daily Patriot*, May 11, 1861, 2:3; and New York Bureau of Military Statistics, *3rd Annual Report of the Bureau of Military Statistics* (Albany, NY: Bureau of Military Statistics, 1866), 84–88. The Smith Brothers is a probable reference to James S. Smith of 23 Chambers Street, New York City, who advertised "ALL KINDS of military goods" in the *New York Herald*, November 26, 1861.

134 Gouverneur Morris, *The History of a Volunteer Regiment . . . Sixth Regiment New York Infantry* (New York: Veteran Volunteer Publishing, 1891), 31. See also Roger David Sturcke, "6th Regiment New York Volunteer Infantry ("Wilson's Zouaves") 1861–1863," *Military Collector & Historian* 27, no. 1 (Spring 1975): 24–29. An engraving of the 6th New York was published in *Harper's Weekly* 5, no. 229 (May 18, 1861): 309.

135 See *By-Laws of the "New-York Zouaves" (Independent Corps)* (New York: L. H. Frank, 1860). See also John P. Severin and Frederick P. Todd, "9th New York Volunteer Infantry Regiment (Hawkins' Zouaves), 1861–1863," *Military Collector & Historian* 8, no. 3 (Fall 1956): 75–77; Francis A. Lord and Robert L. Miller, "Hawkins Zouaves; Uniform Addenda," *Military Collector & Historian* 13, no. 4 (Winter 1961): 128–129; Peter Harrington, "Colonel Hawkins' Uniform," *Military Collector & Historian* 35, no. 4 (Winter 1983): 188; and Michael J. McAfee, "Uniforms and History: 9th New York Volunteer Infantry (Hawkins' Zouaves) 1861–1863," *Military Images* 10, no. 2 (September–October 1988): 25.

136 "Local Military Preparations," *New York Commercial Advertiser*, May 14, 1861, 3:4.

137 Lieut. Matthew J. Graham, *The Ninth Regiment New York Volunteers (Hawkins' Zouaves), Being a History of the Regiment and Veteran Association from 1860 to 1900* (New York: E. P. Coby, 1900), 47.

138 Charles W. Cowtan, *Services of the 10th New York Volunteers (National Zouaves) in the War of the Rebellion* (New York: Charles W. Ludwig, 1882), 24–25.

139 "The National Zouaves in Camp," *New York Herald*, May 9, 1861, 8:2.

140 "Colonel McChesney's Zouaves," *New York Herald*, June 1, 1861, 8:3.

141 "Interesting Correspondence . . . The Zouaves at Sandy Hook—Their Discomforts and Complaints," *New York Morning Express*, May 16, 1861, 4:2.

142 Cowtan, *Services of the 10th New York Volunteers*, 27–28.

143 Cowtan, *Services of the 10th New York Volunteers*, 50–51.

144 Cowtan, *Services of the 10th New York Volunteers*, 58.

145 See "War Movements in the Metropolis," *New York Herald*, April 30, 1861, 4:3; and "Arrival of the Military," *National Republican*, May 3, 1861, 3:1. See also Richard A. Warren and Roger David Sturcke, "11th New York Volunteer Infantry (Ellsworth's First New York Fire Zouaves), First Uniform, 1861," and "11th New York Volunteer Infantry (Ellsworth's First New York Fire Zouaves, Second Uniform, 1861–1862," *Military Collector & Historian* 39, no. 4 (Winter 1987): 174–177.

146 "Washington Correspondence," *Lowell Daily Courier*, May 11, 1861, 2:1.

147 "Letter from the Rhode Island Regiment," *Providence Evening Press*, May 9, 1861, 2:3.

148 "The Fire Zouaves New Uniform," *New York Daily Tribune*, July 1, 1861, 3:2. Also see Warren and Sturcke, 174–177.

149 "New Uniforms," *National Republican*, July 3, 1861, 3:3. See also "The Fire Zouaves New Uniform," *Evening Star*, July 2, 1861, 3:3. Strangely, a hat store in Indianapolis, Indiana, advertised that it had an example of the fez adopted by the 11th New York as early as May 22, 1861. See *Indianapolis Daily Sentinel*, May 22, 1861—"[H.] Bamberger has at his hat and cap store, as a sample, the Zouave cap worn by Col. Ellsworth's New York regiment of Zouaves. It is made of red felt, without band or peak, and with only a large tassel as an ornament. The curious in military caps should call and see it."

150 "The Maine Troops in the Great Battle," *Lewiston Daily Evening Journal*, July 30, 1861, 2:1.

151 "Garibaldi Guard," *New York Times*, May 26, 1861, 8:5. See Frederick P. Todd and George C. Woodbridge, "39th New York Volunteer Infantry Regiment (Garibaldi Guard), 1861–1862," *Military Collector & Historian* 11, no. 3 (Fall 1959): 83, 85.

152 "Movement of the Troops in New York—Departure of the Garibaldi Guard," *New York Herald*, May 29, 1861, 8:4.

153 "The Garibaldi Guard," *Delaware State Journal and Statesman*, May 31, 1861, 2:4.

154 "Runaway Vivandieres Brought Back," *Daily State Gazette & Republican*, June 5, 1861, 3:2.

155 *New York Evening News*, May 29, 1861, 4; *New York Daily News*, May 29, 1861, 8; and "Local Military Matters—Departure of the Garibaldi Guard," *New York Tribune*, May 29, 1861, 8.1.

156 "Letter from Washington," *Pittsburgh Gazette and Commercial Journal*, June 6, 1861, 3:3.

157 "Letter from Volunteer," *Providence Daily Post*, June 5, 1861, 2:2.

158 See "Military Movements in the City—the Mozart Regiment—Encampment at Yonkers," *New York Herald*, June 10, 1861, 5:2; and Sgt. Fred C. Floyd, *History of the Fortieth (Mozart) Regiment, New York Volunteers* (Boston: F. H. Gilson, 1909), 36.

159 Floyd, *History of the Fortieth (Mozart) Regiment*, 4, 22, and 36.

160 See "More Troops," *Evening Star*, July 10, 1861, 3:2; and "Grand Military Demonstration," *New York Times*, May 26, 1861, 8:6.

161 See "The De Kalb Regiment," *New York Herald*, June 9, 1861, 5:2; and "Movement of Troops in New York," *New York Herald*, June 17, 1861, 8:1. See also Ron Field and Roger David Sturcke, "41st New York Volunteer Infantry Regiment (DeKalb Regiment, or 2nd Yaeger Regiment, 1861–1865," *Military Collector and Historian* 39, no. 2 (Summer 1987): 76–77.

162 "Departure of the Tammany Regiment," *New York Herald*, July 19, 1861, 8:5.

163 "Letter from Maryland," *Delaware State Journal and Statesman*, November 8, 1861, 2:6.

164 "General Stuart's Engineer Regiment," *Rochester Evening Express*, August 5, 1861, 2:1.

165 "Local Military Matters," *New York Tribune*, October 8, 1861, 8:2. See also Michael J. McAfee, "Uniforms & History: Musicians of the Tenth Legion, 56th Regt., New York Volunteers," *Military Images* 17, no. 3 (November–December 1995): 28–29.

166 "The Tenth Legion," *New York Herald*, November 2, 1861, 5:2.

167 See "Military Movements in New York," *New York Herald*, November 8, 1861, 5:1; and "Local Military Movements," *New York Tribune*, November 8, 1861, 8:6.

168 "The New York Second Regiment," *Evening Star*, May 22, 1861, 2:1.

169 "Local Military Movements," *New York Times*, May 13, 1861, 8:4.

170 John W. Jacques, *Three Years' Campaign of the Ninth, N.Y.S.M., during the Southern Rebellion* (New York: Hilton, 1865), 9–10. See also "Recruits for the Ninth Regiment," *New York Herald*, July 3, 1861, 4:6; and Michael J. McAfee, "Uniforms & History: 9th Regiment, New York State Militia," *Military Images* 12, no. 5 (March–April 1991): 28–29.

171 Jacques, *Three Years' Campaign of the Ninth*, 35.

172 Jacques, *Three Years' Campaign of the Ninth*, 77.

173 *The History of the Fighting Fourteenth* (Published in Commemoration of the Fiftieth Anniversary of the Muster of the Regiment into the United States Service, 1911), 213. See also Harry T. Grube and George C. Woodbridge, "14th Regiment New York State Militia, 1861–1864," *Military Collector & Historian* 10, no. 3 (Fall 1958): 80–82; Martin Schoenfeld, "The 14th Brooklyn," *Military Images*. 9, no. 2 (September–October 1987): 24–25; and Michael J. McAfee, "Uniforms & History: 14th Regiment, New York State Militia '14th Brooklyn'—84th New York Volunteers," *Military Images* 13, no. 4 (January–February 1992): 27.

174 "The Fourteenth Regiment, of Brooklyn," *New York Herald*, May 12, 1861, 5:2; and "Movements of the Fourteenth Regiment of Brooklyn," *New York Herald*, May 14, 1861, 8:1. On May 12, 1861, the Relief Committee of the Common Council, responsible for providing the uniform and equipment of the 14th NYSM, reported that the cost of furnishing each soldier was "jacket, vest and pantaloons, $7, 50; overcoat, $9; cap, 75 cents; knapsack, $4; equipments, $8; blankets, $3. Total per man, $33 50." See "Military Affairs in Brooklyn.—Review of the 14th Regiment by the Union Defense Committee," *Morning Courier and New-York Enquirer*, May 13, 1861, 4:3.

175 "Poor Uniforms, *New York World*—cited in *Charleston Daily Courier*, May 25, 1861, 1:2.

176 "Military and Naval Movements," *New York Daily Tribune*, July 1, 1861, 7:6.

177 *History of the Fighting Fourteenth*, 237.

178 See "A Regiment of Highlanders," *New York Herald*, November 10, 1858, 4:6; and "The New York Highland Regiment," *New York Herald*, December 12, 1858, 1:6. See "The Regulation Uniform," *New York Times*, January 27, 1859, 3:1, for a letter from Frederick Townsend, adjutant general of the NYSM, informing "the Commandant of the new Highland Regiment" of the "bill of dress" that would be approved; that is, "The regulation hat and ornaments. The regulation frock-coat. The regulation fatigue-coat for the Light Artillery, which may be worn, if desired, for full dress occasions, as a full-dress coat. Regulation buttons. The badges of distinction and rank according to Regulations. The fatigue cap of the Light Artillery. The pantaloons may be of plaid."

179 See "Military Intelligence," *New York Herald*, September 19, 1860, 2:4. See also William Todd, *The Seventy-Ninth Highlanders, New York Volunteers, in the War of the Rebellion* (New York: Brandow, Barton, 1886), 3; John P. Severin and Frederick P. Todd, "79th Regiment, New York State Militia, 1860–1861," *Military Collector & Historian* 8, no. 1 (Spring 1956): 19–20; Michael J. McAfee, "Uniforms & History: 79th Regiment, New York State Militia," *Military Images* 11, no. 2 (September–October 1989): 28–29; and Joseph Bilby, "Blue Bonnets over the Border: The 79th New York Highlanders in the Civil War," *Military Images* 6, no. 1 (July–August 1984): 5–15.

180 "Grand Military Fete at the Academy of Music," *New York Herald*, February 22, 1860, 7:3; and "The Military Carnival," *New York Herald*, July 21, 1860, 5:2.

181 Todd, *The Seventy-Ninth Highlanders*, 5.

182 "Departure of the 79th Regiment," *New York Times*, June 3, 1861, 8:4.

183 "The New York Regiment of Highlanders," *Philadelphia Inquirer*, June 4, 1861, 5:2.

184 "The City: Movements of the Military," *The Press*, June 4, 1861, 2:8.

185 "Our Virginia Correspondence," *Charleston Daily Courier*, June 10, 1861, 1:3, citing the *Baltimore American* of June 4.

186 "The New York Seventy-Ninth Regiment," *Evening Star*, June 4, 1861, 3:1.

187 "Review of the New York Troops at Washington," *New-York Daily Tribune*, July 5, 1861, 5:3.

188 "The Seventy-Ninth Regiment, N.Y.S.M.," *New-York Daily Tribune*, July 12, 1861, 6:2.

189 Todd, *The Seventy-Ninth Highlanders*,18.

190 See Michael J. McAfee, "Uniforms and History—'the Lafayette Guard,'" *Military Images* 20, no. 4 (September–October 1988): 40–41; "Our Welcome to the Prince," *New York Herald*, October 12, 1860, 4:4; "The New-York French Zouave Corps," *New-York Daily Tribune*, August 20, 1860, 7:4; and "The Zouave Meeting in New York," *New York Herald*, August 14, 1860, 8:1. Of $11,404.69 raised by the New York Chamber of Commerce and Union Defense Committee, $4,150 was spent on uniforms for "nine companies; 200 double blankets, $700; 100 tents, &c., $985; 400 pairs of gaiters, $200; 200 do of red worsted epaulettes, $300; 200 canteens, $80 . . . 600 gun slings and canteens, $166; 475 flannel Havelocks, $103; 35 artillery knapsacks, $100 . . . 400 knapsacks and 400 belts, complete, $3,000." See "Expenditures of the Fifty-Fifth Regiment, N.Y.S.M.," *Morning Courier and New-York Enquirer*, June 20, 1861, 3:6.

191 "Meeting of Scott Rifles, Col. McDonald presided," *New York Daily News*, July 17, 1861, 8.

192 "Local Military Matters," *New York Tribune*, July 18, 1861, 7:3.

193 "Local Military Movements—the Clinton Rifles," *New York Times*, September 10, 1861, 8:5.

194 "First United States Chasseurs," *New York Herald*, July 31, 1861, 8:3; see also Michael J. McAfee, "Uniforms & History: 65th New York Volunteer Infantry—1st U.S. Chasseurs," *Military Images* 21, no. 1 (July–August 1999): 39.

195 "Local Military Matters," *New York Tribune*, July 29, 1861, 7:2.

196 See "Contracts for Army Clothing," *New York Herald*, July 28, 1861, 5:1; and "The Army Clothing Contract," *New York Herald*, July 31, 1861, 8:4.

197 "Arrival of the People's Ellsworth Regiment," *New York Commercial Advertiser*, October 22, 1861, 3:5, 6. See also Frederick P. Todd and George C. Woodbridge, "44th New York Volunteer Infantry Regiment (People's Ellsworth Regiment), 1861–1864," *Military Collector & Historian* 11, no. 1 (Spring 1959): 10–11; and Michael J. McAfee, "Uniforms & History: The 44th Regiment, N.Y.S. Volunteer Infantry—'Ellsworth's Avengers,'" *Military Images* 26, no. 1 (July–August 2004): 33–34. According to a newspaper clipping from the *Utica Morning Herald* in the collection of the New York State Military Museum, dated October 20, 1861, the leggings for this regiment were made by L. D. Rodgers. A Lemuel M. Rodgers was listed as a maker of "Trunks, Valises, etc." at 364 Broadway in *The Albany Directory for the Year Commencing June 1, 1861* (Albany, NY: Adams, Sampson), 120 and 183.

198 "Local Military Matters," *New York Daily Tribune*, October 23, 1861, 8:3.

199 See "Consolidation of Regiments," *New York Commercial Advertiser*, October 15, 1861, 3:9; and "Local Military Matters," *New York Tribune*, September 12, 1861, 8:2.

200 "New York Under Arms," *New York Herald*, May 26, 1861, 8:4.

201 "Local Military Matters," *New York Tribune*, May 30, 1861, 8:3.

202 "The New Zouave Regiment," *Evening Post*, July 11, 1861, 1:4.

203 Roger David Sturcke, "62nd Regiment, New York Volunteer Infantry (Anderson's Zouaves), 1861–1865," *Military Collector & Historian* 35, no. 1 (Spring 1983): 32–33; and Michael J. McAfee, "Uniforms & History: 62nd Regiment, New York Volunteer Infantry, "Anderson's Zouaves," *Military Images* 12, no. 6 (May–June 1991): 31.

204 "Military Movements in the City," *New York Herald*, June 9, 1861, 5:1.

205 "Military Matters," *Commercial Advertiser*, August 5, 1861, 3:4. Earlier, the *Tribune* had reported that the Second Fire Zouaves were to wear "a dark blue zouave jacket, and army-blue Zouave pants, with leggings." See "Local Military Matters," *New York Tribune*, July 9, 1861, 8:5.

206 "Local Affairs," *Baltimore Clipper*, July 26, 1861, 1:5.

207 "Military Movements in New York—Les Enfants Perdus," *New York Herald*, December 7, 1861, 10:5; and "Enfants Perdus," *New York Herald*, December 18, 1861, 3:3. See also Francis Balace and John R. Elting, "Les Enfants Perdus, 1861–1864," *Military Collector & Historian* 22, no. 1 (Spring 1970): 26–27. For a list of officers, see "Departure of Les Enfants Perdus," *New York Tribune*, April 21, 1862, 8:5–6.

208 Michael J. McAfee, "Uniforms & History: *Les Enfants Perdus*—the 'Lost Children' of the Independent Battalion, New York Volunteer Infantry, 1862–1864," *Military Images* 18, no. 3 (November–December 1996): 32.

209 See H. Charles McBarron Jr. and Frederick P. Todd, "3rd Regiment, New York State Militia (Hussars), 1850–1860," *Military Collector & Historian* 10, no. 4 (Winter 1958): 106–108.

210 *New York Herald*, August 19, 1861, 8—cited in Michael J. McAfee, "Uniforms & History: First Regiment of Cavalry, New York State Volunteers," *Military Images* 30, no. 2 (September–October 2008): 42–43. See also National Archives RG 217, Box 2, NA—a contract to A. & G. Arnoux (22 July 1861) for 800 cavalry uniforms, of which twenty were for musicians.

211 "Local Military Matters—Departure of the Lincoln Cavalry," *New York Tribune*, August 27, 1861, 8:2.

212 "Lincoln Cavalry," *New York Tribune*, August 25, 1861, 8:2.

213 *New York Herald*, August 27, 1861—cited in McAfee, "Uniforms & History: First Regiment of Cavalry, New York State Volunteers," *Military Images* 30, no. 2 (September–October 2008): 42–43.

214 Letter from James Albert Hudson, "Headquarters 1st New York Vol. (Late Lincoln) Cavalry, Camp Kearney, near Alexandria, Va., February 3d 1862," Spared & Shared II blog site, courtesy of William Griffing.

215 "Military Movements in New York," *New York Herald*, November 24, 1861, 5:1.

216 See "Uniforms Received," *Rochester Evening Express*, October 16, 1861, 2:4; and "Crooks' Cavalry Regiment," *Rochester Evening Express*, October 17, 1861, 2:3. See also Michael J. McAfee, "Uniforms & History: The First Regiment of Mounted Rifles, New York Volunteers," *Military Images* 26, no. 5 (March–April 2005): 32; and Alan H. Archambault, Anthony F. Gero, Philip G. Maples, and Roger David Sturcke, "8th Regiment, New York Volunteer Cavalry (Rochester Regiment); 22nd Regiment, New York Volunteer Cavalry (Rochester Cavalry), 1861–1865," *Military Collector & Historian* 47, no. 4 (Winter 1995): 178–179.

217 *Westfield Republican*, October 30, 1861, 3:1; see also Newell Cheney, *History of the Ninth Regiment, New York Volunteer Cavalry* (New York: Poland Center, 1901), 18.

218 N. D. Preston, *History of the Tenth Regiment of Cavalry, New York Volunteers* (New York: D. Appleton, 1892), 12.

219 See "The State Military Department—Bartlett's Naval Brigade," *Albany Evening Journal*, May 24, 1861, 2:6; and "Naval and Military Movements—the Naval Brigade," *New York Times*, June 19, 1861, 8:5. According to the *Commercial Advertiser*, May 29, 1861 (3:3), the uniform was to consist of "a blue flannel blouse, blue pants and shirt, and black hat and plume."

220 See "Local Military Movements," *New York Times*, May 30, 1861, 8:2; "The Naval Brigade," *Commercial Advertiser*, June 4, 1861, 3:4; "The Naval Brigade," *Commercial Advertiser*, June 5, 1861, 3:6; and "News and Other Items—Manufacturing of Arms," *Albany Evening Journal*, June 6, 1861, 2:2.

221 See "The Naval Brigade Rejected," *New York Times*, June 4, 1861, 1:4; and "War News—Bartlett's Naval Brigade, *Albany Evening Journal*, June 5, 1861, 2:6.

222 See "Return of the Naval Brigade," *Evening Post*, June 5, 1861, 3:9; and "War News—the Naval Brigade," *Albany Evening Journal*, June 6, 1861, 2:5. According to a brief mention in the *New York Tribune* of June 17, 1861 (1:1), "some 20 or 30 of the Naval Brigade rejected" shipped aboard the store ship *Alabama*, which was renamed USS *New Hampshire* on October 28, 1863. This seems improbable, since that vessel is believed to have remained on the stocks until the latter date.

223 See "Local Military Matters," *New York Tribune*, July 17, 1861, 7:4; and "The Union Coast Guard at Fortress Monroe Formed into a Regiment," *Albany Evening Journal*, August 22, 1861, 1:9. Made by Messrs. Annin & Co., a flag was completed and forwarded to the Virginia Coast Guard at Fortress Monroe by July 26, 1861, which was described as "a beautiful American ensign. . . . On the head of the staff is a gold eagle, from the back of which is suspended an anchor and cable. The silver plate on the staff bears the following inscription: 'Presented to the N.Y. Virginia Coast Guard by J. S. Hyde, on behalf of citizens of New York, July, 1861.'" See "Flag for the Virginia Coast Guard," *Commercial Advertiser*, July 26, 1861, 3:4.

224 See "News from Fortress Monroe, *New York Herald*, June 16, 1861, 5:1, "Incidents of the War," *Commercial Advertiser*, August 23, 1861, 2:3; and "Affairs at Fortress Monroe," *New York Herald*, November 8, 1861, 2:2. On May 18, 1861, a report in the *Hartford Weekly Times* stated, "New London will furnish one company for the Naval Brigade, Col. Bartlett, which is organized on the suggestion of the N.Y. Chamber of Commerce and with the sanction of the Navy Department. Capt. John W. Brown will command the New London Company, which will be mustered into U.S. service this week and at once join the Brigade in New York. They enlist for three years, will wear the Navy uniform, and carry the Minie rifle with sabre bayonet, going through the infantry drill in addition to their nautical training." See "A Naval Brigade," *Hartford Weekly Times*, May 18, 1861, 2:6. Detached to man the frigate *Constitution*, his company appears not to have joined the Naval Brigade.

225 See "News from Fortress Monroe," *New York Herald*, June 16, 1861, 5:1; "Incidents of the War," *Commercial Advertiser*, August 23, 1861, 2:3; and "Affairs at Fortress Monroe," *New York Herald*, November 8, 1861, 2:2.

226 "Burnside's Expedition," *Chicago Daily Tribune*, July 18, 1862, 1:7.

227 Michael J. McAfee, "Uniforms & History: First Regiment, New York Marine Artillery 1861–1863—'the Horse Marines,'" *Military Images* 22, no. 6 (May–June 2001): 31–32.

Chapter 3: New Jersey

1 "Jersey City News," *New York Herald*, May 16, 1858, 5:3.

2 See Todd et al., vol. 2, *State Forces*, 992–993.

3 *Daily State Gazette & Republican*, April 27, 1861, 3:1.

4 *Atlantic Democrat*, May 4, 1861, 3:5.

5 *Daily State Gazette & Republican*, May 1, 1861, 3:1.

6 "Visit to Camp Olden, at Trenton, N.J., April 30, 1861," *Philadelphia Inquirer*, May 2, 1861, 2:3.

7 "The Arsenal and 'Camp Olden,'" *Daily State Gazette & Republican*, April 29, 1861, 3:1.

8 "The Jersey Blues on Hand," *Evening News*, May 6, 1861, 3:1.

9 "More Zouaves," *Evening News*, May 6, 1861, 3:1.

10 See "Call to the Ladies of Trenton," *Daily State Gazette & Republican*, April 23 1861, 3:2; "Active Aid," *Daily State Gazette & Republican*, April 24 1861, 3:3; and "American Women," *Daily State Gazette & Republican*, May 6 1861, 2:3.

11 Letter from Capt. J. Gale to Mrs. C. C. Merrett, June 21, 1861.

12 See "Wilkinson Volunteers," *Daily State Gazette & Republican*, April 29 1861, 3:2; and *Daily State Gazette & Republican*, May 1 1861, 3:1.

13 "Correspondence of the State Gazette and Republican," *Daily State Gazette & Republican*, April 24, 1861, 2:3.

14 See "In Honor of Major Anderson," *Philadelphia Inquirer*, January 21, 1861, 1:3. For further reports on the Camden Zouave Cadets, see *Camden Democrat*, January 19, 1861, 2:3, for possible beginning of this unit. See *Camden Democrat*, March 2, 1861, 2:3 for election of officers. On April 29, 1861, the *Newark Daily Advertiser* commented of the New Jersey troops at Trenton, "Three Zouave Companies in French uniform are here."

15 "Letter from one of the New Jersey Volunteers, Washington, D.C., May 8, 1861," *Daily State Gazette & Republican*, May 13, 1861, 2:2; and "For the Gazette and Republican, Camp Monmouth (near Washington), May 17, 1861," *Daily State Gazette & Republican*, May 20, 1861, 2:2.

16 "More Jersey Blues," *Evening Star*, May 7, 1861, 3:1.

17 *Daily State Gazette & Republican*, May 18, 1861, 3:2.

18 *Annual Report of the Quartermaster General of the State of New Jersey for the Year 1861* (Jersey City, NJ: John H. Lyon, 1862), 13. Born at Ridgefield, Connecticut, in 1816, Nehemiah Perry moved to Newark, New Jersey, in 1836 and engaged in manufacturing cloth and other work in the clothing business, with premises at 294 Broad Street from 1845 to 1865. He was elected a member of the New Jersey General Assembly in 1850 and 1856, serving as Speaker of the Assembly in the latter year. He was a member of the Newark Common Council in 1852. He was elected to represent New Jersey's Fifth District in the US House of Representatives, serving from 1861 to 1865. He also served as mayor of Newark in 1873. See his obituary in the *New York Times*, November 2, 1881. Silas C. Halsey ran a clothing business in Virginia before the war and later opened the clothing firm of Halsey, Hunter & Co, which was on Broad Street in Newark. During the war, he was appointed an aide-de-camp to Brig. Gen. Cornelius Van Vorst, became a major, and was made assistant quartermaster general.

19 *Daily State Gazette & Republican*, June 22, 1861, 2:3.

20 "The New Jersey Brigade," *Irish American Weekly*, June 29, 1861, 2:6.

21 *Daily State Gazette & Republican*, May 3, 1861, 3:3.

22 "Exchanging Arms," *Daily National Intelligencer*, May 16, 1861, 3:4.

23 *Daily State Gazette & Republican*, April 20 1861, 3:2.

24 *Daily State Gazette & Republican*, May 17, 1861, 3:2.

25 "State of New Jersey: Office of the Quarter Master General, Trenton, May 20," *Daily State Gazette & Republican*, May 22, 1861, 2:5.

26 *Daily State Gazette & Republican*, May 23, 1861, 3:1.

27 See *Daily State Gazette & Republican*, May 30, 1861, 3:1; *Atlantic Democrat*, June 1, 1861, 2:4; and *Camden Democrat*, June 1, 1861, 2:4.

28 Camille Baquet, *History of the First Brigade, New Jersey Volunteers* (Trenton, NJ: State of New Jersey, 1910), 11.

29 "The New Jersey Troops," *New York Herald*, June 29, 1861 5:3.

30 "Local Affairs—Movement of Troops," *Delaware State Journal and Statesman*, July 2, 1861, 2:5.

31 *Annual Report of the Quartermaster-General*, 7 and 26. On the basis of accounts published in this source, N. Perry & Co. and Halsey, Hunter & Co. probably supplied the uniforms, and Duryea, Jaques & Co. provided the hats.

32 *Annual Report of the Quartermaster-General*, 7; and "The Ninth Regiment," *Daily State Gazette & Republican*, December 2, 1861, 3:1.

33 "Presentation at Trenton," *Centinel of Freedom*, 3:2.

34 "Local Matters," *West Jersey Press*, November 20, 1861, 3:1.

Chapter 4: Delaware

1 *Rebellion Records*, series III, *Union Authorities*, vol. 1, *Correspondence, Orders, Reports and Returns, Nov. 1, 1860–Mar. 31, 1862*, p. 114. Of 112,000 inhabitants in Delaware, 1,800 were slaves held by 600 owners. See "Slavery in Delaware," *Delaware State Journal and Statesman*, June 21, 1861, 2:6.

2 See "Local Affairs—Come Ladies Arouse!!! Help for the Brave!!" *Delaware State Journal and Statesman*, April 26, 1861, 2:4; "Ladies Ready to Work," *Delaware State Journal and Statesman*, April 26, 1861, 2:6; "Clothing for the Volunteers," *Delaware State Journal and Statesman*, May 14, 1861, 2:6; "Clothe the Volunteers," *Delaware State Journal and Statesman*, May 24, 1861, 2:4; and "Clothing for the Volunteers," *Delaware State Journal and Statesman*, May 28, 1861, 2:5.

3 "Acknowledgement," *Delaware State Journal and Statesman*, May 21, 1861, 2:6; and "The Military," *Delaware Republican*, May 20, 1861, 2:5.

4 "The Military," *Delaware Republican*, May 20, 1861, 2:5.

5 "From Our Volunteers at Bush River . . . Fort Dare, Bush River, Maryland, June 2d, 1861," *Delaware State Journal and Statesman*, June 4, 1861, 2:4.

6 "Correspondence of the Delaware Republican. Camp Dare, June 17th, 1861," *Delaware Republican*, June 20, 1861, 3:5. See also a letter written by Quartermaster William H. Allderdice on July 30, 1861, in response to protests from the men about paying each paying $11.50 for their uniforms—"The First Regiment," *Delaware State Journal and Statesman*, August 2, 1861, 2:4.

7 "Letter from Camp Milligan . . . Bush River, June 23," *Philadelphia Inquirer*, June 26, 1861, 2:1—from "Rennat."

8 "Letter from Camp. [Bush River, dated June 12th—copied from the Commonwealth," *Delaware Republican*, June 24, 1861, 2:5—from "Typo" or W. S. G.

9 "Letter from Camp Milligan . . . Bush River, Md., July 1, 1861," *Delaware State Journal and Statesman*, July 5, 1861, 2:3.

10 "Letter from Camp Dare No. 3 . . . Fort Dare, Bush River, Md, June 9, 1861," *Delaware State Journal and Statesman*, June 11, 1861, 2:4.

11 "Letter from Perryville: Letter No. 9 . . . Perryville, Md., Saturday night, June 29, 1861," *Delaware State Journal and Statesman*, July 2, 1861, 2:3.

12 William P. Seville, *History of the First Regiment, Delaware Volunteers, from the Commencement of the Three Months Service to the Final Muster-Out at the Close of the Rebellion* (Wilmington, DE: Historical Society of Delaware, 1884), 24.

13 "Correspondence of the Delaware Republican: Camp Dare, June 17th, 1861," *Delaware Republican*, June 20, 1861, 3:5.

14 See "The First Delaware Regiment," *Delaware Republican*, September 12, 1861, 3:4; and "Letter from Fortress Monroe . . . October 21," *Delaware State Journal and Statesman*, October 26, 1861, 2:5.

15 "The Military," *Delaware Republican*, September 23, 1861, 2:4.

16 Seville, *History of the First Regiment, Delaware Volunteers*, 30.

17 "The Second Regiment Delaware Volunteers, *Delaware Republican*, August 1, 1861, 3:4.

18 "Still Another," *Peninsula News and Advertiser*, November 8, 1861, 3:2.

19 "The Military," *Delaware Republican*, June 13, 1861, 3:5.

20 "Military," *Delaware State Journal and Statesman*, June 18, 1861, 2:6. This company was organized into the 1st Regiment of Delaware Volunteer Militia via General Orders, No. 2, dated July 12 1861; see *Delaware State Journal and Statesman*, July 23, 1861, 3:1.

21 *Delaware Republican*, May 27, 1861, 2:5.

22 "Military Parade," *Delaware Republican*, May 6, 1861, 2:3.

23 "Proceedings of the Council," *Delaware Republican*, August 12, 1861, 2:5.

Chapter 5: Maryland

1 Todd et al., vol. 2, *State Forces*, 878.

2 See "The State Arms," *Baltimore American and Commercial Advertiser*, June 10, 1861, 1:6.

3 *Baltimore Clipper*, May 1, 1861, 2:1. The Union movement in Maryland was mainly centered in the counties of Baltimore, Frederick, Carroll, Anne Arundel, Harford, Washington, Allegany, Montgomery, Caroline, Kent, Worcester, Talbot, Cecil, and Dorchester. See "The Union Movement in Maryland," *Baltimore Clipper*, April 16, 1861, 2:1.

4 "Union Badges," *Baltimore Clipper*, April 27, 1861, 1:2.

5 "Headquarters, First Regiment Light Artillery," *The Sun*, June 15, 1861, 2:5. A prominent member of the Baltimore City Guard, Andrew W. Denison was commissioned colonel of the 8th Maryland Infantry in 1862.

6 "The Baltimore City Guard," *Boston Evening Transcript*, August 25, 1859, 3:5. On February 22, 1858, the *Daily Exchange* reported that the Guard appeared for the first time in "heavy blue pilot-cloth overcoats, recently made to order by Messrs. John H. Rea & Co." ("Departure of the Guards for Richmond," *Daily Exchange*, February 22, 1858, 2:6). On September 6, 1860, the *Evening Star* of Washington, DC (2:1), reported, "Two military companies in Frederick, Md., have purchased the knapsacks and accompanying accouterments of the Baltimore City Guard. The articles are of no further use to the Guard since their adoption of the Zouave uniform." See *Daily Exchange*, November 5, 1858, 1:4, for receipt of Minié muskets with Maynard primer. See *Daily Exchange*, September 8, 1858, 1:3, for flag presentation. See *Daily Exchange*, August 16, 1859, 1:3, for receipt of accoutrements for Minié muskets.

7 "For the Examiner," *The Examiner*, October 23, 1861, 2:6. With "a fine battery of four brass pieces, with caissons," the Eagle Artillery tendered their services to the general government on May 23, 1861. See "War Movements," *Baltimore American and Commercial Advertiser*, May 24, 1861, 1:3.

8 "Military," *Easton Star*, July 3, 1860, 3:1.

9 "New Arms," *The Sun*, July 16, 1860, 1:4.

10 "Handsome Uniform," *The Examiner*, August 1, 1860, 2:7. In July 1860, this replaced a full dress adopted in 1858, composed of a green coat with "pantaloons and a very handsome military cap, with polished leather top, ornamented with a black pompon and scarlet flame." The latter was further described as being "designed and manufactured by Messrs. J. L. McPhail & Bro., of Baltimore City, after the direction of First Lieut. [Ulysses] Hobbs." See "Twelfth of September," *The Examiner*, September 15, 1858, 2:6.

11 "Minnie Rifles for the Independent Riflemen," *The Examiner*, February 9, 1859, 2:3.

12 "Attempt to Destroy a Bridge," *The Examiner*, May 15, 1861, 2:4.

13 "United Guards," *The Examiner*, March 31, 1858, 2:4.

14 "Military Movements," *Baltimore American and Commercial Advertiser*, April 23, 1861, 1:4.

15 "Organization of Uniformed Companies," *Baltimore American and Commercial Advertiser*, April 25, 1861, 1:5.

16 "Parade of the Home Guards," *Baltimore Clipper*, September 14, 1861, 1:7.

17 "Flag Presentation," *Baltimore Clipper*, October 5, 1861, 1:7.

18 "U.S. Rendezvous Office in Baltimore," *Kent News*, May 11, 1861, 2:6.

19 *Baltimore Clipper*, April 25, 1861, 2:1.

20 See "Local News," *Baltimore Clipper*, May 14, 1861, 4:2; "The Attack upon the Maryland Volunteers—Statement of Capt. McConnell," *Baltimore Clipper*, May 16, 1861, 1:7; and "War Movements," *Baltimore American and Commercial Advertiser*, May 17, 1861, 1:3.

21 "War Movements," *Baltimore American and Commercial Advertiser*, May 21, 1861, 1:3.

22 "War News," *Baltimore Clipper*, May 17, 1861, 1:2. Out drilling on May 17, 1861, the Union Rifles encountered a company of youths "dressed in fanciful costume" called the "Jeff Davis Rifles." Avoiding "a row," the two captains settled the matter by "consolidating and parading the streets." See "The Camp at Locust Point," *Baltimore Clipper*, May 18, 1861, 1:2.

23 "Military Affairs in Baltimore," *Baltimore Clipper*, May 23, 1861, 1:2. McConnell stopped advertising for recruits on June 6, 1861. See "The First Maryland Regiment," *Baltimore Clipper*, June 15, 1861, 1:7.

24 "Thanks," *Baltimore Clipper*, June 21, 1861, 1:7. This company was commanded by Captain Benjamin H. Schley.

25 "Letter from 1st Md. Regiment," *Baltimore Clipper*, September 19, 1861, 4:1. Elements of this regiment assisted Union troops escape across the Potomac River after the Union defeat at Ball's Bluff on October 21, 1861. See "Letter from the First Md. Regiment," *Baltimore Clipper*, November 6, 1861, 4:2.

26 "Recruits for the Second Maryland Regiment," *Baltimore Clipper*, June 10, 1861, 2:4.

27 "Military Matters—Movement of Troops," *Baltimore Clipper*, June 12, 1861, 1:7.

28 "Gone to Camp," *Baltimore Clipper*, June 19, 1861, 1:6.

29 "Wanted," *Baltimore Clipper*, July 20, 1861, 2:7. "Captain Conway's [*sic*] Company of Zouaves" was still being recruited by August 6, 1861. See *Baltimore Clipper*, August 7, 1861, 2:7. See "The Second Maryland Regiment," *Baltimore Clipper*, August 26, 1861, 2:3, for company list of 2nd Maryland (three years).

30 See "Visit to a Camp," *Baltimore Clipper*, September 14, 1861, 1:7.

31 "Local Affairs," *Baltimore Clipper*, September 28, 1861, 4:4. A regimental flag made by Edward A. Gibbs, who had a "Regalia Store" in Baltimore, was presented to the 2nd Maryland on June 26, 1861, which was described in the *Clipper* of that date (1:6) as "a very rich silk, 7½ feet in length and 5 feet in width, having the full number of stars (thirty-four) richly gilt upon the field. The staff is of handsome black walnut, highly polished, and surmounted with a brass spear head, from which is suspended a beautiful pair of red, white and blue silk bullion tassels and cord."

32 "Second Maryland Regiment," *Baltimore Clipper*, October 8, 1861, 1:7.

33 "Parade of the Second Maryland Regiment," *Baltimore Clipper*, December 31, 1861, 4:2.

34 "Recruits Wanted for the 3d Maryland Regiment," *Baltimore Clipper*, July 31, 1861, 2:6.

35 See Thomas J. Scharf, *History of Western Maryland: Being a History of Frederick, Montgomery, Carroll, Washington, Allegany, and Garrett Counties* (Philadelphia: Louis H. Everts, 1882), 1:307. See also "Gen. Cooper's Maryland Brigade," *Baltimore Clipper*, October 2, 1861, 4:1, which exaggerated recruitment in the 3rd Maryland. The 4th Maryland was transferred on May 7, and the Baltimore Light Infantry on May 24, 1862. Another more successful 4th Maryland was formed in July/August 1862 and served with distinction for the remainder of the war. See Scharf, *History of Western Maryland*, 1:308–309.

36 "Headquarters," *Baltimore Clipper*, November 21, 1861, 2:4. Commanded by Colonel George W. Wayson, the Baltimore Light Infantry, or Dix Light Infantry, was recruited in Baltimore during November/December 1861 for "Guard Duty only" on the Philadelphia, Wilmington & Baltimore Railroad.

37 See "Public Guard Regiment, U.S.A.," *Baltimore Clipper*, August 31, 1861, 2:7; and "Public Guard Regiment, U.S.A.," *Cecil Whig*, September 7, 1861, 3:3. See "McClellan Guards," *The Examiner*, October 9, 1861, 2:5. Other companies included the Hoffman Guards, Siegel Guards, Morgan Guards, Leary Guards, and Lyon Guards—see *Baltimore Clipper*, September 3, 1861, 2:3; and *Baltimore Clipper*, September 7, 1861, 2:6, plus Scharf, *History of Western Maryland*, 1:309–311.

38 "Col. Schley's Public Guard Regiment," *The Examiner*, October 30, 1861, 2:7. A notice in the *Baltimore Clipper*, September 7, 1861 (2:5), stated that "camp equipments, muskets, provisions, clothing &c." would be ready by September 10, 1861. See "Col. Schley's Public Guard Regiment," *Baltimore Clipper*, November 4, 1861, 1:6, for complete company listing of this regiment.

39 "Parade of Col. Schley's Regiment," *Baltimore Clipper*, November 20, 1861, 1:7.

40 "Camp Hoffman," *Baltimore Clipper*, November 21, 1861, 2:4.

41 See "Military Matters," *Baltimore Clipper*, December 6, 1861, 1:7; and "Arms Received," *Baltimore Clipper*, January 15, 1862, 1:6. On November 16, 1861, the ladies of Elkton presented the Public Guard / 5th Maryland with a regimental flag described as "a most beautiful silk banner, with the coat of arms of Maryland painted on one side in the centre of the blue field, and on the other the inscription: Presented by the Union ladies of Elkton, through Elkton Guards, Capt. E. F. M. Faehtz, to the Public Guard Regiment Md. Vol., Col. W. L. Schley." See "Flag Presentation," *Cecil Whig* (Elkton, MD), December 7, 1861, 2:5. Also presented were two marker flags emblazoned with "Public Guard." See "Inspection, Presentation of Colors and Review of Col. Schley's Public Guard Regiment," *Baltimore Clipper*, November 4, 1861, 1:7.

42 "Home Brigade for Frederick Co. Maryland," *Baltimore Clipper*, July 25, 1861, 2:2.

43 See "Correspondence of the Baltimore Clipper," *Baltimore Clipper*, August 22, 1861, 4:1; "Maryland Home Brigade," *Baltimore Clipper*, August 28, 1861, 2:3; and "Home Brigade," *The Examiner*, September 4, 1861, 2:5. Organized in February 1861, the Frederick Zouave Cadets were the "1st company of the 1st regiment." See "Attention, Zouaves," *The Examiner*, February 13, 1861, 2:5.

44 Hunt, *Colonels in Blue: Union Army Colonels of the Civil War; The Mid-Atlantic States*, 215. Johns was discharged for ill health on January 3, 1862. Raised at Camp Carroll, near Cumberland, this regiment included the Cumberland Continentals, commanded by Captain Horace Resley, the Oldtown Company, under Captain James D. Roberts, "late of the Indiana Zouaves," and the Detmold Riflemen, led by Captain Alexander Shaw, and stationed at Annapolis by the beginning of January 1862. ("The Allegany County Regiment," *Civilian & Telegraph*, August 15, 1861, 2:2; and "The Allegany County Regiment," *Civilian & Telegraph*, August 29, 1861, 2:3.

45 "Orderly Men," *Civilian & Telegraph*, September 3, 1861, 2:2.

46 "Equipments," *Civilian & Telegraph*, September 19, 1861, 2:2.

47 "Regimental Parade," *Civilian & Telegraph*, October 10, 1861, 2:1. On November 22, 1861, the 2nd Regiment, Potomac Home Brigade, was presented with a regimental flag made of blue silk with heavy bullion fringe. On one side was "the national coat of arms handsomely painted," and "on the other, the title '2d Regiment Potomac Home Guard Brigade'" was "emblazoned." See "Flag Presentation," *Civilian & Telegraph* (Cumberland, MD), November 22, 1861, 2:2.

48 Scharf, *History of Western Maryland*, 1:317–318.

49 Commanded by James Wallace before the war, the Dorchester Guards became Co. A of this regiment. See "Affairs in Dorchester County," *The Sun*, September 13, 1861, 1:5. Wallace commanded the Dorchester Guards before the war.

50 "Camp Vickers," *Kent News*, October 19, 1861, 2:3.

51 *Baltimore Clipper*, August 22, 1861, 4:1.

52 See "Recruits Wanted for Gist's Artillery," *Baltimore Clipper*, September 2, 1861, 2:5; and "Cavalry Recruits: 100 Men Wanted," *Cecil Whig*, November 7, 1861, 2:1.

53 *Baltimore Clipper*, September 16, 1861, 2:6.

54 "The Purnell Legion," *Baltimore Clipper*, October 7, 1861, 1:6.

55 "Artillery," *Kent News*, December 19, 1861, 2:5.

56 See "Cavalry," *The Examiner*, August 21, 1861, 4:3; "Camp Creager," *Baltimore Clipper*, September 21, 1861, 1:6; and "The Maryland Dragoons," *Baltimore Clipper*, September 26, 1861, 3:1.

57 "Seizure of Arms," *The Examiner*, August 28, 1861, 2:5.

Chapter 6: District of Columbia

1 "The Inauguration of Abraham Lincoln, President of the United States," *Evening Star*, March 4, 1861, 3:3.

2 "Celebration of the Twenty-Second," *National Republican*, February 25, 1861, 3:2.

3 See "The Inauguration," *National Republican*, March 5, 1861, 3:2; and "The Inauguration of Abraham Lincoln, President of the United States," *Evening Star*, March 4, 1861, 3:3.

4 See "Celebration of the Twenty-Second," *National Republican*, February 25, 1861, 3:2; and "The Inauguration of Abraham Lincoln, President of the United States," *Evening Star*, March 4, 1861, 3:3.

5 "The Inauguration," *National Republican*, March 5, 1861, 3:1; and "The Inauguration of Abraham Lincoln, President of the United States," *Evening Star*, March 4, 1861, 3:2.

6 "National Rifles," *Evening Star*, September 4, 1860, 3:3. See also Michael J. McAfee, "Uniforms & History: The National Rifles—District of Columbia Militia; 'A Matter of Loyalty," *Military Images* 19, no. 3 (November–December 1997): 31–32.

7 "National Rifles," *Evening Star*, September 4, 1860, 3:3.

8 "The Zouave Corps," *National Republican*, February 27, 1861, 3:2. See "Movements of the Military," *National Republican*, April 17, 1861, 3:1, for reference to Ellsworth drilling the Zouaves "for several days past."

9 "The Military Here," *Evening Star*, May 2, 1861, 2:2.

10 "Military Parades," *National Republican*, May 2, 1861, 3:2.

11 "Camp "Jim Davis," *National Republican*, June 18, 1861, 3:2.

12 See "Celebration of the Twenty-Second," *National Republican*, February 25, 1861, 3:2; "The Inauguration," *National Republican*, March 5, 1861, 3:1; and "Parade and Target Firing," *National Republican*, May 28, 1861, 3:1.

13 "The Inauguration," *National Republican*, March 5, 1861, 3:2.

14 "The National Guard Battalion," *Evening Star*, May 26, 1861, 3:1.

15 "Celebration of the Twenty-Second," *National Republican*, February 25, 1861, 3:2.

16 "The Inauguration," *National Republican*, March 5, 1861, 3:2.

17 "Presentation of Havelocks," *National Republican*, June 10, 1861, 3:3.

18 See "Flag Presentation," *National Republican*, March 7, 1861, 3:3; and "The Inauguration," *National Republican*, March 5, 1861, 3:1.

19 "The Inauguration," *National Republican*, March 5, 1861, 3:2.

20 "The Inauguration," *National Republican*, March 5, 1861, 3:2.

INDEX

R

S

T

U

V

W

Z